Tim Page is the most celebrated phot
After his years in the front line, he n

TIM PAGE

Page After Page

Paladin
An Imprint of HarperCollins*Publishers*

Paladin
An Imprint of HarperCollins*Publishers*
77–85 Fulham Palace Road,
Hammersmith, London W6 8JB

Published in Paladin 1990
9 8 7 6 5 4 3

First published in Great Britain by
Sidgwick & Jackson Ltd 1988

ISBN 0 586 09013 4

Set in Times

Printed in Great Britain by
HarperCollinsManufacturing Glasgow

*For all the people, all my frendz who have benevolently
put up with me though, enfin, most especially for Lindsay*

You get by with, you get high with a little help from . . .
Laureate Lennon

Contents

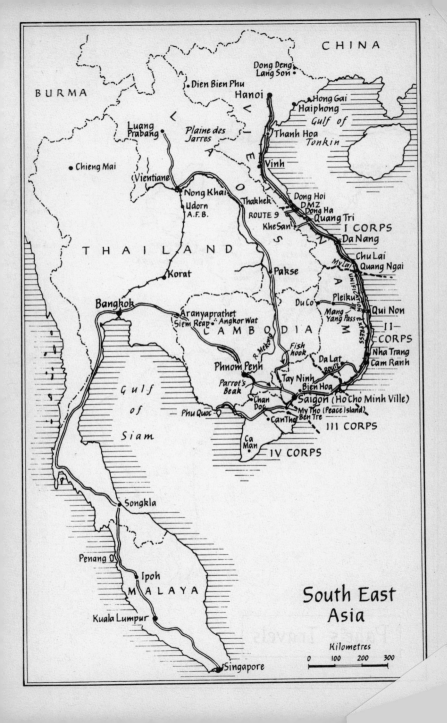

South East
Asia

Kilometres

0   100   200   300

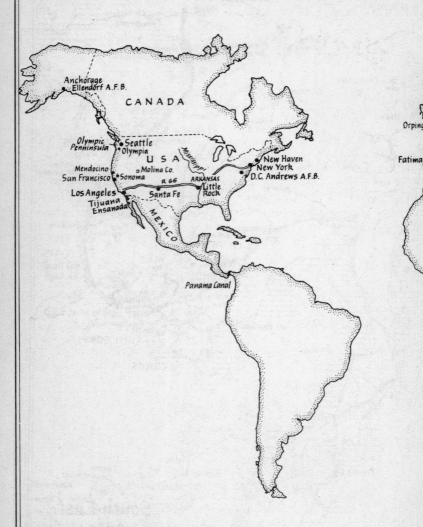

Page's Travels

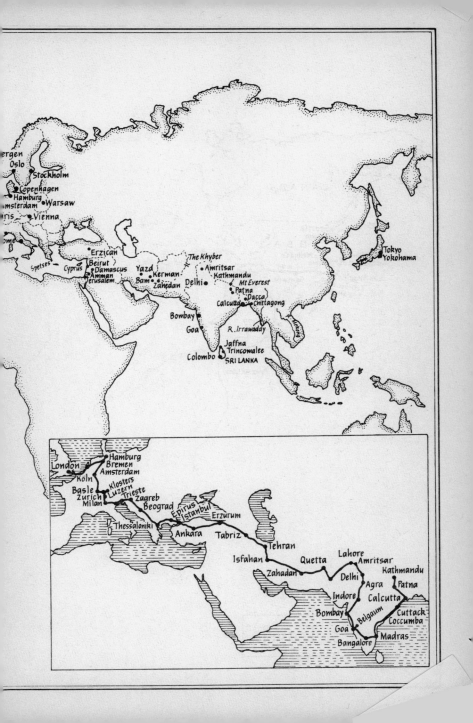

Prologue

I happened to be in London on the opening day of Parliament in 1985. The streets flooded with all kinds of security, especially in Trafalgar Square, abutted as it is by South Africa House with its ever swelling, persistent group of anti-apartheid pickets. Two winos were leaping about harmlessly in the middle of the empty road when, out of nowhere, two cops in crash helmets and waxed riot coats leaped at them, lashing with batons and boots before dragging them, struggling limply, to the church steps. It was like a movie of an accident about to happen, the perfect Pulitzer action frame, freezing into focus.

I had all the time in the world to start shooting. Nam had never been so giving in its action. I ran logics and techniques through my head, not reaching for the camera. Approaching the beating scene I saw blood pouring from the unfortunate down-and-outs, the pigs wading in. I was still not shooting. As I strode past, I heard the whack of a truncheon cracking a bum's shoulder blade. No flinch, nothing. All the way to the corner traffic lights, 20 yards on, I fought the urge to turn back and start shooting, trying to convince myself that the 200ASA film in the box was too fast for the shot.

I'd chickened out and for hours, days and weeks I was still kicking myself. The violence meant nothing, my mind was elsewhere. I was thinking words, silent protests. I was not there. I had failed myself. Maybe a landscape now meant more to me than a front page.

The past gathered at the Seventh Regiment Armory in New York on 21 November 1986.

1

It was not a party, it was not a celebration, it was not a wake. It was the first and probably last reunion of Vietnam correspondents to be staged. We had been together before in another lifetime, 12,000 miles away in Southeast Asia. Now we were reconvening to mull over the enormity of our past, and to renew the friendships that had endured the most difficult post-conflict traumas.

The bus from the airport landed me on a gale-swept pavement behind Grand Central Station. I had no hotel, only the homely but narrow couch belonging to Art Greenspahn, who shall be hereafter called Garspon for Mike Herr, who wrote *Dispatches*, had labelled us Garspon and Nub (for my mutilated left index finger, which I tended to brandish).

It took Garspon twenty minutes to find me outside an anonymous brokerage building somewhere near the station. It had three entrances and I was jet-lagged and confused. It took another forty minutes to find an empty cab, hustling others rudely – Apple-style – out of the way. It was a cold Wednesday night and the whole city was heading home for a long Thanksgiving weekend. We jerked back to Art's crib on the Upper West Side (four floors up in a single room with a view of an air shaft).

Like myself, Art had gone through the cycles of junk and pain, alcohol and depression, confusion and desolation, but he had paid a heavier price. Leaving Vietnam after he was wounded, he had lost his job, he had hit bottom. In New York in 1969 when I was in the Neuro-Physical Institute for Rehabilitative Medicine at 34th and 1st Avenue, he had been a regular bedside visitor, and afterwards virtually camped at my sublet on 25 East 20th Street helping to smoke up the five keys of Lao green that had got back to the US via the USAF evac flight and American Express.

Maybe that was what this reunion was all about, renewing old and dissipated personal ties. The real reunions did not take place in that mock-Tudor drill hall on Park Avenue, they happened at the parties and dinners before and after the event. There the sadness could dissolve to tears and pain to laughter, the banter could be loaded, the conversational shorthand acute.

Before leaving the UK I had heard rumours of who would and who would not be there. Horst Faas, the Associated Press photo chief in London who had presided over their pix in Southeast Asia for a decade, would be going, together with his stable mate Edie Lederer, who had run the AP from Phnom Penh in 1972. That was to be the sum total of the English-based delegates, though there are a good century of us here. Since much of the publicity had been by word of mouth, it was not bad that 350 people turned up. Nearly 3000 of all nationalities, excluding the Vietnamese, had been in that ubiquitous foreign press corps during the 10,000 days of conflict, though some older members went back as far as World War II.

My cab driver, whom I had pulled after a cold, wet wait on the night at the corner of 81st and West End, was old enough to have served both in the Second World War and Korea and was sure as hell aware of Vietnam. He might even have been able to put his finger on a map and point it out. However, he wasn't sure where the Seventh Armoured Regiment Armory was on Park. I had it from the organizers that it was at 68th. I had got it from the horse's mouth of the Overseas Press Club, an erstwhile intellectual, snobbish body of elitist overseas hacks who string it together once in a while over a few jars and plead for the noble causes and for freedom of our kind and its access to material. It was their choice, this arbour of the military, not the fittest locale in the circumstances. The place drowned one in the despair that British troops fighting to retain a lost dominion must have felt, their backs to the wall in this very fort. Now it is the glorification of all that is great and right and American. A1 uniformed Marines guarded its portals, ushering conventioneers to the sundry ballrooms and conference chambers, directing guests to welcome counters to be issued with those plastic ID tags announcing how high you are.

We had come from as far away as Japan and Russia. Mostly the clan were now back home in the USA. Peter Arnett, who had won a Pulitzer for his dispatches for the AP in 1968, was now with CNN in Moscow and won the prize for having come the farthest.

Most folks had that emergent big-bang city look on, three-piece suits, button-down collars, a look of dentists, insurance brokers, corporate hackers. Only five of us were without ties, all but one photographers; image people can get away with bending the book. Everyone else looked as though the boardroom loomed in the real future. The Vietnam Veteran's Coalition, who were demonstrating outside, wore their cherished jungle fatigues with an unforgetting pride, but most of us had relegated our safari suits and field gear to attic trunks and Goodwill chests. I had expected there to be at least a token dressing of yesteryear in the same vein as the panoply of costume at the veterans' wall in Washington on Memorial Day. I had even packed my old olive-drab greens,

3

though at the last minute I switched to my oldest tweed sports jacket sporting a VVA (Vietnam Veterans' Association) pin. Camis or fatigues were definitely not *tenue de soirée*.

It was perplexing. Though all the faces appeared familiar and I could often put a name to them without referring to the damn tags, most people seemed different. Age had overgrown us all; gone were the sportif moustaches, on had come the blow-dry, the thinning, and greying. Back then, except for the superstraights in their television suits, we could have passed for a band of mercenaries, flushed from the Congo – and some were.

The babble was subdued; it wasn't quiet, it was thoughtful. Periodically long-lost mates would raise a hoot or a holler and the wash would ripple down the room. People would turn their heads and mumble, identify the celebrants, remember an anecdote from the past, and swing back into their own rap.

The free-for-all of getting seated at the tables was akin to that of getting all of us into choppers to go on an operation. Dirck Halstead, who had been my UPI photo chief in Saigon, tried unsuccessfully to get me to the photographers' table among the luminaries of then and now. I opted for the heads' table. There was my host Garspon with Jim Caccavo, a freelance from Los Angeles who had nursed me through catastrophes and traumas when I had been destitute in southern California. During the war he had freelanced under a Red Cross contract. The most stunning woman present was accompanying Paul Brinkley Rogers, once at *Newsweek*, now living in the Arizona desert writing for the *Republic*; we had touched bases often during the seventies. The previous day Paul and I had been interviewed by a couple of star-struck Boston-based public-radio types. This had been conducted in Art's tiny crib, smoothed by the Colombian shake the supplicants had scored for the occasion.

The organizers had provided a series of pre-dinner speeches as entertainment. Initially they had asked General Westmoreland, Bob Hope and Tom Brokaw (a starlet newsreader on NBC). What Westmoreland or Hope had to do with the press was never made clear; both were ridiculed by the media or at least those of us neither overly patrician nor deluded by the whole scene. Tom Brokaw had once spent twenty minutes in transit at Ton San Nhut.

David Halberstam, another invited speaker, refused to take the podium beside these pretenders and bowed out of the whole shindig, deriding the reunion as 'a trivial event run by trivial people'. Horst Faas had countered with 'Maybe the best, but not the brightest'. The event became a cause célèbre in the New York media. Westmoreland had sued CBS the previous year and the federal court had recently found in their favour; this sealed his political fate. There were going to be a lot of CBS hardcore tonight.

The OPC had got Westmoreland, Hope and Brokaw to retreat, and also managed to ditch Graham Martin, the last US ambassador to Saigon. They filled in with Robin Moore, retired Admiral Elmo Zumwalt and Barry Zorthian.

Robin Moore? many of us asked ourselves. Isn't he the dip that wrote the film *Green Berets*? You know, where John Wayne and the Special Forces win Vietnam just about single-handedly against a bunch of dumb gooks dressed in red pyjamas, and the sun finally sets in the east over Da Nang beach. Damn it, the guy swanned about playing spook as a government guest, surfing on the Berets' newfound popularity. Not even a bad excuse for a reporter, not even a good writer.

Zumwalt was a different quotient. Sure he had run the Muddy Water Navy, the in-country Mekong Naval Force, the poor buggers who were glamorized in *Apocalypse Now*, riding in fibreglass water-jet boats along impossibly narrow and densely undergrowthed waterways. Then he had been naval chief of operations and introduced a system known as Z Grams, allowing beards, beer and long hair in the staid and puritanical US Navy, traditionally rolled tighter than a Senior Service.

His son had commanded Swift Boats in the Delta under him, running elite, counter-terrorist SEAL teams into the Viet Cong's R & R (rest and recreation) centre on the Ca Mau Peninsula. Then the admiral had ordered vast areas of mangrove-clad southern provinces to be sprayed with dioxin, better known as Agent Orange from the band painted around the 55-gallon drums that Dow Chemical shipped it in. During the war thousands of tons of it were sprayed over millions of hectares of South Vietnam by C-123 flying boxcar tankers whose motto read: 'We Prevent Forests.' They called themselves 'ranch hands'. Unfortunately Zumwalt's son, Elmo III, contracted strange cancerous diseases that this odious stuff appears to trigger, and had to suffer endless therapies and excruciating bone-marrow transplants. Dioxin also causes genetic damage and his son Elmo IV had become another victim. They had combined to write a book, *My Father, My Son* showing the yin and yang of the Vietnam experience under a

5

chemical-biological lens. I thought the admiral was apropos and waited in anticipation.

Disconcertingly, he was overawed, out of place, and his final conclusion was that 'not controlling the press in Vietnam was the downfall of the United States'. He finished by saying, 'You can keep them fully informed and lose it or have censorship and win it.' I knew already that the gathering here was the first and last to cover a war freely. Since Nam, you need a press tag even for a high-school basketball game. The clapping thereafter was only just audibly polite.

The other replacement speaker they had dug up, Barry Zorthian, had run JUSPAO (Joint United States Public Affairs Office), which was the umbrella organization for all information disseminated from both the US military and civil sources. It was also where you had to go to get accredited, and it ran the five-o'clock follies, the daily exercise in information theatre staged at the Rex in Saigon.

Zorro, as Zorthian was called, was still sporting the medal given him back in 1965; it read; 'Ambushed at the credibility gap.' He had left JUSPAO and gone to work for Time Inc and later that night gave me his business card for a consultancy in suburban Washington DC. I suspect that once a spook always a spook, but tonight he was a roguishly lovable one, the bonhomie was thicker than the old beefs. He had the same unenviable task now as back then, that of trying to explain away, or justify, the official role in the war.

Here his address had to follow the uproar generated by Robin Moore. Moore claimed that 'should the war have been left to John Wayne and myself' it would have been won. This did not go down well. He tried to buddy it up with, 'Why am I always in trouble?' Audible chair scrapings. He droned on, digressing to – of all places – Rhodesia and a story of 'wild-eyed spearchuckers or whatever'. At this point we had had enough, the rumblings swelled and George MacArthur (who had been in Saigon from 1965 to the end), seated near the dais, yelled out, 'Sit down! You're an asshole.' There was much applause. George carried on, 'You are the first certifiable loony in this place.' There were cheers, catcalls, boos, shouts of 'Get out!' Moore was by now flapping like an exasperated hen, mumbling on with his anecdote. 'Let's take a vote.' George pointed at Moore. 'Is he an asshole?' Tumultuous applause. A functionary from the OPC tugged at Moore's sleeve, he grinned tightly and left. The man was a blow to our professional egos, even Zorthian, who had attempted to control us, had to respect that.

Hugh Mulligan, correspondent par excellence, summed up the incident in a wire-ready headline: 'Vietnam Journalists' Reunion Erupts Over Zimbabwe Issue.'

Eddie Adams, the well-known photographer who had been in Vietnam from 1965 on the staff of Associated Press, opened the after-dinner speeches. Eddie and I had spent a lot of high times together in and out of the field. He was always the model of patience and tutorship, nearly always beating me, but always praising my efforts with a little superior put-down pat on the back. He became a true friend in the best of buddy ways through the proximity that war imposes. Our paths had kept crossing until we both got out of that quagmire: I on a stretcher, he with laurels pyramiding. We met again in Saigon in April 1985, on the tenth anniversary of the liberation of South Vietnam. The rooftop bar where we used to sit and watch the war in a 360-degree panorama was still serving, though the skyline was not alight and rats frolicked in the ornamental fish pond.

The ambience of tonight's gathering reminded me of that watering hole. The banter, arguments, stories and emotions that had begun there were now getting warmed up again in an atmosphere rekindled by those memories parked carefully out of harm's way. The cast of characters trimmed down somewhat by the war and that old enemy, time.

Eddie used to be low profile, dapper, continually dour, trim and compact. Now in New York he was the quintessential big-time photographer. He wore a chic black velvet suit, silk foulard and black fedora, from the back of which protruded a five-inch ponytail of grey hair. He was to be the first speaker. He was our hero; he had won the Pulitzer Prize for the picture of General Loan's execution of a VCS at Tet 1968. As he went up to the podium, to address us, I called out, totally zonked, 'Adams, you hippy, get a haircut!' The table at which I sat broke into uncontrollable laughter and sundry guffaws echoed round the room. Later Eddie was kind of cool to me.

Eddie spoke more eloquently than most would expect of a photographer, and conjured up the images that we had shot, the pictures that had probably changed the course of history. For before the advent of massive television coverage in the late sixties, the still photographs which had flashed almost instantaneously from the combat zone to the world press had screamed the

7

madness that prevailed. These frames had become the rallying banners of youth's consciousness, erupting in 1968, lit by strobe, fuelled by acid rock, leaking round the world, causing a nation's attitude to change towards a more peaceful awareness. Eddie's voice was almost hypnotic as he verbally held those images up to us, understanding what we knew and had tried to communicate to the outside.

The sobering side of it was that many of those frames had been made by men no longer here. Vietnam had seen an extremely high ratio of newsmen killed in action. It was a war covered by civilians rather than civilians in uniform enlisted to distort the news: almost sixty of us never got home and another twenty are still listed missing. Many others who had once been functioning photographers had been so blown away by what they had witnessed that they had quit the game completely. Eddie eulogized Art's award-winning frame of the 101st Airborne evacuating their wounded out of dense jungle by skyhook: their arms reaching up to secure the wounded body, the dejected, battle-weary survivors clumped in the foreground. It remains one of those haunting images that Nam was, and always will be, known for.

It was moving to hear Eddie recite the roll call of photographs and the men and women who had died making them. We paused for a minute's silence, our heads bowed to their memories.

Coming on after Eddie was the unenviable task assigned to Keyes Beech of the *Chicago Daily News* and later the *Los Angeles Times*. They had been out there in the forties, reporting the French flailing about, watching them turn a free election, one that was supposed to hand over the country to a band of nationalists headed by Ho Chi Minh, into a despotic war, initially of liberation from colonialism before becoming the war we all knew, though not necessarily loved.

Keyes opened, 'Vietnam was the great mistake. We should have won the war. That was the mistake. That is the extent of my reflections on Vietnam.' Nobody knew what was to come next, had we all turned so heavy? But Keyes went on to rap more memories than a dozen field marshals. He was still his wiry self with the same droll, quick wit which can have you mirthed out at the heaviest of times.

In America people tend to regard Vietnam as their personal trip, it is too caught up in their egos. The Vietnamese seem to have been forgotten along the way, a sideshow of colonialism's dilemma. Their lament was not taken up until the last by an ex-

CBSer, David Schoenbrun, now with INN. He pleaded socialist-ically for normalization of relationships.

Tad Bartimus preceded him, the only woman to speak. She represented the hundred-strong contingent, over the years, of men and women who had covered Kampuchea during the Vietnam saga while its American-backed regime tottered to its climax. Nixon and Kissinger's policies had reduced Cambodia from an orientally corrupt, basically content, Buddhist monarchy to a state of tyranny and ruin. B-52s had smashed down a country where the wats were the largest buildings and where the people eked a gracious living out of the abundant fields, forests and waters. As the horror reigned, Tad had run the AP bureau in Phnom Penh, reporting from a battlefield that fluxed with the monsoons. The Khmer Rouge/NVA controlled virtually all lines of communi-cation. During this madness, the press corps had taken a great many casualties, fifteen were ambushed and assassinated, five were captured and came out after weeks or months with incredible tales, and another ten were captured and never came out.

War is not practical for women reporters or photographers. They require separate facilities, latrines, quarters and so on or the officers running the units they visit think they do. This makes for all kinds of implausible situations not really appropriate to combat conditions. The women that mixed and got along with the grunts – the enlisted men – and the Asians were a rare breed and brought a compassion to their reportages that most of us macho dudes were too hardened to exhibit.

Tad came with a plea for acceptance of her sex, to be compared on parity. Equal rights was an established thing among the Viet Cong; their heroines echoed the exploits of the Partisans behind Axis lines during the Second World War. In the US there was heavy prejudice against the ladies and, as Tad said, 'We came with a flower in the hatband of our helmets.'

She evoked the mysterious languor of Cambodia before the genocidal post-liberation period run by Pol Pot's Khmer Rouge and its even more mysterious Ankha. 'My memories,' she said, 'are not of foxholes.' Back in the early seventies 'there was the three-day debate by the Cambodian cabinet over which orchid to honour as the national flower. This as Phnom Penh was under daily rocket attack.'

Twenty or thirty of the assembled survivors in the Armory had returned to Vietnam during the multimillion-dollar bash that the networks had fronted to the Vietnamese for the privilege of beaming live, via a mobile British Telcom-installed dish, their 1985 anniversary celebrations. I was surprised that the keynote speakers, Eddie included, barely touched on the suffering that the Viets had gone through, the millions of dead, countless thousands missing in action, the destruction of one of the most beautiful countries on the planet. What to the military had been nothing but a yellow body count to them represented souls. Asians with their Confucian Buddhist precepts believe that when a dead person is not buried in the traditional family plot, the spirit will wander homeless for ever. US troops continually desecrated village cemeteries and family graves next to rural hamlets. Their understanding of oriental beliefs was based on a cursory briefing on getting in-country and a naïve little pamphlet on customs and habits of the natives.

I had sat in Los Angeles recovering from my second bout of corrective neuro-surgery, down and out, while Cambodia was crippled and Vietnam conquered. I cried for my inability to be there to share in its death throes – theirs, mine a form of mental suicide. My most treasured memory from all those years had been sleeping out under the eerie presence of thousand-year-old Buddhas four storeys up on the Bayon at the Angkor Wat complex. Crippled like the Khmers, I was invalided out of the scene where I most desperately wanted to be.

The New York reunion was a substitute for being there, it offered the security of shared experience. As Keyes stated, 'We came not for the war, but for the friendships. It was the first symbiosis of the first professional colony that has a spirit that links us worldwide.'

It had been an incredible rush then and now.

1

Growing

Someone said that you come through your parents and not from them. This struck a chord deep within me, as at nineteen days I was adopted. To many people who have been adopted, it is a bone to worry for their whole lives. Though genetically I bear no physical resemblance to my folks, my powers of reason are akin to those of my father, my honesty more attributable to my mother. My frankness sometimes shames me and must be from them both.

I was born on 25 May 1944, in Tunbridge Wells, Kent, a Gemini born in the Year of the Monkey, the year one of the first V2 rockets fell in nearby Orpington, off its central London target. My parents informed me, when I was six or seven, that I was adopted, which meant nothing then. Somehow I gathered that my genetic father had been torpedoed while serving on a Russian-bound convoy for Murmansk or Archangel, but I knew nothing of my real mother. It was only years later, when I was clearing out the attic after my father's death, that I found out more facts including my original name.

John, my adopted father, was born the middle son of three to a poor family whose head worked in a tailor's shop in Aylesbury, Buckinghamshire, just west of London. It is now very fashionable, but back in 1907 it was rurally poor. Aylesbury's claim to fame was its breed of ducks. Of that grandfather I know little and even in the family albums his image ceases to appear by the middle thirties. Grandma Page had retired to a boarding house in St Leonards on Sea, East Sussex. Grandmother was the perfect Victorian lady, black dresses, frilled lace collars and cuffs, buttoned shoes, bunned white hair, who held audience whenever we visited for the day. The fun then was tearing around the enormous house with its kitchen full of gigantic ranges and larders, where there were always pies, cakes, puddings or meals simmering for the retired gentlefolk lodgers who supported this residence. With my cousin David, whom I never really liked because he was a better swimmer and had Prince Charles protruding ears, I used to take over the basement, and I know he turned me in for picking at the goodies on the serving tables.

Still, it was a place for a free holiday, where I was often consigned and allowed to go play on the beach – uninteresting, as you could not build sandcastles out of pebbles. The pier was super, decadent, full of slot machines where for a penny you could attempt to control the equivalent of a JCB construction machine to grab junk prizes of plastic watches and whistles; usually the only reward was a stale aniseed ball. The real bitch was being forced to go down to the salt-water baths near the magnetic pier. They were home to a bunch of keen kids who ploughed lengths up and down the pool, questing for poxy little trophies. The chlorine and the salt, combined with my cousin's ardour, left me not only cold, but uncomfortable and frightened. David, I believe, is now involved with VW spare parts.

Uncle Frank had run off to sea and seen out a hazardous war running convoys on merchantmen. He was a cook with a fantasy of owning a land-based nosh shop so he acquired this Gothic Victorian monstrosity of five floors on the Mount on the chalk cliffs on the south coast when he got out of the marine.

The other wing of the family, Uncle Dick, also on ships but as a wireless operator, had ended up in Australia after the Second World War and nobody has seen him since. He is now reduced to sepia memory. His daughter, my cousin, periodically dispatches her accountant husband and pallid children to London so that they can check out their fading Angloid roots. All my relatives disappoint me and I suspect they do my mother too. She comes from a straight background where sailors are not to be entirely trusted.

Both my grandmother and aunt had lived nearby when I was growing up, Gran in Crofton, a mile and a half away, Aunt Margaret, Uncle Kelvin, cousins David and Judy at Chelsfield, a ten-minute walk through a recreation ground and across a rutty field, hedged by great blackberrying tangles. I liked Margaret, an outdoor person with a predilection for keeping weird pets. Just after the war, Kelvin and Margaret had a nanny goat, answering to Daisy, which took delight in consuming washed linen off the clothes line and wrapped chocolate bars, a luxury during those lean, rationed years. When they were evacuated to Northern Ireland during the war, we inherited their tabby cat, Dick, with whom I had great rapport. I always get a mog wherever I have temporarily settled, most recently a fixed ginger tom, who emerged from the hedgerow, meeping, a month after I moved in. (It would be possible to relate one's life story through the eyes of the cats that have stared, mesmerized, me at them, them at me, neither knowing who was the more stoned.) Try to hypnotize your cat and you end up zonked yourself.

My father was an international chartered accountant but none of his mathematical skill infiltrated me. He confused me by issuing my pocket money on a lunar-calendar basis, which worked to my advantage and was incremented by 10 per cent every fifty-two weeks. Somehow this malfunction did not extend to chess, taught me by my grandmother from the age of five. My grandfather had been a grandmaster and teacher of physics and mathematics at the London School of Economics. Chess had a romantic edge, the stuff that war games were based on. My gran let me win to learn the game and to my surprise, even today, I can pull off a victory. I played an unorthodox, unthought-out, commando-type match; a series of adventurous thrusts with no overall plan. I sought adventure also in comic books, progressing from the *Beano* (when I was five) to the *Eagle* (around seven), *Hotspur* and others, where boy warriors controlled battalions of model planes, ships, tanks, guns, trucks and mini-robot men. How I craved to run those legions of modern mayhem! They stopped short of nuclear, biological and chemical gear; this was, after all, the late forties and early fifties.

There is no cause for shrink concern over my childhood. It was an idyll I would wish on most Third World kids. I had love and respect.

My dad used to read me to sleep. The first novel of consequence was *Children of the New Forest* and though the details are forgotten and sadly never reread, it was a story of survival in the woods with fascinating tips on trapping and cabin construction – neat things to get up to, I thought, since I was denied my desire to join either the Cubs or the Scouts. My father thought wearing uniforms was a fascist trait. This tends to hold theoretical water; the putting-on of uniforms creates undesirable characteristics in most men and women. By the age of four, through his efforts and those of Mrs Duncan's play group and nursery school, a five-minute toddle from home, I could read myself and no effort was spared to provide the printed page. The first books, like *Thomas the Tank Engine*, hooked me to trains. Steam trains still ran regularly through Orpington station on the coastal routes to Dover, Whitstable and Hastings. In the winter, the trees bare, they made romantic silhouettes chuffing along the embankment on the other side of Orpington Hospital, half a mile away. The trick was to catch the Golden Arrow pullman, pulled by a green Battle of Britain class loco, nonstop from Victoria to Dover. Every time I spotted the train, I mentally rode to the coast and on beyond the French ports. Paris seemed no further than the embankment. A few years later, I got parental permission to roam the southeast, train spotting. Once a pre-teen friend, his mate and I dragged my mum to Ashford and Tonbridge to crawl around the loco sheds there, swarming up on to begrimed footplates and playing train driver with the real goods. This first fantasy career lasted until I was about twelve.

Orpington Hospital had been built to accommodate the Canadian troops wounded in the First World War; there were thousands of the poor buggers. The wards stretched for half a mile alongside the embankment where the casualties were discharged straight out of the ambulance trains. Seventy years later the same tar-paper and asbestos-sheeted buildings still stand, functioning as the local hospital. My first visit there was in 1946, bawling the place down with third-degree burns on my chest, causing me to become an in-patient for six weeks. At that time, all children were issued with a ration of halibut orange, a foul-tasting nutrient booster which was taken diluted with hot water. One day my mother had put the boiled water into a jug on the kitchen table to cool, and somehow I pulled myself upright and, groping along the edge of the table, encountered the jug handle, lurched back and brought a quart of scalding water down my front. I remember nothing, though I now know pain leaves indelible mental scars; the real ones stretched, as I grew, to resemble an emu-like chicken surmounting an oblong egg on my chest. Hair is unable to grow out of them, and they never really get a decent tan.

My next accident happened when I was four, crashing at high speed on a scooter belonging to the girl next door and getting the handle in my eye. I was held overnight in the eye unit at Farnborough Hospital a mile and a half away, and dispatched wearing a bulging patch over one side of my head.

On my fifth birthday, in addition to a copy of *Swallows and*

Amazons, I got an 18-inch BSA bike. In thirty-eight years of riding I have only come off twice. Learning to ride a bicycle came easier than learning to swim (which I had to be bribed to do: five bob for 30 metres of witnessed length at Eltham baths). My father took me to the nearest stretch of flat road in Gleasons Avenue and ran beside me holding the little maroon bow-shaped frame up, and on the second or third pass I was on my own. Later that year, in the corner of Warren Road Primary School, I rode in a miniature village with roads, shops and traffic lights. Here the entire class went out to play at real life, pre-Thatcherite shop-keeping with cardboard currency, learning the highway code.

My father, meanwhile, resuscitated his ancient Rudge fire-service bike. During the war he had been in the local auxiliary fire brigade and during the Blitz was called up to town, where, during the day, he held his regular job as a junior partner at Crew & Turnball, a now defunct auditing company. It was always a bit of a disappointment to me that he did not have an illustrious war career like Biggles or like my mother's cousin from Derby, Uncle Reg, who had served as driver, mechanic and gunner on a long-range reconnaissance vehicle with the Desert Rats. My godfather, another Uncle Reg this one, had been in the navy and then commanded HMS *Endeavour*, moored on the Embankment in London.

With the Rudge restored, my father and I took to the road, further afield on each outing. At first we made gentle trips around the lanes, getting off to push up hills, but as we both gained strength and confidence we ventured into the Weald and eventually got as far as Hastings, returning by train. My father's bike was enormously robust with 28-inch heavy-duty wheels, as befitted a machine designed to haul ladders, buckets and stirrup pumps – a creation such as the Vietnamese win wars with. He was for ever waiting for me to catch up on my toy velocipede. Neither of us had gears or lights, so the expeditions were confined to fine summer days. We saw most of Kent, often stopping at a pub, with me waiting outside for a fizzy drink and a packet of crisps with salt in a blue paper twist, and Dad supping slowly on a large shandy, claiming it soothed his throat after having swallowed all kinds of flies and bugs, once even a bee, while careering downhill, his mouth agape. All I seemed to collect was the habitual midge in the eye, which was dutifully extracted with the corner of my father's white handkerchief. On one of these balmy evenings I had my first sip of beer and loathed it.

My mother had once ridden, but steadfastly refused to take up cycling. She is peculiarly nonphysical, never having learned to swim, ride or drive, quite helpless at putting anything mechanical together or taking it apart. To her, a screw is verging on astrophysics, while my dad spent endless hours trying vainly to repair or adjust sundry defective household items. He didn't really enjoy messing about with things, preferring to sit back in his chair with a book or *The Times* crossword puzzle, listening to obscure classical recordings. His one concession to luxury was his gramophone and extensive collection of records. He belonged to Orpington and District Gramophone Society. On club evenings I drifted off to sleep with 'Greensleeves', *Peer Gynt*, *Peter and the Wolf* or another of my favourites echoing up the stairs.

It was a peaceful, loving time. I grew healthily, catching every known childhood disease except mumps. Due to my habit of sucking my left thumb (to this day flatter than my right), I was obliged to wear a rat-trap construction across my front upper gnawers. The worst part was the fittings, with the Vaseline-coated moulds metallically cloying the mouth for what seemed like days; I gave up brace and thumb when I got to grammar school.

Fane, my mother, besides keeping us physically together, was principally concerned with our spiritual welfare and is an ardent church-goer, a believer who, without doubt, will go to her heaven, having probably never lied or knowingly had an orgasm in her life. A pillar of involvement at the local Protestant Norman church in Farnborough village, she belongs to Bible-reading fellowships, the Mothers' Union, the brass-cleaning detail, church flower rota, parish-magazine delivery service, and the church missionary society, and recycles waste paper for blind dogs and milk-bottle tops for lepers.

In my early years I was taken to ten o'clock Sunday-morning service, Dad staying at home with the Sunday papers or to mow the lawn. There, I mouthed meaningless verse, knelt painfully, trying to think why I was there, or sat on a pew, even more uncomfortable than a fold-down school desk, listening to rambling sermons. I had no friends who went there. All my mates were spiritless souls spending Sunday mornings mooning about the Green under a big old oak tree or building trolleys in someone's father's garage. I was the only one obliged to keep going to Sunday service, even when my mother ceased accompanying me. Threepence out of my pocket money was ordained for the collection, another threepence was meant to go into my papier-mâché model thatch African hut missionary box, and I was supposed to say my prayers. There was even a time when I was also sent up to Farnborough village to cop the afternoon Sunday school. I revolted early on that and refused to go through with the confirmation business, much to my mother's displeasure. Religious festivals have always degenerated in my mind to pagan ritual, food and offerings, Easter boding the arrival of my other godfather, Uncle Austin, who always brought splendid presents including, once, his boyhood double chest of Meccano. By the time I got to grammar school, dogmatic pressure lifted and I was left freethinking like my father.

Because I was an only child, friends gradually supplanted family in importance, except for my parents, whom I only got to know when I came back to England after seventeen and a half years on the road. Family has always been those individuals with whom I have been sharing a space. My first friends were imaginary, grown out of my wish for a brother or sister. They were called Mr Buxton and Mr Gumshoot and I'm told I enjoyed long, muddled conversations on diverse subjects with them both. I ceased this abstract communication when I became aware of the little girls next door, Jenny and Julia. Jenny was three years older than I, Julia six months younger, and I only wished they'd been boys. Jenny was bossy and much into dolls whereas Julia could be coaxed into activities with hammers, saws, bits of wood and abandoned toys. My folks thought it creative.

At five I got inducted into Warren Road Primary School a quarter of a mile away and Julia was packed off with her sister to a convent school for girls at the other end of Orpington town. There ended my first friendship and romance, though through the creepers which have since sprouted in the sexual-activity jungle I can say that Julia's was the first thing I ever saw, a naked, reddened line of no allure, rubbed raw by fifties Izal loo paper. That was a few summers after the first days of school.

School was great. From the back balcony of the house, I had already heard the cries and shouts from the playground at breaks. The joyous, raucous noise held no fears, it just boded lots of friends. Anyway, I had got on fine at nursery school. At drawing and painting I had been declared a virtuoso. The first year at Warren Road was basically play. I could have got a PhD for sandtray and quickly got promoted to milk monitor, which involved leaving the classroom to collect the class's thirty-eight third-pint bottles of the then free milk. There were always extras, which it was the milk monitor's privilege to guzzle. You always came back from the duty smelling fatty and rancid, stomach and bladder bursting, shirt splashed with telltale stains. The same odour permeates Tibetan huts, where the diet centres on rancid yak butter. At Warren Road the missing element was the smoke from open grates burning yak-dung sticks and moss. The unwashed bodies and feet dominated both environs. Coal was still rationed in Britain and Fridays were bath nights, hair washed fortnightly. It was not surprising that the district health nurse periodically found lice on kids' heads during the ritual mid-term examination. Those body MOTs included an eye test; I got progressively fuzzier but refused to wear those wire-rimmed spectacles John Lennon later made famous. Even more disturbing was the fact that my balls steadfastly refused to manifest themselves. At the turn-to-the-left-and-cough signal, a cold hand found nothing hanging, another cough and still nothing. A small note was dutifully written in my dossier. Somewhere in the Kent County Council medical records I suspect I am still undropped.

I made friends fast. Playing in the street was not encouraged; the back garden was playground, cricket pitch, imaginary forest and battleground. There was a spooky cavern under the house's back balcony which stank of cat pee and mildewing wood. Dungeon, tunnel complex, cave or mine, it was full of sharp, corroding objects and junk guaranteed to cause minor injury. Playing there was *verboten*, Band-aids put on with an 'I told you so'. Out of the rotting fruit boxes, ripped roofing felt and sundry rubbish there I constructed a hut on the balcony outside the french windows. The eyesore abutted the neighbours' fence as a common wall, a tea towel made a respectable curtain. I cadged old crockery for a tea service and, though the roof leaked worse than a sieve, I passed many an hour in the grandeur of my own abode.

It was under the balcony that Dad had recovered his fire bike and I found sufficient old pram carcasses to construct my first trolley.

It was made of two-by-four wood, an orange box, nails, a bolt for the steering machanism, and recycled pram wheels and axles. Gangs of local children caused havoc on the hilly pavements of the Davis Estate. We were Fangios and Mosses crossed with derring-do jeep-borne raiders, often getting the contraptions to lofty speeds of 20 miles per hour. Alarmingly their wheels would shear the retaining pins or the entire chassis would collapse but that made it even better. When no pram wheels were forthcoming, we would retreat to the back garden and construct dangerous little fires to melt scrap lead into unidentifiable slabs we liked to think were soldiers. It was recycled in an endless, formless way; the fires were the most important part of it all.

On my seventh birthday I was given my first camera, a box Ensign of fixed capability. It consumed four or five rolls of 120 black and white in its entire life, mostly in the back garden (the cat was a favourite subject) or pictures of locomotives at Orpington Station. The films were processed around the corner at the chemist's. My father, who had bought himself a Rolleicord on a hiking holiday in the early thirties in the Taurus Mountains, made little prints in a darkened bathroom. Foolishly I did not take the camera to the coronation in 1953, a day of pouring rain passed on Pall Mall on my father's shoulders before scuttling between the crowd's legs (an age-old photographic technique) to emerge into the front row next to a friendly policeman. Queen Salote of Tonga, your quintessential black mammy, was the only one in an open carriage. The amount of horse shit staggered me. Afterwards we came home as far as Catford on a double-decker tram.

A piece of the garden next to the compost, the chalkiest soil, including an apple tree, was designated mine. The fruits it produced – only gooseberries and rhubarb would tolerate the flints – could be sold to my folks for a few bob a year. From an early age my father tried to instil in me the value of money, how to get it and how to spend it wisely. None of it really registered except the spending, which I do with aplomb. My Post Office savings account increased only when relatives sent savings stamps instead of book tokens at birthdays or Christmas. Those few seeds sown and untouched served to fund my first overseas wanderings once I got out of primary school.

In my class were three other children born on the same auspicious day as I. I had a childish crush on Pauline; John was a fellow adventurer who left soon for South Africa with his parents; the third, Pete, was overweight and spotty. A mess that invited bullying, his grey flannel shorts were always stained, one shoelace loose. Towards the end of the summer term, all the forms in a given year put on a play in which every child got cast as something, sometimes only as a bush or a flower. The seven-year-olds that year got assigned *Robin Hood*. The year before we had done *Treasure Island*, in which I was a pirate. This time round I got star billing as Little John, while plump Pete became an unlikely

19

Robin. Little John had the role of defeating Robin Hood in stave combat at a river crossing. The river, placed strategically in the corner of the school's grassed quadrangle, was a rescued RAF bomber-crew survival raft in bright yellow, filled with water from a hosepipe disappearing into the girls' toilets. The crossing was a gym plank. At rehearsal, I played it cool without the staff I was laboriously whittling. During the performance proper I was able to deliver a whack so mighty that Robin described an arc from the gym plank, bumped the yellow doughnut side and slid into the six-inch water, staining his lower self green from the home-dyed ex-mum tights that were the standard costume of all the male cast. Only pride was injured.

The only other time that violence surfaced in those tender years was on my way home one afternoon, in an argument with Johnny Tyler – a bit of a wide lad who lived up the hill on Oakleigh Gardens. He started throwing bits of gravel while retreating uphill, where he turned round and started lobbing horse turds, freshly delivered for his dad's roses, in my direction. I reacted like a Gurkha caught in an Indonesian cross-fire, downed satchel and charged young Tyler with my recorder, wrapped in a yellow duster, awhirl in kukri fashion, bringing it down on his head. This caused it to shatter into three lengths, ending my musical career.

I grew, my progressive height notched in pencil marks on the kitchen door frame. A larger bicycle was saved for, a Hercules of 24-inch wheels with a Sturmey Archer hub, three gears and built-in lighting dynamo. I could go for ever on this machine and stay out after dark. The world widened to take in the back lanes of Kent and Surrey. Toys were there for dismal days, winter weekends for a Hornby OO model railway and Airfix kits that occupied my father more than me. A colleague from his office used to come regularly at Easter and play with him at it, bearing lots of exotic rolling stock and track in magic navy-blue Meccano cardboard boxes. It got too complex with the remote switches, timetables and signals. All I wanted to do was to put little lead people on the tracks and derail the whole Flying Scotsman.

My cousin on my mother's side, another David, was a quasi-hero of mine, seven years older than I. He was always prepared to take me out and teach some outdoor skill. With him, I conquered the fear of small boats on the North Sea on a choppy day. And I vividly remember a pre-teen holiday in Whitstable when he had come by a giant Buick ex-army staff car and he took me to Dreamland, Margate. At that time the amusement park was still in its infancy and by today's standards the rides were tame. We rode everything vaguely daring – spiders, crabs, tea cups, roller-coaster, dodgems and racing cars. Stuffed full of greasy food and candy floss, sickened on Tizer and cream soda, we finally got back around midnight. I felt ill for days but that thrill from dangerous rides stays lurking like a residual case of jungle rot. Every time I pass a fair or amusement park I want to dash in and soak up the atmosphere. The cheap rush, the painted scrubber birds that hang out, the magic of pulsing rock beat from the rides, the smells of unhealthy, smouldering grease, the edge, allure, and danger are all there. I often think that I should have run off and joined the metaphorical circus.

Primary school had been a doddle. We had no homework. I did just enough work in class to stay in the bottom half of the top stream, stayed out of trouble, loathed the lunches but went back for seconds. Suddenly I was ten and the dreaded eleven-plus exam came. I scraped by. At the end of the summer of 1955 I was to start the daily six-mile journey to Chislehurst and Sidcup Grammar School for Boys.

I got my first passport that summer. The photo shows me in a new school blazer, *Eagle* club and Ian Allen Loco Spotters badges on the lapel, grinning foolishly at W. P. Marchant's high-street studio plate camera. Britain was starting to go through an economic boom, and my pocket money had now reached the staggering wealth of a guinea a month.

It was time to get out of shorts into long, grey flannels, the work of growing up was at hand. That was probably my father's idea in taking me on a fortnight's tour of the Benelux countries after the eleven-plus exam results came in. It was a travelling lesson in simple things; catching foreign trains and buses, not being put off by strange people or their tongues, packing and unpacking, budgeting – the basics of how to get by abroad. He was a good guide. We ate at all his favourite haunts where previously his firm had footed the bill; he coughed up for both of us, with no looking at the prices on the menu first. I got to meet his foreign colleagues and their children and go round sundry glucose and corn-starch factories. We went on harbour cruises, canal *rondfaart*, to the opera, and to see old masters which I was too young to appreciate. The best was the miniature city of Madurodam outside the Hague, with trains and ships, trams and

21

street lights, acres of miniaturized reality, ticking like a perfect model-railway set.

The hour-long flight home, my first international hop, was mind-blowing. A couple of years previously, at the Biggin Hill open day, we had taken to the air in an antique De Havilland Rapide twin-engine biplane. It had a nine-seater cabin, but you could still sense the thrill of flying as the wind whistled through the wing-bracing wires. For ten minutes we circled the aerodrome, passing almost over our back garden. I was not sick or frightened, and we all went home pleased.

As first-formers we had to sit blazered and capped all the way home on the 51 bus, ensconced on or as near as possible to the upper back seats, the discomfort eased with chocolate bananas, honeycomb bars and bottles of Tizer. We thought we were veritable hooligans, throwing caps and smoking the odd cigarette, but by today's graffiti-writing, Evostik-inhaling standards, we were nearly angels. Anyway, a prefect who dared to reprimand or report someone or issue a detention for a minor infringement could end up as unsympathetic NCOs and officers did in Vietnam; fragged. The *Lord of the Flies* element was only a millimetre under the surface.

The following year I was allowed to take a Saturday job, the proceeds spent on a pukka full-size (26-inch wheels, cable brakes) bike. Henceforth there would be no more bus passes, but an allowance of 12 shillings a term maintenance along with an allocated slot in the cycle sheds. Already I had earned money in the summer picking fruit for backbreaking wages. On a good day a ten-year-old could make as much as two pounds. The best chocolate bar was only sixpence, a Dinky Toy five shillings and Tizer ninepence a quart. The easiest picking was apples, the fallen ones, which went for cider and jam. Unseen wasps were the set-back. Berries and currants stained your fingers as deeply as the nibbed wooden pens had at school.

The attraction of the Saturday job around the corner at the Co-op butcher's was that most of the work consisted of pedalling a bike around in the morning, delivering meat to those customers prepared to give tips. The bike was enormous, uncomfortable, with a huge basket built into the frame over the smaller front wheel. Gearless, it had to be pushed up even a shallow hill, and became my challenge in training.

Cycling had become more than a hobby, it was an obsession, an escape to wider horizons, actively encouraged by my parents.

Weather permitting, I spent every spare hour on the road, pumping resolutely along. Most of my local friends preferred loafing about on a piece of greensward under an oak tree. I kept a diary, carefully noting all the mileage accrued during the day and week. The yearly tally was similar to that done in a small family saloon today. There was no more attendance at school sports – rugby in the winter, cross-country in the spring, cricket, tennis or swimming in the summer. Instead, every Wednesday after lunch I was allowed to pedal off. Remarkably, I did not skive off, but pushed myself to my limits, getting to the south coast and back by dinner, habitually served at seven o'clock just after my father got back from work. Wednesdays were the day of the week when a chop and two veg always graced the table. Thursdays, liver; Fridays, fish. My mother had a fixed pattern and exotica did not enter the menu, though Mondays often were curry – or the British concept of it then – using leftover beef from the Sunday joint, diced apple with dried fruit and raisins. I was ill-prepared for the hot rush served in the subcontinent a few years later. I consumed everything, I was famished and growing.

From eight in the morning to mid-afternoon I slugged the trademan's bike around Farnborough Common, Chelsfield, Green Street Green and Cudham. Afterwards I stayed on at the butcher's scrubbing blocks, sweeping out the shop and finally swabbing the 14-foot-square freezing cold room out. When it was done, all the globs, blobs and bone-chipped blood puddles swept into one heap, coagulated with sawdust, I could go home, knackered. An ordinary Saturday saw me five pounds in pocket; Christmases with extra time put in plucking, gutting and making sausages earned me £25 for a couple of days' abhorrent work. The tips added up to £10 or £12. I had enough for a month on the road in Europe. Dutifully I gave 10 shillings to my mum, usually accompanied by whatever bits of offcuts or sausages I had salvaged with the permission of either Frank, the manager, or Arthur, his assistant.

I got on well with Frank and Arthur. Arthur's stories still haunt me. He had spent the war as a POW building the Japanese railway in Burma. His health was much impaired by it, although he always had a Woodbine burning at the back of the shop and a cup of tea to hand. Apart from two schoolmasters and my father, he was the first man I knew as a friend. Over the years that I was away, Frank and Arthur enquired almost daily about my progress around the globe, my mother often dropping in for a chat even when not buying meat. Frank has retired, still phoning my mother at Christmas. The Co-op closed and is now a tacky chain store. I still have an endearing image of Frank in a striped apron, arms crossed, standing outside the clean façade ruddily smiling.

Chislehurst and Sidcup was a radical school where new approaches to teaching bright boys were tried out. I was only bright enough to stay in the B grade near the bottom of the form, I scraped through exams and loathed homework as an impingement on my time to read and cycle. Geography was the only subject in which stardom was possible; the year I took my GCEs, 1960, I had one of the highest scores in the country. Cartography was my forte; the European and British maps, abstract to most classmates, were a reality that I had pedalled or hiked over. The geography master also took us on the official school ski trips every Christmas. I went two years in a row.

Art was encouraging, the master there gave me free rein, but I had to drop the subject. My maths needed more attention. French classes were entertaining, the comfortable teacher spent many lessons instructing us how to make baguettes, choose wines and order from menus rather than getting on with past irregular tenses and weird genders. He tolerated the foursome at the back of the class who continually masturbated whenever possible. A Mr Lovell tried to imbue us with religious knowledge but had no control over the class or the subject, his only defence was to rush to the back of the room and rap the wankers over the backs of their hands with a steel ruler. I don't think he believed in what he taught and digressed easily into foreign culture and philosophy. I wrote poems for assigned work and got awarded high marks, to my surprise. The German master looked like Hitler but smelled of delicious pipe tobacco. Everything got sent to the end of the sentence, but German made more sense than algebra and was to come in handy very soon.

Mr Side taught us physics with a skill that let me understand the nature of mechanics, of optics, the mysteries of the toys that fascinate. We learned about balance, pressure, leverage, what made things work; more importantly, we were told about solipsism. He was a freethinker and threw open the class to philosophical discussion. His instruction more than any other demonstrated that education should teach how to learn for yourself. I had the lowest consistent marks in the class, the maths failed me, but I invented a simple electro-magnetic uncoupler for model trains which earned full marks.

24

As I grew into puberty girls ceased to be merely inferior opposites to lob gooey things at on the bus. I started to have crushes on certain regulars who waited at the same stop daily on their way to our sister school, but it got no further than exchanges of looks. Whatever energy there was to consume was put through the chain drive of the Campagnolo gears hanging on the rear sprocket of a 27-inch Mafac-rimmed bicycle wheel.

I remember nothing of my first sexual dream, only the awakening to a sticky mess in my sleeping bag at Hastings Youth Hostel in Fairlight on the Rye road. I was twelve. I did not capitalize on this revelation until over a year later, due, I recollect, to the embarrassment that I would suffer should my mother discover the telltale stains. It was an era before Kleenex. I was neither furtively off to the loo for a quick pull nor an overt back-of-the-class stroker. There was never any question of not knowing what it was about but the most erotic stuff I saw were lingerie ads in the Sunday papers or grainy slides in biology class.

The first gropes, not orgasmic, were at fourteen, unfulfilling but narcotic, even when practised on cold, rainy nights in unlit alleyways. The moment my cherry disappeared was blurred out. So many summer afternoons, then winter evening and weekend cider parties happened, where we would all be pseudo-exposed, entwined on couches or the floor of someone's house when their parents were out. The moment of penetration and orgasm never became a defined event. The second one did, I peed instead of climaxing. A sodden mess which had to be cleaned up before my folks got home. Fiona, the poor girl, still saw me, until an older boy snatched her away in a car. The crushed love of a fifteen-year-old.

With passport and youth-hostel card, I had licence to travel. The first circuit, during my thirteenth summer, was with a group of fellow bike freaks from the fourth form around Belgium, Holland, Germany, Luxembourg and France. We covered 400 miles in three weeks without mishap. We all shone in French orals the next term and proved that you could live on wurst, *frites* and milk.

The next summer, my fourteenth, set the tone for the future. I did an endurance run of 2500 miles in just over five weeks, with one companion. A short, wire-rimmed, pebble-spectacled but tough kid, Rex was later to race the circuits in France for a living. For our age it was a masterpiece of logistic planning, no parental help. We booked the Newcastle to Bergen ferry, youth hostels for every night between Bergen and Ostend, and the ferry to Dover. The bikes were primed and each carried a spare wheel and two tubeless roll-on spare tires besides chains, sprockets, cables and assorted special tools designed to adjust the expensive machinery we bestraddled. Everything was stowed in two panniers and a saddlebag. From Bergen we crossed the mountains to Oslo and cycled to Stockholm, Copenhagen, Lübeck, Hamburg, Bremen, Oldenburg, Groningen, and across the polders to Amsterdam. I was still walking round somewhat robotically, legs bowed, when the new term began.

I was inclined to leave school and take to the open road, but had not a clue what kind of life or line of work I wanted to pursue. I scraped along, getting passes except in maths, late on homework but never playing hookey, hardly a day sick. Bored and emergently horny, like every other fifteen-year-old schoolboy in the world.

Rock and roll was stirring. Radio Luxembourg could be scratchily tuned in, the Everly Brothers, Buddy Holly and Fats Domino had superseded skiffle and trad jazz. Rhythm and blues ruled my beat, perfect accompaniment to sexual stirrings. My father, owner of 2000 classical records with the latest valved hi-fi to play them, forbade the use of his equipment to play my burgeoning collection. 'Little Bitty Pretty One', 'Blueberry Hill', 'Dream Lover', 'Summertime Blues' – the best of certain fifties songs still stop pulses and chills. The rush of realization, the chrysalis cracking open.

I was becoming a dire wanker, my looks not improved by the orthodontic brace on my upper teeth. Gawky and prone to using my father's hair gel for quiffing, constantly picking at dirty nails with broken matchsticks, I shot up. The handlebar stem and saddle pillar on the Holdsworth lengthened, a 25-mile time trial was over in just over the hour, the 50 in two ten. On the one-and-a-half-mile circuit I placed last, unable to get my feet in the toe straps until the pack was half a mile away, Instead, I started cyclocross but I finished 47th out of 137 in a 250-mile road marathon.

Having a good time, the consumption of any available liquor became obligatory. We were too young to consume legally in pubs but beyond the suburbs publicans were lax provided you didn't throw up by the dart board. Brown and mild, rough cider, blackcurrant and rum at Christmas.

Grinding up to O levels was hard work, outside temptations lured constantly. I failed all but two of my mocks in November 1959. Cramming was left until the final three weeks the following summer before we were sequestered in the school hall for a week of life-decisive testing. I was sure I had done miserably in everything but geography and the English essay. The results would not be known until way into the summer holidays. Depending on those results, I would graduate to the lower sixth or be another candidate for the job market, still with no idea of what line of employment to take.

That summer, 1960, was a fine one. The parents gave permission for a hitch-hiking and camping trip to Italy. My companion, Bob Baker, and I had become bored by the pedals' speed and range, so, rucksacks draped with primus stove, sleeping bag and tent, we thumbed off to Dover. Continental Europe was a soggy camping experience, living on barely warmed food out of greasy aluminium pans. The tent was damp to put up and stow away. We warmed ourselves with cheap, legally purchased schnapps and wine, bloating our guts on stolen fruit from wayside orchards while awaiting lifts. After a week we were in Italy. We had not been molested, the rides had not left us stranded at autobahn cloverleafs. South of Milan we split up, Bob towards Rimini, I towards Genoa.

We had not quarrelled or fought, we both probably imagined we could have a better time solo. Though I had the tent I used it only three nights of the remaining ten. Two British servicemen let me share their camper for three days, a lost younger brother. I was picked up by a young Italian woman on the outskirts of Ventimiglia. That was a romantic score and she drove me out of Turin onto the St Bernard road two days later, sated with home cooking, clean clothes and ravished body.

The next lift was from a trio of middle-aged nouveau riche Sardinians. The myth of Latin women, or at least their infatuation with young northern lads, continued to the Swiss side of the Alps. The next driver was a gay German in a new Porsche Spyder, which he even let me drive. He wined and dined me in splendour and I saw my first hardcore porno pictures, Gestapo-clad male troilisms. My fifth-form Deutsch was strained repelling his less and less subtle advances. I abandoned ship outside Saarbrücken in the pouring rain, leaving the kinky Kraut to zoom back to Hamburg. The adventure dulled, funds gone, I fell in with an English family of five crammed into a Ford estate car. They were doing the continent on the cheap. Canned sausages, baked beans, fried bread, endless tea was the fare until they dropped me at the bottom of the drive two days later. Ten pounds had bought a

27

seventeen-day, six-country holiday. Bob reappeared the next week with other tales of teenage self-discovery.

To my surprise I had passed all my O-level GCE exams except maths, with distinction in English, history and geography. I entered the sixth form, where the boys had the privilege of wearing a sports coat and not wearing a cap when coming or going to school. I developed a vague notion of entering a profession to do with trees or forest products, maybe after reading Orwell's accounts of being a forestry officer in Burma. To this end I wanted to do botany, Swedish and cartography as my three A levels, but they lumped me with English, German and geography. School soon became untenable.

I plotted a way out without really consulting my folks. How would I get to Burma with no qualifications? I sent away to the Forestry Commission, who replied that maths was required but I could join them at a practical level working in the woods for a year and a half before going to a special forestry college in Aberystwyth or Aberdeen. By now even the thought of homework was too regimenting. Most friends had jobs, money, motorcycles, girlfriends. Fifties giddiness was over, the progressive sixties had dawned and I wanted part of the action.

My mind was not in the classroom, it was out in the street, on the road. Alcohol habitually made Monday morning German class or biology lab a throbbing nightmare. I made an appointment for an interview with a forester who ran Commission lands along the North Downs, based on a yard near the top of Pol Hill, three and a half miles from home. I took the day off from school without asking, my first ever truancy. Mr Vickery, the forester, promised to take me on the following week. At school the next day I was summoned to the headmaster's office – another first. The head, a puffy, red-faced man named Pedley, insisted on an explanation for the day's absence. My reply was that I was leaving. He told me to stick out my hand for six of the best. He delivered one and I retreated, my stinging palm pointed at the little, balding man, and said, 'One more fucking stroke and I'll wrap that cane round your bloody head.'

He said, 'You're expelled.'

I left then and there. The sixties were barely in first gear but the pattern was hewn: I had dropped out.

Work was bloody hard. For ten-hour days, five-day weeks, with optional fire-watching summer weekends at double time, the wage was £4. Everyone except the gangers and the district officer worked piece rates. For every hundred oaks planted, we got four shillings, every sack of larch stuck out, ten; in summer it went by the acreage we weeded in spring, chains of fence installed, ditching dug or pre-teen trees brashed (that is the lower branches trimmed to head height down the rows). Everyone buried hundreds of young plants in specially dug holes or would use their planting spades to make an extra large slit and pop one or two oaks in the slot before leaving one healthy one perfectly planted. Except for planting there were no scams. During the summer, as we weeded the bracken and brambles from around the baby trees, barely more than a foot high, we would pick the delicate wild strawberries which even then fetched 25 shillings a pound in Maidstone market.

Our normal ganger, Charlie, turned a blind eye to the alternative activities and joined in, whereas the other ganger would putter up unexpectedly on his BSA Bantam. Ron the ferret would skulk nearly out of vision, checking for plants buried, saplings amputated, shortchange us on the chainage measured and then dock our tickets. In Vietnam he would have been fragged; here his brakes were loosened, tyres deflated and tank doctored. On my first day at work he issued me with an unwieldy, blunt fire axe to clear out scrub for replanting. For three days I struggled with this impossible tool, never making my day rate, until fellow workers lent me a spare and showed me how to use a honing stone. The gang laughed at my blisters and childlike ways, but in weeks I was as tough as the rest, proud wearer of heavy gumboots and an ex-army jacket topped with an Aussie campaign hat.

In the winter we had to check in at 6.45 to start work at 7 a.m., in the summer everyone was on the job at 6.30. We slaved until four in the winter and 4.30 when the days grew longer. Only a typhoon would stop play; drizzle, which penetrated every layer of clothing, was simply tolerated. My mother got up before me and made a classic lumberjack breakfast of eggs, bacon, fried potatoes, porridge, tea and toast before getting my father off on the 7.10 train to Cannon Street. I left on my bicycle with three thermoses, an oxo sandwich box, sausages and apples stuffed in an army pack.

The rest of the gang, except for Fred, waiting for his retirement, were in their late teens and early twenties. All came from within a radius of a few miles and commuted on motorcycles. Paul, fifteen, came on the pillion of his brother's 1953 250cc BSA. That machine radically altered my life expectancy. I bought it for £20, reluctantly strapping L plates back and front, although well hidden around the suspension units. By this time, all the local lads I hung out with had divided into mods or rockers, translated as lovers of scooters or bikes. Bikers wore heavy gear, leathers, Barbours and boots; the scooter crowd posed about in duffle coats and suedes. Back then it was not obligatory to wear a helmet. I did. Usually.

Getting to work was a dream now, a five-minute ride, though often the Beezer was a bitch to kick into life. Once it burst into flames at the yard, when the ancient electrics shorted out over the flooded carburettor with myself astraddle. Another co-worker, Bob, three years older, ex-public school, doing the same training I was, had a Triumph Tiger 500cc machine and weekends went sidecar grass tracking on a home-made rig. He took me along occasionally riding the chair as monkey. There was no money to get into it seriously, nor for my other passion, scrambling, although I spent weekends standing at cold, muddy circuits all over the south-east. We went to the Dragon Rally in north Wales in the depths of winter, with over 1000 bikes thundering around the Welsh lanes at night. Tucked in behind the dustbin, streamliner fairing, we came down the just opened M1 at nothing less than a ton up, blown to a 45-degree angle by the cross-wind when coming out of underpasses. Only two Jaguars passed us. My bicycles were forgotten in the quest for speed.

Saturday lunchtime dad habitually went down to a local pub in Green Street Green, half a mile away, for a couple of pints with his mates from the fire-service days. The Saturday of 7 October 1961 was like all others. I had speeded through my meat round on the motorized wheels and got home early. My father, running late, asked for a ride down the Green. We rushed out, carelessly not grabbing our helmets, and rode down to the pub. I dropped him off and wheeled off home. I got halfway back. The next thing I remember is waking up in Scott Ward of Orpington Hospital, very painfully, every limb seemingly immobile, my head feeling as though a bomb had gone off inside it.

I had been puttering along at between 20 and 30 miles per hour, the weather fine, wind in my face, a perfect day to be out, two wage packets in my pocket, a roast-beef lunch waiting on the table. Evidently a fool had decided to hook a right turn across my bows, no signal, no warning. I had gone straight into the left side of the car and had been dragged 15 yards under my mangled 285-pound machine. My hip ground into the asphalt, my left hand entwined in the brake and choke levers and handlebar and was hamburgered. The main problem was my head, which had hit the road at a velocity of nearly 100 miles per hour, slashing a length from temple to topknot out of my skull, parting the temporal artery. It was a gusher; seven pints of blood spurted before an off-duty surgeon on his way home from Farnborough Hospital pulled up and put his thumb on the mainline. He held it there during the half-mile ride to Orpington Hospital in the back of a passing minivan. The saving graces were the heavy gloves and leather jacket I was wearing. Without the gloves they would have had to amputate my left index finger.

They passed me full blood for twenty four hours, a drip feed for two more days, and then unplugged me to go to the toilet for my first crap in what seemed like a month. I swam nervously upright, nurses standing back encouragingly, put my legs over the side of the bed slowly, took one pace forward and described a perfect arc straight into the floor. The admitting casualty-room folks had been so worried about my precarious DOA (dead on arrival) status, head open, that they hadn't bothered to X-ray more than the obvious damage, simultaneously putting on clamps and getting out the sewing kit. My left hip was on fire.

I came round, aware of my mum and dad holding my hands, but it was very blurred. I slipped under again, to be reawoken by a probing flashlight as someone pulled up my eyelid checking for signs of life. Then black again. I woke later to a bedside of sympathetic friends and girls who had never given me a second glance prior to the wreck. There were flowers, sweets, illicit cigarettes, magazines, even a couple of bottles of stout. After the statutory half-hour visiting period, I was left bemused by the attention, feeling changed in a way I would not comprehend for many years.

I had died. I lived. I had seen the tunnel. It was black. It was nothing. There was no light at the end. There was no afterlife. Nothing religious about any of it. And it did not seem scary. It was a long, flowing, no-colour wave which just disappeared. The mystery was partly resolved, all the fearful church propaganda took on its true, shameful meaning. I was content. I was alive, I was not dead, and it seemed very clear, very free. This was the dawning, the overture to losing a responsible part of my psyche. A liberation happened at that intersection. Anything from here on would be free time, a gift from the gods.

Recovery was a drawn-out affair. I fainted when my left hand was unwrapped from its bandage. It was a purplish, red and black stitched mess with the fingers at odd angles. The index finger looked like something seen run over on the motorway, the odd bit of bone visible. I was issued crutches, too short but free, courtesy of the NHS. Bored with the food and the short visiting hours – shared between my parents and the hardcore friends, especially two fifteen-year-old girls, Terry and Lynne – I got myself discharged sooner than the staff wished, with admonishments not to miss therapy.

The hospital had omitted to teach me to climb stairs. I was installed on a divan in the dining room downstairs at the back, overlooking the garden. Accrued sick pay purchased a powerful portable radio, Luxembourg blared around the clock. Visitors came by after work, after school, it became a regular party. My parents retreated to the front room and a new 12-inch black and white TV. My mother would always cautiously knock before entering to count the heads for the inevitable cuppa. Terry took to dropping by every afternoon on her way home from the girls' grammar. She would often stay for dinner. I bought an autochange Dansette record player on which we religiously listened to Eddie Cochran, Fats Domino and the Everlys; we even had a jazz collection of Brubeck, Mulligan and the MJQ. With great contortions we performed the heaviest petting in a high-backed chair, broken hip notwithstanding, dodgy hand at elbow's length. The bar fire was inches away, scorching exposed portions. We could not be seen within the confines of the chair's wings. There were some spectacularly excruciating orgasms besides a selection of interruptuses when a tea mission dropped in. In the period vernacular, we were going steady. We were birds of a feather, both of us adopted. She had been adored by her father, a war cripple, and resented by her mother, who later bore a younger brother. Her father had committed suicide and she had found him. She was out of a home, out of love. We sensed deep things in each other, together we could run free. She stayed by me right through the four-month recovery.

Except for a drunken topple onto a wine glass at a Christmas binge, requiring four stitches to the left elbow, I was fit enough to go back to light duties at the Forestry Commission. A new machine, a blue and chrome-tanked 250cc AJS, was leased on a promised settlement from the insurance claim. Before that Christmas we had been summonsed to Bromley magistrates' court where the driver – I never got his name – was found guilty of driving without due care and attention. Fined £20, suspended six months' jail sentence. The damages had yet to be haggled out.

Pegging chestnuts, fixing fences, I was let off the seasonal clearing and planting jobs. I took days off, meeting Terry, who skipped school. We took the AJS or walked in the woods, made love on the damp spring grass, laughed a lot, never mentioned the future. I was back on the job proper after six weeks but had no compulsion about doing it; the whole rigmarole of getting up at an ungodly hour around the year for minimal money had no more appeal. The career which had been vaguely mapped out held no real attraction, a slog towards a faded goal. I needed space, time to think.

I went absent, got on the AJS and headed north, sleeping bag and tent on the carrier. All the way to Yorkshire, where failing light and nine hours' riding left me thinking of pitching camp, it had poured down. Towards the end of the afternoon, at a tea stop, another biker pulled over and we teamed up, finding a barn to crash in. We travelled north for two days, circling back through the Lakes before heading for his parents' place in Glamorgan. I stayed for three days down there, an in-country R & R. It was March 1962. In an early-morning thick, patchy fog I set off for Kent. I got as far as the Neath roundabout, which I mounted at 50 miles per hour, grinding to a halt, front wheel hub deep in mud in the centre of the obstacle, spotted too late. The bike was a mess, a nasty dent in the front wheel, twisted bars. I somersaulted 40 feet and sprained my right thumb. I walked away and started hitch-hiking.

I was not going home. I intended to go stay with a mate from the Forestry who lived with his wife in Sevenoaks, and call Terry to come down. I needed to rap it out with her, for a week earlier she had announced she was two months pregnant. I was stunned and slapped her. The thought of children was totally unreal. She was fifteen, I seventeen. The biking R & R had made it all too clear; run, leave home, ditch the whole caboodle.

Terry convinced me to take her with me. Picking up a new youth-hostel card, a couple of bits of camping gear, I paid a visit to the post office to get whatever was stashed: a total of £8 12s. I packed a duffle bag, Union Jack on top, folding in my Barbour motocross suit, gum boots – for I believed I could get agricultural work in Holland – the tent and sleeping bag still rolled up from Wales. The following morning Terry and I took the 51 bus from Orpington Hospital bus stop to Crittalls Corner, a fourpenny ride.

With due respect and loving consideration, I left on the kitchen table, for my mum, who had gone shopping, the following note:

Dear Parents

Am leaving home for Europe and perhaps navy and hence the world. Don't know how long I shall go for.

Pay back bike from birthday money and also money for possible fine from accident in South Wales.

You would not understand the reason for going, do not contact authorities as I shall write periodically. Don't worry about me.

TIM

PS Pay postage on parcels and cancel driving test.

2

Journey to the East

Terry and I got a lift within five minutes of sticking out our thumbs, 100 yards from the 51 bus stop. Two rides took us all the way to Dover in time for a late-afternoon ferry to Ostend. We were segregated in separate dorms at the Bruges Youth Hostel, having taken the train that far, sick of waiting for a lift in a Belgian drizzle. The plan was to get to Rotterdam and cadge our way on board a ship bound for South America, a Conan Doyle-inspired destination. If not South America, anywhere. We were too naïve not to believe we would be taken on. Terry had done dance classes so the pregnancy was not obvious.

We hung out together in bars and cafés down by the port for a couple of days unsuccessfully trying to catch a sea-going officer's eye. Then I tried it alone with no more luck. The camping *platz* was surrounded by autobahn, cold and hard, our money was disappearing whiling away time in the bars. It was a miserable start to a great plan, our tempers short after sleepless nights crammed into a single sleeping bag fully clothed. We were down-at-heel runaways fast becoming hungry. We took the train to Amsterdam and checked in at the hostel there where things were more liberal; cohabitation and a kitchen open round the clock.

There we were put on to the student employment office. I had to lie about my age, but two days later we both had bottom-of-the-ladder jobs at the Academica Hotel. I was downstairs tending an enormous washing-up machine, Terry upstairs cleaning rooms.

We moved out of the hostel the next week, life took a turn for bliss. I even bought a second-hand Bromfijte moped.

The honeymoon lasted a little over a month, before we were unceremoniously handcuffed on the job and marched out to a

35

green and white Opel police car to be whisked down to the central jail. Thrown into solitary, stone-floored, iron-walled cells neither of us had a clue what was going down. For the next thirty-six hours I had no communication with anyone except the trusty who pushed a food tray through the door slot. Claustrophobia dripped from the graffiti-scratched walls. People screamed and bellowed from the other tanks, banging doors and walls. The only light was behind a heavy wire grille beyond reach.

Late the next afternoon the cell door opened and I was invited to accompany the warders. I was given back my shoelaces, belt, watch and odd pocket possessions. I was free. It transpired that Terry's mother had put pressure on the authorities and they had got us on the technicality of being underage without work permits. My father had vouched for me, though I was still underage at just turned eighteen, but Terry was shipped off in chains back to the care of an aunt in Hertfordshire to wait out the pregnancy. Mrs Bird could never bear to see her daughter free or happy.

I returned to the hotel, free to stay with my parents' blessing. Although I had not been in contact until the arrest, I was to see my father once when he came on business to Holland. That time, I was able to wine and dine him after a long run to Arnhem to visit World War II battle sites.

Free, I worked my butt off overtime. The management rewarded my enthusiasm with better positions and I graduated to sous-chef. I dug the cooking, and the chief chef, Kookije, spent hours improving my culinary vocabulary. Within weeks I had an old 350cc Matchless motorbike set up for motocross, a 1950 maroon Morris Oxford, and shared a large room in a young couple's flat with Don, a Dutch guy. Having no licence and no clue how to drive, I had a Canadian girl drive the £20 banger out of the lot back to the apartment. The following weekend, an Israeli and I biked down to Antwerp and bought Belgian *permits internationale de conduire* for bikes, cars and trucks. We were fully qualified by the Automobile Association of Belgium for the gross sum of 80 francs. In my first week of driving, unable to find reverse, I had to resort to pushing the car out of its parking slot before taking off experimentally around the surrounding quiet, suburban streets. Amsterdam is luckily flat and had few traffic lights; the only danger was bicycles and trams. Within ten days I could brave rush-hour downtown; in another ten I was making courier runs to Paris in vehicles bought for one round trip. The spare tyre came back full of 30 kilos of prime Moroccan hashish.

When the settlement from my motorcycle accident the previous year arrived from the guilty driver's insurance company, £783 6s 3d, I opened my first bank account in the Nederlandse Handels Maatschapij. The first cheque went to the export department of Volkswagen. The Kombi bus was picked up in Krefeld a week later, but due to my misunderstanding and a goof-up between the Dutch and the Germans, I was not issued the triptyque carnet, the international tax-free car papers which went with the white oval Z plates. Lack of papers was to be the bugbear of the next year and a half.

At the hotel an Israeli studying naval architecture at Dordrecht had a brother Michal who was a radio operator on the ZIV lines ships about to go into German ports for the first shipments of reparations to the Jews since World War II. We drove off following the tramp steamer along the coast, buying second-hand BMW motorcycles at good prices, passing them to Daniel on board, falsifying the dockets of purchase price. Import tax in Israel was running at 600 per cent. He made sure we got some nice Lebanese honey-gold hash for our trouble. The fights the crew got into with the first Germans they had ever seen, we steered clear of. On a trip to London to score more machines when the boat picked up Centurion tanks, I saw Terry in Harlesden, slept in the VW truck when her aunt threw me out, but deliberately did not go home, though I drove past the house to check it out. It hurt all the way back to Dover; the Channel easing the pain with distance.

This was the time of the beginning of the Provo movement, a forerunner to the yippie radical groups to come on line elsewhere in the late 1960s. There were the Kerouacs like Jan Kramer and Simon de Vinkenoog, the architect Theo Niemeyer who went on to design Brasilia, a whole sub-society of hipped-out artists and professionals. They started the white-chimney programme for cleaner air, white-bicycle plan for free bikes, white-virgin scheme, whereby all girls could get the pill; they got on the town council; theirs were the voices heralding the revolution in the offing. The rock 'n' roll beat was picking up; cool jazz reverberated around the bars off the Zeedijk in the red-light area. I was learning to swim a completely new stroke, reality had dissolved into a stoned, subconscious state. People came and went on mysterious missions to exotic parts, returning with strange potions and higher yarns. The Dutch government had virtually legalized soft drugs but frowned on trafficking.

*

I had fallen under the spell of a quixotic Australian Jewish guy, Steve, a jazz drummer who had dropped out of the *West Side Story* touring troupe via Melbourne and America. His main claim to fame when I met him was the old corncob pipe he smoked his dope in, which he said Dizzy Gillespie had bestowed on him. The thing was old enough, with a hole burned in the base of the bowl. Steve used to block it up with a thumb when he fired up, and turn it round, blasting you shotgun style, his mouth over the glowing bowl. Guaranteed orbit. When someone we knew got busted on the Belgian border, the grapevine alerted the survivors. It was time to bug out.

Steve convinced me we should head for Switzerland to work out the winter. I would pay the gas, the truck was mine; he had no money but he had the stash.

In a Klosters chalet pension, late at night, drinking thick Swiss chocolate, Steve offhandedly said, 'Let's drive to Australia for Christmas.' It was mid-October 1962, we had no map and no vaccination shots, much less visas or insurance. I agreed.

The next morning we skipped out of the hotel bill and sped down to Zürich to transfer my funds from the Amsterdam bank, a grand total of £135. We hoped it would be enough for gas, food and smoke for the supposed two-month trip. We were to sleep in the bus, on the rear two bench seats turned facing each other, my Paris fleamarket chest spanning the gap between them. I christened the truck Thérèse and traced our route on the rear panels above the engine grilles; 'Bombay or bust' was scrawled by Steve on the rear bumper. The motor had not even been run in properly.

From Switzerland we drove straight down to Trieste. In Trieste we had to wait for the Yugoslav consulate to open for a visa on the Monday. Steve had been driving when we passed Venice, so my view of the city was one of lights across the lagoon. The autostrada tolls were an unexpected expense.

It was dismal drizzle at the striped-pole gate leading into my first communist country. Mud seemed to besmear everything.

The *autocesta* to Belgrade proved to be a cobbled motorway interrupted by potholes. Night driving was decidedly dangerous with numerous unlit horse-drawn carts and stumbling, drunken peasantry. The onset of winter gave everything a grim proletarian look of despair. The colours were rich and dull, the trees stripped by autumn gales. Southern Yugoslavia had just been hit by violent

38

earthquakes, tremblers still rippled. Skopje was in ruins, digging out, we couldn't even buy bread.

I would have stayed in Greece for a long time: the people were friendly, the food great, the sun shone and no tourists lurked. Steve sold blood; the truck got new vital fluids. Yugoslavia had been a testing ground, now new shock absorbers had to be installed at the back end and sundry electrics replaced. Kavalla on the coast was straight off a postcard. We were parked on the fishing quay, eating *kalamari* from the boats overlooked by the Roman aqueduct, sipping pastel colours, thinking Lawrence Durrell. Near the last township in Greece, Orestias, the road deteriorating, we suffered the first puncture. Awaiting its repair in the village centre we adjourned to the *kantina* getting into a retsina-sampling session. Pissed out of our minds we climbed back aboard, determined to make Istanbul late that night. Two kilometres up the road we stopped to give two Greeks a lift, both dressed in their Sunday finest. They were on their way to a wedding taking place in a hamlet just shy of the Turkish border at Edirne, which we had bad reports of. Steve's minimal Greek endeared us to them and we found ourselves shuttling marriage parties around the northeastern neck of Greece for the next three days, sleeping it off in the truck whenever the party ebbed.

The 19 November 1962 saw my first entry into Asia. Turkey has always seemed a mysterious place inhabited by gollums, more Arab and more Asian than European. The frontier officials in Edirne stamped *Pazakule Nodut Kapisi* over a full page of my passport. Both the Slavs and the Greeks had been more than reasonable about the absence of the triptyque for the car. The Turks demanded vast sums, but after hours of wrangling conceded a passage across their country of no more than ten days – very tight.

On the other side of the frontier pole waited two disconsolate travellers, enormous packs bearing Welsh griffin and Union Jack prominently facing oncoming traffic. They lifted their thumbs, we pulled over, and they asked where we were going. Melbourne for Christmas. They were overjoyed. Ez and Brynn were two of a trio making it overland to Oz. The oldest of them, Jim, had gone to Stamboul to await the others at the renowned travellers' hotel, the Oriental, just off the main bazaar. Jim was their leader, a wiry little ex-RAF corperal, while Ez was a shaggy six-foot drop-out. Brynn a casual, innocent boy destined to teach in a classroom after this one stray down the hip path. Their resources were minimal.

At this time there were no organized overland trek and bus groups, but there were probably some 500 folk underway between Sydney and London, mostly Brits and other Commonwealth citizens, then French, Germans and Americans. I saw double-deckers, *deux chevaux*, scooters, mopeds, London taxis and bicycles creeping east and west. A lot of second-hand Mercedes, Peugeots, VWs and Land-Rovers were bought cheaply in Europe and sold on the black market in Afghanistan or Nepal to pay the drivers' way out and on.

We found the Oriental Hotel in the smog, down a filthy alley with no secure parking. It was a stack of dirty wooden boxes with one communal latrine out back, of the squatter variety, raised above earth-floor level and overflowing. Jim was waiting in the coffee shop which also served as the foyer, kebabs grilled on a fire on the front stoop inundating the whole building with a delicious aroma. Coffee and mint tea served, Steve chased down our floor boy to cop a score. The lad's prices were outrageous but we coughed up for a conker-sized ball of black hash so hard it needed shaving off; the muslin it had been dried in still marked the outer skin. It was opiated Anatolian stuff, we were zonked after the first pipe puffs.

Though the weather was foul, we all fell a little in love with Istanbul. I got lost for hours in the souk. Even common objects seemed really foreign here, often crudely handmade. Manufactured items commanded high prices. Turkey was not yet on the tourist beat and the influx of Turkish *Gastarbeiter* to Germany had not begun. Steve and I bought black leather jackets, having few winter clothes. And we were heading for the Anatolian Plateau; the truck was unpanelled, the heater feeble.

The taxis in Stamboul had ingenious slot record players in the back seats, for which the drivers handed you a stack of 45s to play. Mournful tracks, half belly dance, half rock, angst-ridden in an Islamic way. The same music can be heard throughout the Middle East, even beyond the Indian border. It echoes from coffee shops, truck stops, street corners and every passing vehicle. It is often interrupted by martial announcements, extolling the Muslim ideal.

We ate fish thrown up from the boats beneath the Galata Bridge, grilled fresh on charcoal braziers and sandwiched in pita bread. We ambled up and down the five-and-ten-lira streets, gawping at the painted, obese women, clad in scanty veils, selling themselves for the price of fish and chips back home. We dared each other to have a go, but there were no takers, it was just too sordid. A few more months on the road would change our minds. We checked in at a friendly but useless British consulate to determine conditions ahead. For a finale we went to St Sophia.

There was a service going on in the Blue Mosque. The suffused blue-tinged light heavy with incense smoke, the chants to Allah from the congregation echoing up in the bellied dome, made it ethereally eerie. As in Notre-Dame and other old cathedrals, and later at Angkor, Mandalay Hill, and Kelaniya in Colombo, I felt a nearness to things unexplained. I left feeling light headed, confident and overjoyed with life.

We were the first vehicle on the Bosphorus ferry, mixed in with a handful of cars, horse carts and bicycles. Before leaving Amsterdam, I had bought a small red wooden Buddha in an Indonesian curio shop. When we landed in Üsküdar it had gone. None of us had been more than a few paces from the truck and nothing else was missing. The Buddha had got me to Asia.

A pattern was established: Steve or I driving, a navigator also up front and three people seated around my trunk in the back, keeping the four-extension hookah bubbling. We ground on to grim Ankara, a necessary stop to get an Iranian visa, stuck behind black-belching, overloaded trucks and buses all the way, our carburettor wheezing harder as we climbed. The next few days were an acclimatization to rough winter conditions. We had to leave Turkey before our deadline. The route lay through Sivas, Erzincan and Erzurum to the Iranian frontier. The Asian Highway was but a figment in the minds of the planners, the first survey crews were just starting to theodolite their way over this land. This eastern region of Turkey had not even been properly mapped, much less signposted.

Rounding precipitous, ledged stretches of track, we would find boulders the size of trucks, potholes deep enough to lose a VW Beetle in. There were few signs of habitation, just rock and stones, wandering goats and fat-tailed sheep. We got lost, the road became a path, we forded metre-deep rivers in high spate, got stuck in one river and waited until way after nightfall, wolves howling, for a tow. The last bus on the Erzurum run pulled us out; we dried out the electrics and got to town at three in the morning. We were all smitten by the runs the next day, having consumed the same dross at the bus-station tea stall. Down a long

41

unlit flight of stairs, you could smell the public loo before you spotted it. The locals had ceased trying to get into the stalls or urinals. The floor was a sea of shit, piss and worse, starting at the bottom step. Luckily it was frozen. Only Steve used it and then went off for a ten-minute clean up at the tap behind the bus station. I lost a pair of underpants that day. We just couldn't get out of town quick enough.

Ararat rose on our left flank, Russia was only a few miles away. The area was saturated with military patrols, gruffly stopping the truck every 20 or so miles. There must have been a flap on, but with no functioning radio or newspapers we were oblivious of world events. We spent the tenth night in the dormitory of the Bazargan border post on the Iranian side, where I had to buy £20 worth of tax stamps in lieu of possessing a valid triptyque. The customs official used one page of my passport for a block of beautiful blue and orange imperial peacock-throne stamps plus another two pages of Farsi script permitting a crossing to Pakistan. It took two and a half hours to put it all together, requiring four separate stamps and signatures.

It got warmer and we descended from the hills, the road improving all the way to Tabriz. The bazaar yielded a stinking Afghan waistcoat and an improved hookah. Here we met our sixth crew member, or rather he introduced himself to us. Graham was gay, headed home to Australia with a married couple in a Morris. Well-to-do and with a tendency to leave the party in search of young delight, he was, in his casual smarts, a contrast to us vagabonds. The couple had obviously got sick of his company and abandoned him near the bus station. He had over a thousand pounds with him, and a driving licence. Crammed in, he effectively paid the petrol.

We lived on yoghurt, naan bread and dates. In Isfahan we stopped to service the truck and got so ill that we had to stay for four days, gradually recovering. Somewhat nervously we went sightseeing. The shaking towers did their bit, one wobbling when a person mounted the other minaret 40 feet away. The souk was the most beautiful I had seen, spilling onto a vast piazza faced with a stunning mosque. The city was a dusty oasis with honking traffic and flashing neon. We detoured for a couple of hours to Persepolis before charging off across the high Dasht-e-Lut desert.

You could touch the stars at night; the shooting ones looked like tracers, they were so close. It was so cold that rocks, heated to 130 degrees Fahrenheit in the day, split with battlefield percussion throughout the small hours. I remember the joy of being on the road, the night halt, lying in the sun-warmed sand, staring straight up, the others spread around the truck, the motor ticking as it cooled down. Not a sound save those we had imported, not a soul for miles.

Near Yazd we ran into a sandstorm, an absolute nightmare. It was 110 degrees in the shade. The cloud of sand choked us and powdered everything an inch thick. We could not drive, we could not breathe and we had no water. The roof rack collapsed, forcing all the extra luggage inside. We sat it out in the dark.

When the storm abated, we found ourselves less than a mile from a tea shop and caravanserai. They offered minuscule eggs, unleavened bread, tea and coffee. We had eaten all they had when in walked three individuals looking like brigands. In previous weeks, we had heard foreign travellers' vehicles had been ambushed, their passengers robbed, raped, killed or abandoned. These three dudes in flowing robes, beards and headdresses were travelling in a jeep and the youngest sported a submachine gun, the elders shotguns. They took up residence on a raised shelf at one end of the tea room, ordering tea before opening up an intricately carved chest, the sort of container my mother had her sewing things in. From the box they produced pipes and lamps, needles and odd-shaped tools and a jar of treacly yellow goop. Settled comfortably, they called for charcoal and proceeded to place little bubbling blocks of the goop in the small bowls of the pipes. We sat entranced at our table by the door, six sets of dilated pupils awaiting the outcome. Steve, the sassiest of us, got up and ambled over, sniffed the air and mumbled a guttural, vaguely Arabic-sounding opinion. It was the open sesame. The three brigands turned into benevolent gentlemen and invited us to participate.

It was my first opium. The heady, honey-flavoured smoke was almost creamy, the first toke hot and sickly, then the somnolent ease slipped from end to end of the body and the soul. The earthen surface of the dais floated, no longer hard. Opiated hash just was not the same thing any more. The smoke is as evocative as the smell of frying onions, bacon or coffee. The slightly sickening richness of it promises a mellow, dreamlike voyage.

The sun was setting when we left the adobe hut to continue the 2000-mile desert crossing. The road had a roughly graded, corrugated surface and the dust kicked up by other vehicles hung about for hours. Without so much as a shovel on board our rig, whenever we got bogged down in sand we had to wait for a passing truck to haul us out. We had no accurate map and carried no water. The temperature soared to 140 degrees.

Having heard that petrol was scarce further east and five times pricier in West Pakistan, we bought twenty four-gallon containers of it in Kerman, carpet capital of Iran, and lashed them up on the badly re-welded roof rack. This was theoretically sufficient fuel to get us to New Delhi. Before we had gone 50 miles, the thrice fixed rack collapsed with a sickening thud and stench of leaking petrol. We were obliged to stash the whole lot inside, adding to the space problem. The danger of the charcoal-fired, smouldering hubble-bubble did not occur to us. The leaking four-gallon tins were a joy to empty and abandon. The roof rack is probably still lying out there.

The frontier post at Mirjaveh had leaped out of a page of history: a turn-of-the-century mud fort building with balcony, a couple of slit windows and a barracks with a red and white pole barrier. The surrounding desert is gritty rock, hard rolling plateau. The same parched rocks stretch each way from the Arabian Sea to Tibet; Afghanistan is in between, West Pakistan a mere spur. Innumerable smugglers cross the wastes hereabouts, transporting weapons, gold, hash and heroin. Precious items are often secreted in the humps of camels, done by slicing the fatty tissue, stuffing in the goodies and plopping the dome back down. Camels are said to recover well after this operation and much of the opium then in Iran was smuggled in this way.

It was nightfall before we had cleared the frontier. I had the first spell at the wheel. Before midnight, the stars bright, bumping merrily along, navigator at my side humming, I was suddenly aware of a cliff or mountain dead ahead a few hundred yards. It was like seeing a ghost, it was not supposed to be there. I stopped and we all climbed down and marvelled at the sight of a wall of rock. We then started to search for the road and could not find it. We turned around and headed back four or five kilometres to the highway which, at that point, had taken a sharp, unmarked turn. A missing headlight, courtesy of a Baluchi stone-kicking bus, had not helped.

The first Pakistan town of Nok Kundi served us a boiled egg and chapatti breakfast. On the road again late morning, in the middle of hilly scenery, the temperature over 105, we called a stop at a small tea shop with tables and chairs on the sand by the road. The small community was at a crossroads of caravan traces.

Trails led north towards Afghanistan. Everyone wore grubby pyjamas and acres of dingy blanket cloth with furry hats.

Steve and I sat down and ordered tea. Steve removed his thick, tinted specs and gazed at a speck of dirt on the table, which was very cruddy. With one forefinger he prodded the piece of grit, stabbed it with a blunt finger and raised it to his mouth. I stared as he put it between his teeth and gently chewed. He removed it, held it aloft on a fingertip and, just at the moment that the pyjama-clad boy arrived with a tin tray loaded with glasses of tea, proclaimed, 'Charas!' The boy, astonished, plonked the tray down and scuttled back to the shop. The others from the truck came and sat down. We became aware of a large crowd watching us from inside the building, grinning madly. We were to be raped or pillaged or . . .

A spokesman approached us, beckoning us to follow. We ducked through the front room between rotten-toothed smiles, weapons propped along the walls, curved knives in belts, into the kitchen. The heart of the Urdu cookhouse is its large, earthen tandoori ovens, hive-shaped mounds into which the unleavened breads are slapped to bake. In this furnace room were two such stoves, one traditional, one flat-topped with a girth of four feet, around which stood three bare-chested, sweaty, bearded wildmen. A young boy was acting as gofer. They were busily kneading an enormous brown mass on top of the tandoori. The smell that hit us had the sweetness of the purest hash. Every so often one of the men would pour from an amphora a liberal tot of blood, alternating with one of dust and resin, or summon the boy to ladle in a few scoops of amber desert honey. Their eyes had red spider webs.

We salaamed each other with spontaneous giggling smiles. Another cup of tea was produced, and a long kitchen knife. Cookie then sliced a corner off the steaming loaf, adjusting his cut while chanting rupee figures. For thirty bob we got a chunk the size of an Italian panettone loaf and dense as pumpernickel. Had we had scales they would have tipped at a key and a half. It had to be sampled.

The goat curry with pilau rice we had eaten to appear hospitable was the cause of Ez's finding a cave. It was late afternoon when we got out of the hamlet. We were climbing over rocky spurs, the road curving along precipitous ledges, when Ez had to go. He scrambled up to the side of the road behind a boulder and disappeared. There alongside the 'Ali loves Ahmed' chipped

45

graffiti, were friezes direct from an Athenian museum. We perched in the opening, hundreds of feet above the valley floor, gazing west as the red sun sank into Persia.

In Quetta, the first town of any consequence, we recuperated from the Baluchi cooking drinking endless cups of sweet, dark tea. The second night, feeling stronger, bathed and in clean clothes, we took a stroll down to the street of loose ladies. Amplified Urdu film music blared down from speakers on power poles. The painted, overweight women sat, back-lit by diffuse amber light, behind split stable doors, a classic scene like a Cartier-Bresson study of *putas* in Mexico. A lot of frontier-force army lads cruised the block-long brothel. Graham naturally abstained; Steve, followed by Jim and Brynn, plunged in for a three-bob fling; Ez and I hung back watching our pockets, wishing.

We cruised to Lahore in three days, out of the barren hills to the fertility of the Indus valley. The plains were green, the cane tall, the palms no longer just dates; Scanderbeg's armies had loved it here. We found a munificent palace of a place to stay, the Hotel Lahore, just off the Mall, an establishment which had seen better times during the Raj. The six of us were accommodated in a cavernous ground-floor room, beds surcharged at five rupees per charpoy. These rope-hammock mattresses suspended in a bed frame are the coolest way to sleep in this region but leave a cat's-cradle impression all over the body. They are, however, vermin-free and luckily it was not the season for mosquitoes. Afternoon tiffins in the bar attracted former army officers, mumbling over weak beer and G & Ts. One major had a black panther with jewel-encrusted collar which sat like a piece of Dresden china inside the doors, its owner at the bar chatting on. At the slightest move towards its master the creature's ears pricked up and the fur bristled.

I went to the AA of West Pakistan to verify the carnet requirements for India. A triptyque was necessary. There would be no importation of the VW, however temporary, without a massive deposit or the required vehicle *laisser passer*. We were blocked. Thérèse and I could go no further. The others were free to do what they would.

Graham, the freest and richest, was the first to go. We took him to the railway station. He would fly home from Delhi. Generously he laid 500 rupees on me. The five left took to cheap pursuits, long walks to the Shalimar Gardens, the mosques, the bazaar, the smoke shop. Jim, Brynn and Ez had to move on next.

46

A P & O liner was leaving Bombay on Christmas Eve, and they had tickets. I drove them to the border crossing and gazed longingly across. That left Steve and me. Steve decided to off, money or no. I didn't even bother to drive him out of town. The bugger took off with 150 rupees from the communal fund.

I cried as I moved my few possessions out of the large room to an airless box in a far wing with no toilet, just a tap outside on the flat roof. The hotel made me a deal of 100 rupees per month, for it looked as though I was in for a long wait. Either my father would post a deposit in the UK with the AA or I could try to make a profitable sale of the truck. I felt desperately alone, hungry and 6000 miles from what I had called home. I became something of a feature at the British consulate, daily checking to see whether any letters had arrived from my parents. One rather splendid retired government official took it upon himself to be my patron. Nawob Malik lived in a rambling, run-down old British mansion in Islamia Park, a once exclusive neighbourhood. An old man, in his seventies, with a twinkling eye and Afghan *jinnah* at a jaunty angle, he invited me regularly for superb traditional Punjabi meals, always bestowing a red 100-rupee note on me when I left.

At the receptionist's suggestion I made an appointment with the British trade commissioner. He invited me out to his bungalow on a Saturday to discuss the matter of my vehicle sale. I arrived punctually in the upper-class cantonment, where the streets were clear of rubbish and the verges trim, and pulled into the acre of grounds, manicured into hedges of flowering bushes and palms. Verandahs ran around the house, a pool twinkled through the french windows. A liveried house boy showed me to the back terrace to await the sahib. I had actually shaved, shampooed and put on my best togs, though the desert boots had split open somewhere along the road. After a twenty-minute wait, Her Majesty's government's marketing man strolled out of his study and sat beneath an umbrella at a poolside table, gesturing me to take the other seat in the full sun. Once I was seated, he ordered one beer, a Heineken, which arrived pronto for him to sip, pulled out a pack of State Express, lit one without offering them to me, and asked, 'So what are we going to do?'

Manners maketh man, my folks had always reiterated. I drew out a battered pack of Charminar, the cheapest local smoke, fired one up (and they stank like burning, rotten rope) and blew the cloud at HMG.

His only offer was to repatriate me once I had donated the

47

truck to the local Red Crescent (the Pakistani equivalent of the Red Cross). He told me I would be better off back home, doing something useful or going to college. I got up, leaving the chair where it had fallen, stormed out round the bungalow, jumped in the VW, revved the motor and popped a really neat wheelie circle over his lawn and back into the drive. In my rearview mirror I caught a glimpse of a flapping house boy.

I started selling what few chattels I had. I fell in with a shady lot of merchants in the bazaar who proposed to drive up to the Khyber Pass area. We returned in three days with 200 keys of prime Afghan hash in my fleamarket trunk. They paid for the petrol and the Lahore Hotel got its rent. I got 500 rupees and a brick of goodies; I also got taken to the house of the dancing girls.

Before Christmas I was introduced to an Anglo-Indian family, retired from the army and railways, who lived in a run-down smallholding on the trunk road to India. The Nicholsons had lost their own son and adopted me. Though I kept my rooftop box, I spent more and more time in the spare room, their son's, still full of his toys, gear and kit. We went out hunting snipe and duck in the *geels*, the salt pans northwest of the city, and when I had become learned in the ways of hunting birds, we went out for wild boar in the canebrakes, with single-shot twelve-gauge shotguns. It was not so much for the sport as for the food. The whole extended family and entourage survived on pensions two decades out of touch. Life at 28 May Gardens was one of faded grandeur. They talked continually of the old country but would never get there except in their fantasies. I was made to feel at home and would miss them for a long time afterwards.

Christmas dinner was a lump of cold roast beef and a bottle of local beer; my last dollar went on a bar of Toblerone. The hash brick eroded and then the letter came from home.

My father had put the house up as security for a loan to obtain the triptyque to get the car into India. To get his money back I had to guarantee that the vehicle would leave India intact. In the letter was a square black-and-white snap of two infants in a pram. On the back in Terry's handwriting it said, 'Christopher on the left, Verity on the right. All my love.' I was now the supposed proud parent of twins. The mind boggled. I reached for Dizzy and blew a lazy large cloud of smoke.

It took six weeks to get out of La Whore, as I now called it. I was itchy for the road and my father had been generous enough to

48

send £100, enough, I reckoned, to get me to Bombay, nearly 2000 miles away. I bought the nawab dinner and a beer, and took chocolates and a tin of Capstan tobacco to the Nicholsons for the last dinner. The day before I left, the merchants took me to their favourite fortune teller who, after sharing a shopfront narghile, prophesied that my lines were 'all crazed up' and by five-and-twenty years I would be rich and well-known. The whole crooked merchant ensemble was outside the hotel the following morning for my departure. With a knowing smile Azad Sheikh handed me a large present wrapped up in old newspaper, 'for the tripping'. I salaamed, hugged everyone and cried.

I flipped on the ignition and was at the border in forty minutes. I was alone and frightened of I knew not what; only the goal of Bombay and a ship to Australia spurred me on. Steve had promised to send me a ticket from Melbourne.

I stopped for a short gander at the Sikhs' most sacred shrine, the Golden Temple in Amritsar. Delhi was a coffee and petrol stop and took for ever to get out of. I was making up for lost time. Near Agra I pulled over for a back-seat sleep and got to the Taj for sunrise. Trapped in a time warp, the building commanded the pools reflecting the brightening light. I lingered past midday. The spirits seemed to touch me in the light breeze. I felt a magic I could not place. When I got back on the great southern trunk road I was glad to be alone.

I had heard this stretch of road was plagued by dacoits, highway robbers, who put rocks on the one-lane, macadamed roadway before storming trucks, buses and preferably private cars. The Sikhs at the evening's truck stop advised me most sincerely to travel in convoy with them. The Sikhs control most transport in India, even the taxis. Their Tata Merc 10-tonners ground along at 40 tops on an unpotholed stretch, I ate dust next to last in a line of six. Periodically the whole convoy would halt at a tea shop run by a friendly Sikh, where I got my petrol at commercial rate and food for nothing. In exchange the odd truck driver, mate or helper would get to ride with me for a spell. There was no traffic after dark, even the police patrols laagered up.

The third night of this slow progress was a Thursday, a second Thursday and thus marked by a bi-weekly religious ceremony. This was preceded by the passing of a chillum full of ganja. The chillum is a pipe looking like a miniature upside-down power-plant cooling tower, three or four inches long, made of terracotta or stone. A small stone is dropped in the funnel to prevent the smoking mixture falling out. A wad of finely chopped tobacco is then inserted, on top of which the ganja is crumpled, perhaps with a twist of charas. A wallbanger mix, fired preferably with a little glowing piece of sandalwood charcoal. The mouthpiece is wrapped with a hank of wet cotton cloth which acts as a coolant filter for the hot smoke. In lieu of a piece of cloth, peasants will ball up some wet straw or grass cupped round the mouthpiece. The whole process is somewhat akin to loading an old muzzle-loading musket. The chimney is held in an arrangement of two fists like that a small boy will make when blowing a note from a blade of grass. The chillum is traditionally passed clockwise around the assembled group, replenished by the host after each tour. The first sucking blast is enough to blow your head off; the rush is as pulsing as for a junkie shooting smack or an alkie downing a double scotch in one. Then you level off and cruise. The French have a great word for it, *enplane*; low high level.

To their surprise, I blew the chillum with an accustomed grace, even reciting the ritual chant before inhaling. It toured thrice, reddening the eyes of the whole tea shop, easy creased grins around the room. We were one. A large, bearded trucker got up, came across to me, called for soap, took my hand, lengthening and massaging my fingers and wrist, easing them thinner. He produced a kara, the bracelet worn by Sikhs, and gently but forcefully squeezed the steel ring over my right hand. The pain of the band's progress disappeared as he hugged me, kissing both cheeks. I was an honorary Sikh, the kara could never leave my wrist. The thing is so strong it is virtually impossible to squeeze it into an oval though it is only half a centimetre thick. Once they had served as a last-ditch weapon but were kept only symbolically.

The rest of the journey into Bombay was a bumpy drive in tandem with an Australian naturalized Indian on a Lambretta. Seyd rode in front, beeping his horn, clearing a path along the cluttered trunk road. Bombay loomed in two days.

At the P & O shipping office I found no ticket waiting, although Steve should have been back in Melbourne after two and half months. I sank into a bewildered blue funk, which deepened when I took Seyd down to the departing liner I was supposed to have caught. Adrift with only a few rupees left, I had to find a way of getting some money. I had found an English family camped next to the football stadium behind the beach with access to the washroom in a private college across the road. Their green and white Bedford coach was parked on waste ground strewn with rubbish and faeces, both human and animal. There was no shade or privacy. This is where I parked the Kombi. I hung towels over the windows on one side, attempting to sleep even with curious faces peering through the windshield.

Finding a job was dodgy. No one wants to know about a down-and-out young white man in a country riddled with caste and unemployment, and I knew what any high-commission employee would say. I taught the manager of the Kwality Ice Cream Parlour to drive in the VW. That lasted three overpriced lessons, I was too terrified to take more, being in a left-hand-drive car in a crazed city with a total novice at the wheel. Then a gig as an extra as a blind student in a Bombay talkie; my movie debut. I got handouts from various people including the Houselips in their camper. They had been stuck there for three months, trying to dispose of their bus and secure passage to Australia.

I took to hanging out at the Gateway to India, the marble arch outside the Taj Hotel, wistfully watching the shipping. I would chat with the hookers, and passers-by, hoping to find a foreigner I could con a meal out of. One evening I met a couple of wealthy, middle-aged, upper-class gays, a Dane and an American, cruising the world. They sat in the truck door and smoked with me; they bought me dinner and I played paid guide and chauffeur. The following evening they asked me to invite one of the hookers into the back of the van. It almost turned into an orgy right there on the waterfront, the evening throngs strolling by. Discretion prevailed and we drove to the couple's flat. The lady unswathed her surprising yardage of sari, revealing a plump, pox-scarred body. They produced porno books for the whore's titillation. I went first while Johannes and Bryan fumbled in the corner. The woman was to my inexperienced body a veritable *Kama Sutra* sex machine.

I never saw any of them again and went back to a starvation diet. Sugarcane juice with a dash of lime and ginger, the occasional cup of tea and rarer chapati. A bad case of dysentery, complicated by a strained back from pushing a fuelless VW back to its parking place, weakened me further. My trips across to the college became yo-yo frequent, piles developing since the only toilet paper around was copies of *Road & Track* I had taken from the trash at the Hotel Casa Academica. Taking a leak was becoming excruciatingly painful, I was peeing blood and pus and my left testicle had grown to the size of a tennis ball.

I met Harry at the Gateway to India and he moved right on to the waste ground in his black 1949 Austin Ten, a hole cut in the passenger-side floor as a toilet and rubbish chute. Harry claimed to have spent a week sick in the middle of downtown Isfahan, parked with his curtains drawn. He also claimed to be a full-fledged gourmet chef, learned, he said, while doing his national service, catering for a staff officers' mess at Clermont-Ferrand. Then he had worked at Maxim's, been a boxer, smuggler and had other sundry jobs before splitting for the road. He was tough, craggy, thirtyish, with a large Gallic *nez*; he was also definitely a bit touched, unpredictable. We got on from the very first hit. I poured out my woes, and he insisted he take me to hospital the next morning.

We went down to the Queen Victoria public hospital, a Gothic Christmas cake of a place behind the main railway terminus. A gaggle of doctors appeared in grubby smocks, curious to see a sick white face. After much delicate probing, prodding and taking of pulses, temperature and vital signs, they proclaimed that I had clap, testicular elephantiasis, bacillic dysentery, malaria, blood poisoning, and weighed 105 pounds. I was sicker than I had thought. I was admitted to a common male ward on the top floor of the building. Since there were no available beds, they put a stained mattress on the floor in the hall between ward and bathroom. The intravenous stand stood on the bottom of three unwashed steps leading up to the squat toilets and three ever dripping faucets, the only washing facilities.

I was dosed megashots of medicine with a blunt reusable syringe and given a large glass of quinine juice to knock back plus a handful of pills. A pretty Goanese nurse administered this, returning to ask me to shave my offending balls for further medication. I had no toilet kit, not having expected to be admitted, and the hospital did not have a safety razor. She hurried away, returning within ten minutes with one of those people you see squatting in public places in India who are human chimney sweeps: they clean noses, ears and other parts of the body with miniature brushes, clippers, shears and needles from their bus-conductor satchels. Clad in a dirty dhoti, with filthy fingernails, he squatted barefoot beside the mattress, stropping an antiquated cut-throat razor and grinning as he assessed the objects of his attention. I remonstrated enough to obtain a passing doctor who fetched his personal safety razor from his quarters later that evening. I operated on my own pubes, laying them bare to the Goanese for a heavy coating of purple gel. I felt like Yossarian in *Catch-22*.

Someone died and I got a bed in the ward. It was like being in a zoo. Pigeons and starlings flew free around the room, occasionally zapping into the turning fans. Rats scurried at night and cockroaches lurked everywhere, including in the curry. Harry discharged me after four days of watching the Indian health department blunder along. He had sold his car to the shipping magnate whom I had been procuring hookers for. His triptyque was clean, the deal had been done at a profitable rate into French francs, and we were off to Goa to recuperate on the beach in Panaji.

Goa, a former Portuguese enclave 250 miles down the coast from Bombay, had just been liberated by the Indians. You could still get olive oil, a loaf of bread or a VW part. We got there in a day and tarried two weeks, bronzing, fattening, breathing clean. I lazed on the red pyrite sands or in the shallow warm sea, and consumed Harry's Cordon Bleu fresh fish. We were the only foreigners there, no hippies, no druggies, just bemused Goans still unused to the occupying Indian troops. We decided to drive to Madras, using the money from Harry's car sale, where we would ship on the monthly ferry to Penang in Malaya. There the vehicle could be sold with ease, we had heard. We bumped across the southern part of the subcontinent via Bangalore and Vellore. On our simple diet of fruit, veg and chapatis, dried fish and pulses enhanced by Harry's magic and the Goan olive oil, my weight crept back to 130 pounds.

One night outside Bangalore, near some Vedic ruins, we camped in a grove of wild mangoes. The stove lit, the tea on, we brought out the coconut water pipe, settling in for a beautiful, sultry night. We would sleep out. We had begun to eat the ratatouille, spooning it up with the flat chapatis, when a curious monkey came and sat half a dozen paces from us with no fear whatsoever. It chattered away, inching closer. Bemused, we clucked back at it, not discouraging, not encouraging – monkeys in India had been known to be rabid.

Then there were half a dozen monkeys, then there were twenty or thirty, then there were literally hundreds, all with long proboscis snouts, mean black eyes, long tails and very pink-purple, protruding bottoms. They got bolder, climbing on the truck, edging closer, darting little hands out to grab our dinner things. We tried lobbing bits of food to the outer fringes of the crowd, but it served only to draw more of them closer. We packed up *super vitesse*, throwing the gear back into the truck, hopped in and locked the doors. The monkeys swarmed over where we had been, searching for whatever. Then they started to beat on the side panels and roof. It became a din of pummelling tiny but strong fists. A windshield wiper and a side mirror went. Our consternation turned to anxiety. We climbed into the front seat and started up, hooting the horn. The little buggers kept up the skirmish. A few heavy male adults picked up green mangoes and were bunging them at the truck, others picked up rocks. We thudded out of there in a shower of missiles.

The beach in Madras was a paradise: rolling surf, large dhow fishing boats with tuna and swordfish. We parked in the YMCA cricket grounds; it was out of season. The *chowkidar*, or concierge, thoughtfully unlocked the changing rooms after he was slipped a pack of cigarettes and 20 rupees. The bad news was that not even the Bank of India would change Harry's French francs. The black marketeers were only too happy to buy our foreigner's liquor-permit ration chits at exorbitant sums but refused to look at the strange foreign notes. I sold my camera and two shirts (nylon, drip-dry), Harry his radio and jeans. There was still not enough to get us on the ferry. We went down to the pier to watch it sail away. We would go to Kathmandu, it was only a couple of thousand kilometres away; we would be able to change the francs in Calcutta. It was rumoured heavily among fellow travellers that vehicles could still be sold in Nepal; more importantly, the triptyque would be redeemed and my father's deposit restored.

Plugging up India's east coast, the truck began showing signs of impending breakdown. Money was low and the people, though not hostile, not overtly hospitable. Harry was getting more and more agitated and upset when faced with the habitual staring crowds, largest in rural villages. He took to staring back at them, his bulbous eyes red-lined from the ganja, breaking into little threatening charges accompanied by wild waving of arms and fists.

Wherever you stop or sit in the subcontinent, even in a civilized urban environment, a crowd will gather to watch you. Eventually someone will detach himself from the mass and approach you. Often the first query is, 'And what is your native land?', followed by enquiries such as 'And who is being your Pee Em?' This may continue for a couple of dozen questions and answers before the inquisitor invites himself to be seated, offering tea. They will usually even pay for the refreshments to better their conversational English powers. Harry and I would daily change nationalities and factual reality. My favourite was to say we were from Cosmopolita, 'halfway between England and France.' 'Aha, I'm knowing it well. And your Pee Em being?' Our reply might be 'Peter Ustinov', to which there would be much waggling of heads and huffing in awe and respect. This drove Harry mad. He would just bellow and rant, flying at the innocents. I tried to keep a diplomatic anglo *noblesse oblige* together.

Harry took to jousting oncoming bicycles with my Pakistani camel stick. The VW had left-hand drive and Harry would wind down the passenger window and lean right out, stick at an Uhlan's angle of attack. The road was a paved strip wide enough for a single vehicle, and Harry had countless chicken runs with approaching overloaded lorries and buses. Buffalo carts tended to hug the dirt borders, unlit at night; cyclists wobbled down the narrow macadam, hundreds of pounds precariously balanced on carrier or head. These were Harry's targets. Usually just the threat of a poke in the eye with a brass-ferruled camel stick was enough to send the dhoti-clad riders of the big black Indian bikes wobbling off into ditch, brush or, twice, a canal. Periodically, the poor peasant would not chicken out and the chattels on his head would take a direct pierce, Harry's arm would double back in pain with a screamed '*Merde!*' or 'Fuckin' *merde!*', and there would be the most awful mess on the road behind us.

Once I misjudged a cow that changed its direction three times. I ended up with another smashed headlight and badly dented door. The cow was left writhing, bare broken bone at the rear end. We dared not stop. In India you can get lynched for killing a sacred mother beast. The country is full of them, wandering everywhere, eventually you have to hit one.

The trek took us a week of wrong turns. Ferries marked on the map turned out to be nonexistent; we strayed into the Mahanadi delta near Cuttack and then into the Ganges south of Calcutta. We arrived there in the middle of a cholera epidemic. They were using old-fashioned English dust carts to pick up the dead from the streets twice a day.

Going to an immunization point to get inoculated I met a well-spoken student, obviously of means. Though Harry was reluctant we went back to his family home. His father, a wealthy gem and bullion dealer, had a four-storey palace in a quiet area downtown. We were soon installed in a rooftop room leading to the terrace. It was de luxe, carpets and cushions, old Moghul decor; there were servants and free delicious food, sometimes taken *en famille*.

The paunchy, sweaty head of the clan, who dripped gold and chewed betel endlessly, wanted the VW. (I was not to realize how much until 1000 miles further on.) He tried every venue of approach to its illegal sale: no dice. We searched the town in vain for filters, plugs and points to service the ailing truck. It was Nepal or bust. We set out on the Great Trunk Road to Benares and Patna. Thirty miles per hour was our top speed, beyond that the motor produced a cacophony of disaster-knelling noises.

Within sight of the last Indian town of Rauxal on the border with Amalgunj, the engine started to emit the loudest bangs and backfires so far, accompanied by a loud clatter. It was given to stalling, refusing to start unless it had been allowed to cool off for a quarter of an hour. A few miles later we missed another turn-off, the strategic one to the border, completely unmarked, and sailed up a B road for another four miles before, with a wheeze, lurch and bang, the Kombi packed up.

Pushing an even partially loaded VW microbus in midday heat is not so funny. A rare tractor happened along, the driver a former Hurricane-engine mechanic from the Second World War, employed by the local bigwig. Pandit Tiwari owned an entire cluster of hamlets. He came to inspect us and sent the mechanic back with the ageing Massey Ferguson to tow us to his manse. The Pandit was a Brahmin with an enormous family but a closet queen. It was me he was interested in. The mechanic took the motor apart, and made an attempt to order valves, pistons and other parts from Delhi; fat chance. After a week of boringly plain vegetarian food, yoga lessons, and parrying the Pandit's advances, Harry read the old boy the riot act. We were towed to the frontier post and cast adrift.

The Parekh gold merchant's revenge came at the customs post. He had told the customs that I was smuggling gold, a crime just shy of cow slaughter. The customs lads dutifully searched through our meagre possessions. We were too poor to eat, much less smuggle gold to Nepal, but were invited to spend the night in the clean jail behind their office. The technical reason for the arrest was the expiration of the six-month carnet. I went to Patna, the nearest AA office, where a formal application to extend the carnet was made. It was to take six weeks of bureaucracy to put together. Back to the cells.

Harry got pissed off with waiting and hopped a Sikh-owned Tata 10-tonner to Kathmandu. I was left to my own devices by the border staff, surviving on a diet of lychees, mangoes, bananas and whatever they could spare. The occasional traveller or foreign vehicle brought light relief, even a two-day affair with a Peace Corps girl. No more than a dozen trucks crossed each day, but every half hour or so a buffalo-drawn wagon would plod up. Most of the carts carried grain and this was tested with a special auger. One joyous afternoon the lads tested some grain sacks and withdrew a sample of high-grade hemp. As 'taxes' the staff collected two gunnies of Terai Nepalese grass. There must have been 50 keys; they laid one on me. Their payday came just before my renewed papers came through; a whole wagon load masquerading as straw was found to be a ton and a half of primo crop. We kept two sacks and the carter called his man to bring enough rupees to buy back the rig and load. It was the best sort of prison I have ever had the luck to be in. I was sad when the striped pole was raised and the entire crew helped push me down the dyke road the half-mile to Nepal.

There was no carnet covering Nepal, so the truck was left locked, gathering dust next to the Nepalese customs shack. A Sikh trucker who was interested in buying the vehicle picked me up. In a convoy we made the two-day climb over the Himalayan foothills up to 8000 feet into the Kathmandu valley. I rode a Tata Merc, flattened to the bottom of its sagging springs by a slab of cement bags. Progress was slow, and it was stifling hot in the decorated wooden cab. The door and windscreen had crenellations resembling the Taj, the panels were gaudy with painted scenes from the Ramayana. The vehicles drooped silver chains from their chassis and chrome decor transformed the front grille into a fairground piece. The view was spectacular when not frightening, the overloaded trucks taking two runs to make the hairpin bends when the drivers' assistants hopped out, jamming rocks behind the back wheels to save and preserve the thin brakes. We stopped on the first sub-col at over 6000 feet, dossing down in a tea shop. The washing facilities were a roaring stream behind the café where the Sikhs performed fastidious ablutions, including rolling and netting their beards and waist-length hair; I shaved but was too embarrassed to wash as I had no underwear. On the easy bit on the plateau, they let me take the wheel before the frightening descent into Nepal's central valley from Naubise.

Kathmandu was cut off from India until 1960, when the road was opened over the mountains. Before that, everything was humped in on porter's backs – the British high commissioner's

Rolls-Royce required 136 sherpas. Then Kennedy's neo-colonialist doctrine had USAID build a cable car which goes from near Hitawa nearly into Kathmandu, a span of over 50 miles; it has tank cars, gondolas, cattle cars and plain pallets. Airline services in 1963 were twice-weekly decrepit Dakotas.

The Paras Hotel was a rather seedy four-storey modern hotel. The plumbing was drippy at best, the beds prone to bugs, the linen laundered bi-weekly. Harry was installed there in a room overlooking an open-air market and temple. There was a German working as maintenance engineer at the US embassy who would fix the bus when the parts arrived from Wolfsburg. I had to wait six weeks. Harry and I took to spending hours in the temples, renting bikes to visit the outlying Vedic sex temples at Bhadgaon and Patan. The entrance to each temple contained a vaulted gatehouse with raised platforms on either side. Here usually were installed a harmonium and tabla player. Traditionally one sat and chanted with the musicians before entering the inner sanctum. Chillums were circulated, with the ritual chant of *'Bom bom nosum sunkum ha'* before inhaling. In Nepal they had a wicked way of lacing the ganja with opiated hash – temple balls.

Harry tired of all this, and in a terse scene I gave him half the advance on the truck from a Sikh I had done a deal with, and he split for Dacca. I was to get the balance of the cash when the parts arrived for the VW. A few hundred more rupees were raised by liquidating the rest of my western possessions, then still a rarity in Kathmandu. I held a car-boot sale on the temple steps a couple of hundred yards from the hotel. Plastic beakers, nylon shirts, camping stove, everything went in ten minutes, even a few old bottles, valuable in a nation that doesn't produce glass. In those days travelling overland was simply a matter of starting out loaded down and gradually selling off all one's belongings. The Third and Fourth worlds were craving items from our polluted culture; old magazines would be dismembered and framed virtually page by page. The last *Road & Tracks* and *Playboy*s not used for toilet paper fetched as much as the cooking utensils.

Bored with sitting in Kathmandu, I trekked off towards Namche Bazaar at the foot of Everest for two weeks. Bertrand, an Afrikaaner hippy, was strong company versed in the ways of the hill people, having been in the mountains for nearly a year. One hour we were plodding up 3000 feet of rock-strewn, winding paths, the next descending into a breathtaking valley. The bridges were the most terrifying I will ever encounter. Strung across gorges churning with rock-dashed white water, they were at best suspension jobs of rope and wire with a meagre hand rope either side, a series of branches, poles and slats for a footway. The worst were a log or two, slippery with freezing water, balanced across narrower spurs. My fear of heights was not conquered, just beaten back. Bertrand and the porters got me across with mulish efforts. We ate like peasants, a revolting gruel called tsampa; ground roasted barley, tea, salt and rancid yak butter stirred into a sort of porridge with hot water. At night we would crash in cow byres for a few rupees, too tired and strung out from the altitude to be able to think, the highest highs ever. Villages, stupas and monasteries were surrounded by walls niched with prayer drums. It was obligatory to pass round the walls three times, spinning each drum and thinking big Oms following the sherpas' example, for onward auspicious passage. The cow sheds were ridden with bugs, the glacial streams torture to wash in, though never have I felt so on top or in touch with being. This trek touched parts of my spirit I had been unaware of; the parting with the truck and the possessions was a mere step on a larger path.

That year Royal Air Nepal had lost two aircraft, one after the other, when they failed to gain altitude from the strips ringed with ragged peaks. Indian Airlines had a marginally better record. It was good to fly back to the sticky plains of India. It was good to know the triptyque on the car had been restored to the AA in Patna, so that the deposit would be returned to my father. I was free of responsibility once more, on the road to wherever, dipping reverently into a dog-eared Tagore or Yevtushenko.

I was travelling with a stolid German guy in his early twenties. Hans-Dieter Darmstadt from Düsseldorf had the dimensions of a professional bodyguard, he must have been six foot five and loose in a Negroid way. He looked kind of dumb in his lederhosen, with hairy legs sticking out of climbing boots; his handshake was disarmingly powerful, his forefinger missing, a casualty of American tank-gun shrapnel when he had been sitting on his mother's knee in 1945, aged four. We made an odd pair, I in a battered bowler hat, afghan vest, T-shirt, jeans and split desert boots, Hans-Dieter a huge blond Hun with a jaunty jäger hat perched on his shoulder-length hair. He carried a guitar and a rucksack, I a Bombay-made mango dholl (a double-ended tabla akin to a drum) and a Nepalese sack sherpa style from a headband strap.

It seemed right to blow some of the new-won money, wads of tatty rupees, on first-class travel. We boarded the overnight express mail to Calcutta. It was a step back to Raj times – a luxurious overstuffed doileyed compartment with adjacent mahogany-panelled toilet and hand basin. Four fans twirled at high velocity; the smuts from the puffing steam locomotive did not penetrate the sealed windows. Our fellow passengers, a Sikh colonel and a wealthy, anglified merchant, were chagrined by our bedraggled looks but readily divvied up their tuck boxes. Travelling first class in India is like being the goldfish looking out of the bowl, a distorted view of a disparate reality.

This time round Calcutta was kind. Sipping milk shakes at a table by the window in the Kwality Ice Cream joint where Harry and I had hung out on the way up, I saw an emaciated man keel over on the kerb and die. The crowd merely edged around the prostrate form. Next to me a dapper, nutty-brown oriental gentleman announced, 'Terrible thing that, not happening in my country.' Conversation revealed that he was the Burmese consul general, and we were invited for lunch on the following day.

Burma had long been a forbidden land, visas granted for a maximum of one week, always at their discretion. But after a delicious Burman curried lunch, a milder affair than its Indian cousin, we were ushered into the consular section of the residence where a complimentary entry/transit permit was stamped into our passports. In neat red hand printed at the bottom was written: 'Land route not permissable.' It was valid for sixty days. An overnight wait and two dollars got us a Thai visa.

Howrah Station, Calcutta, has been the subject of countless photographs. It is a city unto itself; people are born and die in the sooty Victorian cavern. The city it serves was then 8 million strong; every day a quarter of a million people pass through this peeling edifice. Getting to the Dacca train was like hacking through unwashed jungle growth. As it was an international train, we had to purchase tickets before boarding. We bought the cheapest, third class, and then installed ourselves in second. A series of bemused, hapless conductors challenged our right to be there. It became a sport to destroy their arguments. The first line of resistance, only *sprechen Deutsch*, brought lots of head waggings, then a renewed assault in an even more simplified Indian English accompanied by gesticulations to produce more rupees. We steadfastly resisted three ticket wallahs before the East Pakistan border, where the combined forced of Indian railways, border guards, immigration and customs officials finally got us off the train. They took pity when we claimed we were destitute, and had a collection among themselves to pay the difference between second and third class. We had delayed the Bengal mail for thirty minutes and the whole border at Darsana had become involved in this international bureaucratic incident.

Dacca was a dump: an overextended fishing village in a swamp of jute and rice, stickier, hotter and more untogether than Calcutta. The cyclone season was upon the overcrowded, underhoused city, the streets swollen with country folk taking refuge from the storms. We struck lucky and met an American aid worker who put us up in style, imported beers, hot and cold running, normal food. We stayed for two days, wandering the city trying to find Harry, who had supposedly ended up in a French Catholic convent here. He was not in, a Bengali nun announced when we found the place. Another friend adrift in the Asian sea, a camaraderie consumed and drained. I was sad not to see Harry again, we had laughed and learnt a lot together and my French had become street hip. Now I was speaking *Deutschlish*, larded with local vocabulary picked up from Urdu, Hindi, Nepali and Bengali.

The aid man drove us to the station to catch the express to Chittagong, 130 miles down the Arakan Gulf. We used the same ploy, third-class tickets, second-class compartments, and took up four seats; we were becoming more imperialistic the longer we stayed in the ludicrous grip of the Indian subcontinent. The more timid Bengali ticket inspectors soon passed the word to ignore us: 'Too much bothersome.' We settled back in the stinking, hot train, buying cups of tea at the frequent stops. From the Iranian border to the Burmese border, every railway station has a throng of vendors who cluster trainside, hawking the region's short eats and titbits and always tea. The tea is milky, sweet and strong, served in little terracotta cups containing an espresso-size shot of brew. The used cup is smashed between the railway tracks. The cup cost two annas – less than a penny – in 1963. We virtually lived on them. The only safe food to eat was chickens and eggs and precious few had survived the tempests.

It took thirty-six grinding stop-and-start hours to make that journey. Cyclones had cut the track, a 10,000-ton ship had been heaved by the winds five miles inland. Riding any train in the region is an experience in endurance, but that ride produced the most haunting view of any.

One becomes immune to the endless parade of beggars, blind and crippled, diseased and damaged, like mutants in a grotesque *Star Wars* bar sequence. East Pakistan – now Bangladesh – is still one of the ten poorest nations. Many are deliberately crippled to beg. Too poor to give, but begged from since we were white, we found it difficult to be unaffected by the horror. On this train there was a continuous stream that passed through the cars, creeping, crawling, dragging along from car to car, being thrown off at the next stop. Second-class passengers came under heavy attack. We rebuffed all, save one. At the spittle-drowned 'Baksheesh!' I opened one drowsy eyelid; two hands, two feet, no stick, no problem. I looked up. Looking back at me was a hole spiked with two teeth. A black, red, frothy hole of leprosy temporarily arrested. There was no nose, just a sort of gristle bridge and more hole. The teeth sat at the bottom of the major hole. A fist could have been swallowed in it. The man kept on pointing at the hole and trying to make a cogent sound. Finally a fellow passenger said, 'But sir, he is a regular, all he is a wanting is a cigarette, then going along!' Hans fished out a rumpled Charminar and lit it. He passed it to the leper, who stuck it in the gristle and puffed away, his face leaking smoke like a bonfire. He went on down the carriage and into my subconscious for ever.

Chittagong had been ravaged by the recent disastrous weather. No hotel was open, a decent place to eat almost impossible to find. We took up residence in the first-class gentlemen's retiring room at the railway station, foraying into the muddy streets for the odd meal and to check with United Burma airlines as to the probability of an onward flight to Rangoon. The airstrip, only partially tarred, was mostly awash and no one knew when the next flight would arrive, much less leave.

It was a five-day wait before the Bay of Bengal got back to normal and a notice posted in the garden of the airline bungalow announced a 3.00 p.m. estimated departure on the morrow. Their DC-3 had struggled in late that afternoon, too late to turn around. At last I was going to break out of the Hindustan run into the purity of the orient.

3

Sliding Towards Theravada

My feet are dirty, I don't care
anyway right now I don't
because feet are only what
just feet
and feet keep walking
walking on in despair
hoping, hoping
hoping some day that the mind may care

Bombay '63

A lightning-bolt strike on an airplane is a frightening thing. The overworked Union of Burma Airlines DC-3 had climbed bumpily into a black sky full of thunderheads and ominous darts of white light. Getting to 5000 feet took for ever, engines misfiring, puffs of oil and flame. Once there the crew fought to keep us on course. We were scheduled to put down at Akyab just over the Burmese border and to this end, a number of peasant passengers had been relegated to jump seats at the rear among the baggage. They sat there terrified, clutching kitchen utensils, drums and fighting cocks, throwing up over each other as the Dakota lurched. We were blown way off course, missed Akyab and clawed into Minga-ladon airport an hour late, both engines, firing on inconstant cylinders, the oil slicks down the fuselage forming a Jackson Pollock painting on the dented aluminium. Even the crew looked fraught.

Burma runs on a thriving black economy, and the first lesson in it starts at customs. Everything, down to your last filter and film, must be listed in triplicate, all currencies declared in both numerals and longhand (the inadequate forms are not provided on the plane). Old hands simply slip the inspecting officer a bottle of Johnnie Walker, whereupon all forms are stamped and bags chalked. Outside, next to the Union of Burma Bank window, enterprising black marketeers give you wads of kyats (pronounced chats) for your booze, cigarettes or dollars, offering a rate triple that of the bank.

It took three days and nights to chuff up the Irrawaddy plain to Mandalay. It would have been a day's ride but for the stops to repair sabotaged rails. Every bridge or culvert in Burma had two, three or four rails lying broken beside it. To the detritus of the fierce campaigns fought by the ebbing and flowing Allied and Japanese armies, more wreckage had been added by insurgent ethnic groups fighting to gain independence from Rangoon's authority.

Mandalay station had a restaurant run by an Englishman who had opted to retire in upper Burma rather than be repatriated after the war. We played chess till late in a chilly monsoon night and ate home-country curry, white bread, corned beef and rice with cold Mandalay lager. The up-Kachin express pulled out before sunrise, a squad of troops dispersed along the length of the train. Most of them were soon asleep. The train puffed through brilliant jungle over swollen rivers, passed countless hidden temples, *shwes*. 'Express' denoted only that it did not stop between stations to let down or pick up passengers. We did stop at every halt on the line and most bridges were negotiated at walking speed. Illegal fares came and went. We ate, on our fellow passengers' advice, crisp paddy shrimp and fish fritters, baby finch and deep-fried sticky rice balls with hot sauce. It was delicious and cost pennies.

Myitkyina is the northern railhead in Burma, as far as you can get towards the strategic roads leading to India and China. General Stilwell had built his road to connect here. There are no buildings over two stories, the shops have boardwalks; it is like the set for a western frontier movie built of tropical hardwood – mahogany and teak. The unpaved roads were full of puddles, the monsoon ditches full. On the edge of town at the deserted military airfield, old Japanese planes were speared with green bamboo. The camp beds in the Chinese hotel above the only decent café were bliss after forty-eight hours on wooden seats.

Our fantasy had been to try to get back to Rangoon by road, but it was said to be impossible and nobody had heard of hitch-hiking in Burma. We would have to take the post jeeps. The war left Burma with thousands of used American and British army vehicles. These have been incorporated into the country's transport system. The larger trucks have been converted to buses and freightliners, the weapons carriers and jeeps serve as the intertown communal taxis upcountry where the roads have all but returned to the jungle.

Dieter and I, for an extra 10 kyats, bought front-row seats. Behind us there were up to seven souls and their possessions; on the roof were trade foods and the mail. The government contracted with freelancers to run the post through rebel territory. Up here the presiding power was the KIA – the Kachin Independent Army. The Stilwell road is one of the marvels of the world. It crosses ridges and hills in high monsoon country covered in 200-foot-thick triple-canopy jungle. To get over the worst sections there are dozens of hairpins, some to be negotiated in two shots. Since it was built in 1943–4, the elements have done their best to destroy it. We were held up for four hours while a crew hacked through a landslide for 50 yards with only picks and shovels.

We only went 80 kilometres to Hkala Yang in the first day down the road and had to pay the 12-kyat fare for the next day's trip to Bhamo before wandering down to the local government post to have our passports stamped. Having secured Chinese-owned beds behind the only functioning chow house, we sat content at tin tables under naptha lamps that drew exotic moths from miles, eating noodles and curry, rice and fruit. The whole village turned out to watch us and buy us beer. We were the first foreigners to venture down the road in six years who had not been turned back at the first police checkpoint south of Myitkyina.

It rained a lot, slowing progress the next day. Everyone regularly hopped out of the jeep into knee-deep ooze to push us out of tracks which disappeared into 100-yard-long seas of silty red mud. Hans-Dieter was the first to don the traditional Burmese *longyi*, the sarong cloth which male and female alike wear as both official and unofficial dress. A T-shirt and Chinese cotton waistcoat completed his attire. Unable to keep the bloody cloth securely knotted, I stuck out for cut-offs, save for bedwear.

Bhamo is the furthest navigable point north on the Irrawaddy and a large Burman Buddhist settlement, once an important trading and timber town, now cut off by rebel activity. We had time for lunch and a stroll along the shore before the afternoon jeep tried to get to Namhkam before sunset. We were sitting out a shower on top of a steep col when a tattered group of armed Kachins ambled up. Their leader was a look-alike for Castro with oriental eyes, and a red star on his Mao hat. He carried a weapon akin to an air rifle, the others had a shotgun, a Japanese Nambu and a muzzle-loading musket. This was the KIA. Our driver passed over a wad of kyats – road tax. Our German and British passports were admired and returned before the jeep lumbered off to Namhkam.

The hill tribes have mainly been converted from their animist beliefs to Baptism and Methodism. They do not like the lowland Buddhist Burmese and their collective ways. The same spirits, or *nats*, are common to them all and dominate the way of life.

Here there was not even a Chinese-run doss house. The army, who stamped us in, pointed out the hospital at the far end of town. We trudged along the muddy main street and up a steep hill to a British-built hospital complex set under flame trees, facing China across the valley. The Namhkam hospital was run by Dr Stirling Seagrave, son of a missionary who had run the post before. He had been uninterrupted since the war when he had stayed behind to look after both Japanese and Allied wounded. Left untouched by the warring factions, he was needed and respected by them all, a long-lapsed American with a clarity found in remarkable men, a Christian with Buddhist attitudes. He was already in his seventies when I met him but his handshake was firm, his eyes saw into you. After initial caution, he welcomed us in, showed us to the shower and our splendid colonial rooms. After his rounds we sat in planters' chairs, conversing quietly, looking east across the dark mists to Salween in China. The last foreigners to visit him had been in 1956 and 1957, Japanese and then two Dutchmen. Seagrave had created an oasis of sanity in the turmoil of this tri-state area and never expected to leave. He died there in 1972.

From Namhkam south to Lashio there was no regular taxi or bus service. Only the occasional truck made it at its own risk, and monthly army convoys. The area was definitely insecure, we were told to go back. We sat the best part of the day at the town's parking lot where petrol was on sale so any vehicle coming or going had to turn up eventually. An empty log truck, a 1944 Bedford, offered us a lift 50 miles south. The crew happily climbed out on the back deck so we could ride up front in the sweltering cab. After dark we pulled up and camped in the jungle, miles from the nearest habitation. The loggers fed us and over tea offered Burmese smoke. We were led to the sleeping platform, laid down and proffered the pipe – a blob of fashioned stone with a small, indented, conical bowl on a long bamboo stem. A black liquid was stuck in the bowl and the stem turned towards me. The pipe was then lowered over a simmering oil lamp. I inhaled with a long, sustained suck, just as the Iranians had taught us. I floated away instantly. This was legendary opium, Golden Triangle black, long known as the primo. Opium up here is the cash crop run by warlords in alliance with the independence movements.

The delighted Shans clapped their hands and fed the pipe for a couple of hours. There was no language barrier, though the subject of discussion escapes me. Sleep was painless, with complete, half-conscious dreams: that feeling when you wake half an hour before the pre-set alarm and gain thirty minutes of lifetime, to dream, the complete dream with ending, be it good or evil. Fulfilment.

Another wartime log truck took us a further 30 miles into the forest. We were put down on a deserted piece of ancient hard top running through a beautiful teak wood, the morning cool just evaporating as we strode off on a southerly heading, praying for any transport to come by. The nearest settlement, we had been told, was another 15 miles away. We made a good pace, encumbered only by our Burmese shoulder bags and Hans-Dieter's guitar. The other gear was stashed at the Y in Rangoon. He still wore the *Jagd* hat and I the bowler. I had stopped to take a leak on the side of the dapple-shaded road when from the shadows a squad of armed guerrillas materialized, wearing Shan United Army patches, rising sun on Burmese flag. I don't know who was more surprised, but I reached in my pocket and offered a cigarette, then snapped a photo of us all shaking hands. They gave us a cheroot apiece and filtered back into the forest.

We plodded on, to be overtaken by a brand-new Nissan truck laden with hill rice. It stopped out of curiosity, we hurtled back to Mandalay, bounced about on the hard sacks, and by nightfall we were back in the comfort of the railway station's first-class waiting room.

Fifty miles north of Rangoon at Pegu is the largest reclining Buddha in the world, 180 feet long. Playing tourist in Burma is to slow down to the pace of their way of life, to go visiting temples, shwes and Buddhas, paying homage to one of the thirty-seven *nat* shrines. We were soon enmeshed in the throngs meandering round the sedate figure, absorbed in the piety of the place, the quiet, the peace, the camaraderie. Brown, smiling faces everywhere. An American agricultural aid worker on a day trip found us and offered a lift back to Rangoon, after a visit to the temple city of Shwemawdaw nearby. A 100-metre-high hill crowned with a golden stupa, it mirrors the Dagon in Rangoon but stands in isolation on the Irrawaddy plain.

The shwes in Burma hold a spiritual space. To enter the covered stairways was to be steeped in a cool mind; the pain of walking barefoot on the hot marble of the stupas' plinths was overshadowed by the beauty of the curving golden shwe, the wind chimes and gongs resonating.

The UBA Viscount of indeterminate age had two passengers and seven crew. We occupied the very last row on the right side at the back by the galley. The cabin staff dumped a case of cold Becks beer on the seat next to ours, handed us a bottle of scotch, a bundle of cheroots and two in-flight boxed meals, and went up to the cockpit to party with the pilots. We poured our way to Bangkok, breaking only to roll a couple of superbomber joints of cheroot, opium, hash and Bengali ragweed. No one seemed to notice the smoke when they came back from the cockpit for landing. They were as pissed as we were. The landing was not exactly a perfect three-pointer.

At the airport a blur of considerate Thai officials, undaunted by our appearance and condition, affixed the normal two-month permit to our tourist visas, issued in Calcutta. They even held the bus up while they helped us pick ourselves up and out of the customs. We were dumped at the downtown terminal with splitting hangovers and no Thai Baht. I fell out of the bus and said, 'Where are the hotels?' and someone answered, 'Down by the railway station.' We stumbled in that direction, not knowing how to catch the bus. The neo-Gothic station had a stinking klong on one side and across the square was a row of seedy hotels with shops and restaurants on the ground floor.

The Thai Song Greet, five floors mostly given over to a brothel, had an open-air restaurant on the corner. Directly behind a row of sandbags designed to keep high tide away from diners' feet were the ever bubbling cauldrons wherein stewed chicken carcasses, pigs' trotters, veal heads, all manner of stock-making gear. Next to them stood the charcoal- and gas-fired woks and the food safes full of cured pork, dried fishes, eggs and a plethora of exotic green vegetables. The form was to order what you wanted and how much of it, and then how you wanted it done. The chopping, woking kitchen staff brought the platters of steaming food straight to the twenty or so tin-topped tables overlooking the choking traffic intersection. Thais eat every two or three hours, delicious titbits between the three daily meals. All imaginable flavours – spicy, tasty, curried, sweet and sour, salty – anything that is edible they consume, and prepare it exquisitely.

We moved in above this. There were a dozen resident girls in the Thai Song Greet who rotated between their rooms, the restaurant and the more sedate coffee shop. After the privations of Hindustan and the austerity of Burma, we were in hog wallow. Even the beer was cheap German-brewed, though laced with enough formaldehyde to pickle a cadaver. Thai stick, the local weed, was abundant although theoretically illegal. Round the corner was a pharmacy and grocery shop where prescription drugs were sold across the counter and the sidewalk-fronting fridge displayed liquid speed beside the Mekong whisky, Coke and soda bottles. Bangkok in 1963 was a stoner's paradise. The Indo-China War was picking up all around, except in tranquil Cambodia, and the city was just beginning to receive an invasion of foreigners. White devils – *farangs*, as the Thai call us round-eyes – were flocking into the country to exploit the emerging business-consciousness of the locals. Cokes and Fantas were sold up-country where freshly squeezed juice or tea had once been the norm. As a strange concession to western influence, the Thais made fingers of white-bread toast to dip into their satay sauce, and sprinkled white sugar on the fried noodles and rice. My favourite east-west cross was griddled pancakes doused in condensed milk. We ate fluffy rice and coconut-milk-based curries and mango ice cream. We started to get fat again at the Thai Song Greet.

Within days we bumped into a cheerfully mad cockney, Dave, his mate Ivan, a Welshman, and a third Brit, who went by the name of Jim, then. They were overlanders who had strayed north of Malaya in search of employment and chasing the legendary Thai largesse. All three moved into our room on the third floor back, having sampled the fare downstairs. The train from Singapore daily delivered strung-out travellers to our corner. The scam at that time was to voyage down the peninsula to Penang or Singapore and stock up on cheap watches (sweep second hands a must) for about six dollars. Back in Thailand, especially further upcountry than Bangkok, you could get upwards of twenty bucks for them. Codliver-oil pills had a similar markup but were bulkier. Going back down to get a new Thai visa, you took dope and pills

– an over-the-counter market at either end. Hard cash, no hassles.

We spent a lot of time in our room, gobbling tubes of twenty Pep-Pil and Pep-Tab, rolling endless reefer, eating into our dwindling reserves. The room cost 20 baht a day – a dollar – meals took another buck. The speed was a shilling a tube, the stick was given away. The resident hookers were fascinated. This novel form of *farang* was worth investigating. They did our laundry and on slow days were not averse to sacking out for an hour or so. We were a big happy family; everyone was obliged to use the communal bathroom, of the splash-bath Thai variety. They are a fastidious race, wash as often as they eat; they are heavily into matters of the body.

I got my first real job, one requiring the wearing of a newly purchased nylon drip-dry shirt, slacks and loafers, even a tacky tie. I was the white representative of Ever Retty torch bulbs, a dodgy Taiwanese-Thai pseudolegal corporation, and toured upcountry in a large, fancy sampan, flogging flashlight bulbs to gullible country-store owners. All togged up in the then flash western gear, we puttered up lotus-clogged klongs for hundreds of miles on five- or six-day trips, eating on board, sleeping on padded mats under mosquito nets in the forward section. We would come across unsuspecting general-purpose shops at canal intersections or in distant villages where cheap plastic goods tangled with strings of dried fish and seaweed. Sacks of pulses, rice, cans of oils, outboard gas tanks, nets and tools cluttered the interiors. Our high-powered sales team would try to persuade the poor local to invest in at least a gross of their inferior bulbs. I mean, how often does your flashlight bulb burn out? Anybody who bought bulbs got a very cheap transistor radio. The more they promised to purchase, preferably for cash up front, the better-looking present they could choose. We kept a stack of prizes in a couple of cartons on the boat. Should anyone buy fifty gross, there was even a promised television, although not the one we had on board. My duty was to officiate at the sale and put my somewhat illegible signature on the foot of the gobbledygook contract. I opted to sign Timothy Dieter Napoleon. It was a scandalous rip-off. I made another circuit in a giant old American car doing the same number, staying in small upcountry hotels which came with hot and cold running girls. All compliments of the half-Chinese Cheng family who ran the bulb lark.

The next job was just as much a rip-off but it had redeeming cultural and educational aspects: selling the *New American*

Encyclopedia. A set of basically teenage US remainders, simplified, in twelve volumes, bound in vinyl and hence washable. Some volumes had plastic inlays like flip charts of maps, anatomy, stellar systems; Volume Five, which we carried as a demo model, had a transparent skeleton in black and white on an acetate sheet. I never saw a complete set, so I could not definitely say whether other volumes fulfilled the sales spiel. The set cost 6000 baht – about $285 – we got 10 per cent, roughly $28 dollars on that deal. I sold two.

The worst night was in the newly developing upper-class suburb of Sukhumvit. I had gained entrance to an enormous, guarded, modern Thai-Chinese merchant's dwelling. I was shagged out, having speeded all afternoon, hardly stopping even for a Coke. With dry mouth I sat gabbling to this educated gentleman in his parlour, as he poured enormous tots of Glenfiddich over Polaris-water ice cubes. I was energetically demonstrating the book's finer points, like its washable cover; I spat on it for effect, to rub off an offending blotch. The red and gold lines dissolved and smeared into the white vinyl. The demonstration to prove it was scratch-proof ended when one of the crawling infants received the book on its foot as I hurled the thing to the floor. I had to beat a mortified retreat to the bus back to the Thai Song Greet.

It was a gas riding the buses, speeding on pills, giggling on the weed, chatting up the bus conductresses or cheating them out of the two-cent fare by grinning and speaking only German or French. Stoned swine of a *farang*.

An assistant librarian bought one of the wretched encyclopedia sets, and offered to organize a private class of friends should I want to hold conversational English classes. I dropped the sales pitch and moved on to the language circuit, nattering in a refined way about the world's events to a lovely bunch of Thai twenty- to thirty-year-olds.

We were living a rogue existence, albeit totally enmeshed in Thai society. I became street-lingo proficient enough to score whatever I wanted and chat up the girl I fancied in the cafés that fronted the whorehouses. The girls took me home to stilt houses on klongs, where life was city rural, and we often went to wats, the Buddhist temples that stud the city like pubs in London. It is no stigma in Thai society to be a prostitute; many are married, have children and work to support families in the impoverished northeast of the country. They are, to a person, devout, visiting their wat frequently; an altar shrine is always prominent in the bar or café. The girls were happy to take me on their secular visits, to lay gifts of flowers in front of their patron Buddha.

The Thai wats were frenetically busy after the tranquillity of the Burman shwes, though the same peaceful vibes emanated alike from the Shwedagon in Rangoon and Wat Po in Bangkok. The wat is the centre of Thai society, propagating traditional learning and the morality of the entire population. Young boys normally enter the monastery for a year or so at the age of seven or eight, just as they are drafted later into the national service. The lessons learned last for ever; it establishes the dharma, or path, that everyone will follow. It teaches the balance of karmic living, the balance between good and evil, life and death. Just being in a temple has a healing effect. The Thais are happy to help you understand their culture and language, thrilled that you dig them for what they are. The Burmese are more reluctant, being too xenophobically cut off by their successive governments from the outside and foreign perversion; even the British barely scratched their surface.

My two-month visa was about to run out and I was woefully shy of the $500 worth of deposit required for a residency-permit consideration. I was going to have to leave the country, get a new visa and return for another two-month bout. During the course of the teaching I had met a more established group of whacked-out travelling *farang*, and they provided me with the solution.

Simon Dring had originally stayed at the Thai Song Greet nine months before, on arriving in Bangkok after a vaguely similar overland voyage. He had graduated at the grand age of seventeen, not an O level to his prep and technical school credit, to subeditor on the Bangkok *Daily Post*. He had found a splendid, cheap residence in an abandoned night club on the roof of an office building. There were five people, a Brit, Danish and Dutch mixed-sex crew squatting there, beds arranged around the stage and booths. They all stayed in-country for the permitted two months, renewing their visas with long weekends in Vientiane, Laos, 500 miles north across the Mekong. The trip could be financed with a rucksack load of Melias, a Lao-made Gauloise taste-alike cigarette.

The third-class overnight trip was a series of constant stops, the regional food being pushed aboard at each one. Hummingbirds deep fried, locusts, paddy crab, hundred-year-old eggs, mangoes, dumplings – the Thais generously overfed me, for I had two dollars to my name. After Phnom Penh there are no bridges across the Mekong, which traces the Lao border with Thailand. An outboard-powered pirogue took me across to Tha Deua, the official entry port for all overland goods and people. I arrived in downtown Vientiane with precisely 50 cents of Thai currency in my pocket. I strolled to the Thai consulate to get the forms for the visa, which required five dollars, and wandered the back streets of the sleepy town, too broke to go back to complete the application.

Vientiane at its most swollen, war-torn peak has never boasted more than 125,000 souls, struggling along 10 kilometres of the northern bank of the river. There are five paired avenues and no building over four storeys high, except for the stupas, here called *tats*. In the dry season most of the streets are dust-filled, rutted alleys, in the monsoon a quagmire. Monsoon ditches border the dyked roads and serve as drains and sewers. It could be a set for a spaghetti western or a Graham Greene thriller. I stumbled down alleys lined with bananas and palms; stilted houses sat in little plots of gardens; dogs, pigs, ducks and chickens ambled about. Just as it was getting ridiculous, trudging in the heat when it was obvious that the whole country took a three-hour siesta, I bumped into a long-haired foreigner.

Brian worked for IVS, the International Voluntary Service, a privately sponsored Peace Corps type outfit. With its delicate balance of politics the US government did not station Peace Corps teams in Laos, it contracted IVS. Its members were often older blue-collar workers; the team here even had a 67-year-old plumber. We went back to the team house and flopped down under the ceiling fans in a sparse, clean, rattan-furnished common room. Brian turned out to be a jazz drummer from Connecticut bored with the US jamming, in Laos as an English teacher at the training college at Dong Doc, 10 klicks out of town. This was his afternoon off. We sat listening to Gillespie and Monk, toking his stash, drinking cold San Miguels. I even had a bed for the night.

On the team's suggestion I applied for a job at the USAID compound the next morning. American involvement was on the increase, the Kennedy doctrine in full swing. The mission in Vientiane was crying out for semi-skilled third-country nationals. I was in the personnel office as they opened at eight, clad in my smart trousers and washed though wrinkled shirt. A job was mine after the briefest of interviews, conducted by a woman in rhinestone owl glasses on a granny chain. She must have fancied me. The most trying task was filling in a questionnaire about my politics and religion and that of my parents, a series of true and falses. The application took three hours. My little forestry and knowledge of French landed me in the agricultural department. I was awarded a salary of US$164 per month, a quarter to be disbursed locally in kip, the rest in a hard-currency bank of my choice anywhere in the world. I was to be on probation for two months. They took mugshots and fingerprinted me and sent me right over to the agricultural building. The AID compound was set up like an army base with guard towers and high barbed-wire fences. The various departments were dispersed in prefab huts on brick pilings. There was a giant motor pool and aircraft-hangar-sized PX, to which I had no privileges. Only American nationals could enter the tax-free K-Mart portals.

I blundered up the wooden steps to the air-conditioned hut and into a tall, lanky Anglo who said, in a perfect upper-class accent, 'I hear you must be the new fucking Australian?' I said I was a fucking pom and we laughed, slanged each other in a roadsense way, jawed the lunch break away. Martin Stuart-Fox had been on the road from Australia for four years, via Papua New Guinea, Japan, Taiwan. He looked like your quintessential Englishman in the tropics, beetroot face, bleached hair and a body that towered above the locals. Always dapperly dressed, always polite, attuned to Asian ways more than anyone I had yet met. We had an instant affinity; I wanted him to be the elder brother I never had. We were to be patched together for the next two and a half decades.

Martin was on the same scam as I, third-country-national contract, as were half the agricultural department's staff, who filtered back in after the three-hour lunch. The Laos pace of life is just below the stall speed of a bicycle; they work a six-hour day max, and there were, before liberation in 1975, 103 official national and Buddhist holidays (including all full moons, a three-day festivity), so the average week ran to just over three days. It is only possible in a climate where when seeds are thrown out of the windows there is an instant crop. A Lao can pick his breakfast fixings on the way to work. The mean midday temperature is 100 degrees Fahrenheit. Days and nights in Laos are bloodwarm. In the monsoon season it is slightly cooler, but damp.

By 3.30 that day, late in 1963, I had been introduced to the team members. My immediate superior was the senior agronomist, Jim Hawes. A satisfied man, who had raised a family in the suburbs of Washington DC, growing cut flowers at his own horticultural centre, he had opted to do good bachelor duty in Laos and had brought almost his entire library and a collection of chess boards. Between Martin's double first and PhD, and Jim's library, my formal education was to take informative bounds. We sat drinking coffee; at 4.45 Jim gave Martin and me a lift back downtown to the Som Boum Hotel, where a foreign colony had formed on the top of one wing.

The Som Boum had in its better days been no more than a temporary lodging for French officers. The French had never thought of Laos as being anything but a garden to their Indo-Chinese empire. The fans on the wooden ceilings moved at the same languid speed as they had in the thirties, electricity supplies permitting. There were four floors and three wings, two of which fronted a tree-lined dusty lane backing onto the Ministry of Education. All the rooms had access to a long wooden balcony running along the wing. Windows and doors were louvred, pastel green, paint peeling. The ground floor contained a combined bar, café and restaurant, which was excessively grubby but had verandah tables, and next door was the Lido nightclub – equally insalubrious. The ladies who worked in the club lived in the third wing at the back where the rooms were cubicles and the ablutions in a communal splash bath. The whole building was a small village. On the top of the south wing and in two rooms below on the second floor, there were four French guys, two volunteer workers, two hippies, a German and Martin. I moved into Martin's sitting room, agreeing to split the rent. Next door lived Zabo, the hip cartoonist.

Those of us who worked would gather in the morning for croissants and *café au lait*, made sickeningly sweet with imported condensed milk, down in the bar. The day would end in the Lido, drinking canned Asahi and Saporro beer over dubious ice, a lime on the side. The girls, mainly Vietnamese émigrées, obliged to leave their native Saigon due to Madame Ngu's repressive vice laws, found our strange company fascinating. They presumed that we were hip to the latest western music coming out of the armed forces' radio. When I had left England the Everly Brothers and Buddy Holly ruled the airwaves. Now the Beatles and the Stones were starting to protest. The twist was in its ascendancy, and the girls inveigled us to lead them onto the dance floor. We had all been too long on the road to be aware of the new beat sweeping the west, but we threw ourselves about with rhythmic vigour. The hostesses gravitated to our rooms when the shop was shut to

75

share a pipe or two, intrigued to meet *farangs* who turned on. Traditionally the working girls of South Asia, the hookers, dancers and masseuses, often smoked ganja, a herb considered of benefit to the libido and mental stability. American aid officials and French colonials tended to be juicers who drank their liquor cheaply from the PX or in flyblown hole-in-the-wall bars.

Life became a series of parties and hangovers. A kilo of weed at the Talad Leng – the morning market – cost 10 US cents in real money, ten pipes of opium set you back a dollar. Sex, drugs and the start of rock 'n' roll cocooned our lives, the same girls circulating our cribs nightly.

The days were just as undemanding. Jim had admitted, during that first afternoon, that he had no need for another third-country-national overseer but since he had got me free, so to speak, he had better have me do something harmless. I was instructed to draw a pick-up truck from the motor pool and collect six coolies from the personnel dispatch centre, then to proceed to kilometre 6, the site of the American dependant housing compound, where I was to set up a nursery to provide flowers for the US gardens. I was issued a brand-new, just out of its packing crate, light-green Studebaker six-cylinder truck, the head workman knew a hundred words of French and we set off to the boondocks north of town. Jim would drift out later in the morning.

We had on board shovels, hoes, rakes and *coup-coups*, the locally made machete. In the interest of not offending the residents living either side of the vacant corner lot where my garden centre was to be, the first job would have to be the construction of a latrine for the Laos' use. For this I was to collect the knocked-down crates the same residents' limousines had come all the way from the States in. I had never built anything more complicated than the lean-to on my parents' balcony and no one gave me a plan for building now. I had vague concepts of a cesspit so the seven of us dug a hole of three cubic metres in the hard soil. On top of this I had visions of a platform of four-by-four pine timbers; on that we would have a shed, possibly of woven bamboo. The interior seating could be completed later; the hole was the big thing, all that crap had to go somewhere.

Three days later we were still digging while two of the lads pulled nails out of the shipping-crate boards. They then sat there laboriously hammering the bent ones straight. It was that or requisition some. We had a goodly pile of lumber and a nice mound of dirt. The bottom of the hole was continually muddy, so it had to be bailed at the start of each work shift. Nasty little snakes fell into it and it attracted swarms of insects.

On the fourth day, Jim Hawes dropped by to see what had been going on, hoping to inspect a budding nursery aflame with newly collected jungle blossoms. He did not actually catch us in one of the frequent smoking breaks but just after. It had taken the coolies all of five minutes to suss that I turned on to the *tuc sa*, to their absolute joy, guaranteeing the day's progress at a normal pace. Immediately after we had set up on our corner lot, two of them had ambled off with a mumbled explanation. Nearly an hour later they returned, beaming, dragging an assortment of bamboo and a sarong full of leaves. Luong, the senior man, he with a hundred words of French, squatted down over the pile of bamboo stems and selected a couple of likely pieces. These he trimmed down, one to 15 inches with a knot near the bottom and a hollow tube at the top. He notched a slot just above the knot, and dovetailed in a five-inch piece of slimmer wood. Pee Wee, the squad joker, had meanwhile taken a small knot of wood and had carved a doubled-ended acorn section from it; this was stuck on the short protruding bamboo. The lad I called Karl, since he was Hun-officious and big for a local, had squatted by the truck with his *coup-coup* and was hacking up the semidry pile of leaf. The final touch was a seal made from a blob of asphalt that had oozed from the compound road in the morning heat, squeezed around the stem slot. We had our first USAID-sponsored bong, or water pipe, Indo-China's recyclable answer to the Islamic narghile or hookah. The finely chopped leaf was wadded into the acorn bowl and a sliver of bamboo fired from the tea fire. I was given first blast, disappearing in a cloud of choking, green smoke. Brain went to jelly, then clarity, a huge grin, then the most awful cough, followed by tea and a somnolent high. The lads grinned, burbling Lao small talk. The bowl was refilled by pressing it into the chopped *sa* and passed on. It went round twice and I declared it lunch time. This set the pattern for most of our endeavours henceforth.

Jim found us in a laid-back state contemplating our mounting piles and politely suggested that the latrine was abandoned, a screen erected in the corner of the plot and the hole used for the storage of rhizomes and tubers. Before sending us off to the forests to fill the pit, he sketched out the seed and plant beds he wanted dug. We would have to cut bamboo for shade frames for the seedlings.

77

We took off to the jungle, not difficult when all you had to do was to follow a farm buffalo-cut track until it finished and then walk on a few yards. Each day we struck out in different directions, armed with shovels, hoes and gunny rice sacks, filling the pick-up in a morning of casual gathering. I had little idea what was what, just picked the pretty and groovy-looking things, left it up to the lads.

I sat in the cab reading one of Jim's thousand-plus books. Both he and Martin thought I should become an existentialist, persuading me to devour Kafka, Kerouac, Camus and Colin Wilson. I became an indiscriminate reader of serious books and hardly knew what it all meant, though the space I was in let a lot marinate. Over evening chess games, having got Jim stoned on the AID grass, we would sit discussing till late hours with Martin and the Som Boum hipsters. I had a family.

Some days I would drive way out of town beyond the last check post, not really even thinking of the Pathet Lao threat. Laos was, at that time, divided into three factions – right, neutralist and communist (Pathet) Lao. The leaders of the various parties, all of them warring, were half-brothers and hereditary princes. It was an internecine muddle, with the king in the royal capital up the Mekong, accessible only by air, in Luang Prabang. The communist brother lived at Sam Neua on the Plain of Jars, while the right-wingers, deeply in cahoots with Uncle Sam, ran the lucrative shop in Vientiane. Up in the hills there ruled a self-styled king of the Meos, Toby Le Feng, an honorable admiral in the French navy, and his lieutenant, Kongle.

Although technically at war with the Pathet Lao, the military regime was obliged to let the opposition keep a legation in town, courtesy of the rules laid down by the ICC, the International Control Commision. This had been set up in 1954 at the time of independence from France and the accords were co-signed by twelve nations, which were subsequently obliged for the sake of face to maintain elaborate missions to this backwater land. It bred magnificent diplomatic bashes, binges and faux pas. Before my arrival the neutralists had been in power and were supplied by the Soviet bloc, before then it had been a coalition, French-wooed and supplied. There had always been the reclusive Buddhist monarch and a French military mission advising and training. The Lao navy had three launches and a landing craft, the air force a ratty collection of old propeller-driven planes. It was a front-line farce, the board for a game where the world's powers made side-of-the-table moves that no one usually bothered to report or pick up on.

Around the corner from the Som Boum, on Avenue Samsen Thai, was the Hotel Constellation, from where all Laotian events were reported. This was Vientiane's honorary press club. It was also the main watering hole for all the foreigners loose enough for a daytime drink. Evening saw the off-duty CIA aircrew and the unattached dips – diplomats – lining the bar or playing Cameroon dice at the low tables on the patio. Vientiane had become a catchment for weird characters since the end of the French Indochinese war. Every race and nation could claim at least one representative at the Constellation, and many of their mixed progeny claimed heritage in up to a dozen.

Maurice was such a one and he ran and owned the hotel. Part Corsican, part Viet, Lao and Chinese, he had fingers in all the pies of Vientiane. More business and information flowed at the Constellation than on the telexes of the diplomatic missions. Maurice also did a good deal in demi-pensions: for 1850 kip you got a lunch a day, except Sundays, a full-blown four-course meal with coffee, Algerian plonk extra. It was one of the redeeming features of the pseudo-European existence I was leading and the only guaranteed square meal I would get. The dining was at a communal table where the chat was the background to the power plays of empires. Gun runners, opium dealers, gold smugglers, part-time newsmen, spies, diplomats and hippies shared baguettes, dirty salad, buffalo steak, *frites*, crème caramels. Everyone became a conduit of rumours, half-truths, lies and true nuggets of information.

Dave and Ivan, the speed kings from the Thai Song Greet in Bangkok, came up for new visas and stayed. We crammed them into the rooms at the Som Boum; they shared the girls and the dope and put a little in the rent pot. It was becoming an overcrowded slum. Later Simon appeared to flesh out the throng on the third floor of our rickety palace; the shallow-draft dream sampan that he and the other nightclub residents were restoring – hopefully to sail to New Zealand – had sunk.

Through Martin's AID interpreter, Nan Si, we found an unused Lao-style house behind the compound. It sat on a corner lot, surrounded by papayas and coconut palms. A large, flowering hedge bounded the monsoon ditch. Downstairs was mosquito-screened, but otherwise open-air. We lived upstairs in five rooms. In a separate building was the bath house, kitchen and two rooms for the servants. Water had to be hauled out of a well that was 100 feet deep in the dry season. The crowning features were the badminton court and the rent: US $50 a month. The servants would cost us $20 for a complete family, already installed in the quarters. It was a five-minute walk to work, a ten-minute stroll downtown for lunch or dinner. Both the morning and evening markets were ten minutes away. I continued to receive the weekly letter from my parents, now delighted to have a permanent address to reach me at, via the British embassy. That was in a compound a kilometre away next to the Aussies, Kiwis and the Polish commission.

The Brits, being short-handed, roped me into the Chancellery soccer team that was obliged to put up a show against the Mission Militaire Française at their pitch near Wattay on the airport road. Any Brit in-country, under fifty with four limbs, was needed to make up eleven men. I recruited Dave and Ivan; Martin was dragged in, he had been born in the UK and still maintained a British passport. Calling us a team would be a compliment. Our first kick-about was pre-match. We appeared in a motley array of strip T-shirts, tennis shirts, football boots and borrowed sneakers; the French were in short shorts, cleated boots and matching tops, *très sportif*. I believe the score at half-time was 4–0 for them. The Pep-Tabs we had consumed on our side were burned out, we were exhausted and dehydrated. More tabs and some beer helped a bit but the final whistle found us six against and a conciliatory one for. The real match was to come, a champers tea *chez* the Mission Militaire followed by a booze-up *chez* the Brits. All square at the day's end.

The move from the Som Boum had been made after eight of us had caught the clap from the same bedmate. It was a dose with a vengeance, not easily cured. The French went to their hospital to have umbrellas rammed up their penes pre-injection; I went to the Operation Brotherhood Filipino-run free Lao clinic; Martin went to the US embassy unit. All of them failed to affect the constant drip. The French called it the *pisse chaud*, a sensation of peeing razor blades, accompanied by constant irritation and ever present globule of pus at the tip of one's dong. Beyond anything else, it was boring, since during treatment there was to be no booze and no sex – both nearly free and on tap twenty-four hours daily. Pills, shots, scrapings, liquids, diets and refraining were to no avail, the bloody thing recurred six times. It had armour plate on every bacillus. Finally Zabo, the cartoonist, went on a short trip to Hong Kong and returned cured, bearing a box of ampoules and capsules for our consumption. Sigmamycin and Kanamycin, hitherto unknown in Laos, triumphed. Their potency was to slip once the bar girls started to munch them. Strange rumours were started by a visiting ABC cameraman and correspondent, Neil Davis, that I was selling 'the cure' sitting on an army poncho in the evening market, the only place where strong medicines could be found, no questions asked, for green, kip or Thai baht.

Neil had come to Laos on his first overseas assignment from Uc Da Loi, the big land under, as the Lao call Oz, to spotlight the escalation of the conflict with the Pathet Lao. It was a story hooked on the CIA spook-run airlines; Bird & Son, Continental Air Services and, principally, Air America. They took supplies, including arms and ammo, up to the indigenous mountain tribes who were the principal fighters along the fringes of the central massif, the Plain of Jars. A half-dozen peoples, including the H'mung, Meo and Yao, had been slash-and-burn farmers, working the jungle's mountain terrain, planting hill rice and corn but primarily the opium poppy. They were not self-sufficient in their food production but their opium surplus was in the hundreds of tons, ready to find a morphine-base conversion outlet. The CIA's planes and a handful of Union Corse mafioso bush pilots guaranteed the dispersal of the raw black viscous poppy sap. The Montagnards got carbines and grenades, machine guns and transistor transponders in return. The stuff rained free fall from the back of ageing American flying boxcars, C-47s and Caribous, their markings sandblasted off. Some sat out at Wattay airport, painted ominous, drab black. The dudes in Ray-Bans and bush jackets who kicked the shit out of the rear doors made a fortune, and watered and dealt at the Constellation. Neil needed cut-away shots of smokers getting it on.

There were, back then in 1963–4, at least a dozen *fumeries officielles*, government-approved opium dens. Entrance was free, and at the cavernous one near the afternoon market you had a choice of slabs on which to prostrate yourself for the ritual. An unknown vibration directed you to the pipemaker you believed to be the most empathetic. A red 100-kip note bought a *bidon d'o*, a measure fashioned from the base cap of a 37-mm cannon cartridge. A 20-mm measure was 50 kip. Depending on the pipe person, that gave you between five and eight smokes – a siesta fix or a night cap. The measures were standard at all the official dens as well as the private ones, where the quality of the smoke was often enhanced with imported Burmese or Indian blends. The Lao love to turn you on, like the French are proud of their vintage wine; they are delighted to lead you down their path, the way lit by their philosophy of Bo Pin Yan – an oriental mañana, the French translate it as *Ce n'est rien*, a policy of no sweat.

Opium gives you a slo-mo hangover. I started getting in to get the pick-up at the motor pool at nine or ten in the morning. Lunch hours got longer, the coolies only too happy to nap their twenty bucks a week away. USAID got smart to my nonactivity after six weeks and there were still no beautiful plants appearing in their wives' front yards. Jim Hawes let me go out with Martin on his alternative-crop incentive programme. America had decided that the Lao needed a greater variety of vegetables, so they started to import vast quantities of new American seeds. My nursery served as a test bed for strange, improved Florida watermelons, Californ- ian squash, and okra never before seen. There was an inherent problem with the American goodies; they thrived well at home but without the doses of pesticides, insecticides and fertilizer, plus all-American know-how, they would not flourish here. Home- economics teams then had to go out to villages to show the people what to do with the exotic veg.

The same dilemma arose when the New Zealanders decided to import dairy cows to improve the diet with milk products. The cows had to be fed with lush grass grown in large window boxes; the grass withered, the cows died and the idea was laid to rest. Milk in Laos still comes condensed in cans.

Cruising with Martin became a full-time job after I ran the director of USAID off the road with the Studebaker. We were returning from the teacher training school at Dong Doc, past the housing compound on the narrow dyketop road, the paddies dried out either side. Feeling ornery, I did not give way to the oncoming limo and watched it lurch off the verge in a swirl of dust. Back at the motor pool that night, I had to surrender the keys.

By now my Laotian was better than rudimentary, the lads in my gang had taught me enough to sow, plant and harvest anything. Helping out in the villages was fun. Often we were invited back for feasts and dinners – an enjoyable form of agricultural diplomacy. When the new crops flourished we were introduced to the new IR8 miracle rice for distribution. This was a strain bred in the Philippines which was to green Asia, doubling and trebling the harvested tonnage. Our big hassle was that the Lao did not like its texture or taste when cooked, preferring their age-old sticky rice. The IR8 was distributed anyway, because the government needed a larger army to fight the American-inspired civil war. Better yields needed fewer hands to farm.

Our best invention should have been patented: the recycling of the four-gallon cooking-oil cans handed out to the refugees. These tins were used for storage or beaten flat for roofing. Martin found an enterprising metal worker near the market prepared to work on prototypes, and he remodelled two tins into one watering can, perfect for dousing our improved seedlings twice daily. He also made sieves for fine seed beds, funnels and lamps. In 1980, returning to Vientiane, I noted the same collective of shops still turning out the products we invented. The same cans of oil were still being donated to refugees now by the US via the UN, the US AID handshake logo with stars and stripes on handshaking cuffs still stamped on the packaging.

I was reassigned to do some real work with my gang, under the supervision of a big black guy, Doug Harris, an IVS volunteer from Illinois who was in charge of an experimental pig farm at the training college. Starting from scratch in an area of raw jungle, Doug had carved out a farm where the local strain of sway-back black pig, more wild boar than bacon machine, would be crossed with imported Taiwanese Yorkshires. He hoped they would all straighten up and yield lots of the favourite local meat. The buildings and sties were built out of the same discarded shipping crates as my abandoned latrine. RD (rural development) drilled a well and poured some slab concrete, and we worked to clear the surrounding land for a field of corn. Termite hills too hard to bulldoze were blasted and fired; scorpions, under nearly every pulled stump, were doused in diesel; partly by hand, partly by machine we hacked out 10 acres and planted the first seeds. A blight hit the lot and we had to feed the newly arrived Taiwanese porkers on the bulgar wheat originally destined for refugees but turned down by them as inedible. With Jim Hawes, I dreamed up a way of using the dried-up Mekong river bed for growing short-growth crops for the farm in the dry season. It was approved and I was reassigned an ancient Land-Rover to drive round the river bottom. Corn, sweet potatoes, melons and squash thrived in orderly rows within weeks, though at the cost of rural development drilling a well in the middle of the sandbar which would be lost the next rainy season. The People's Democratic State's pig-breeding ranch of 1980 had been relocated but the inmates still showed their northern English–Taiwanese ancestry and their fodder was grown on the same sandbars.

I made enough money, carefully stashed in my Dutch bank in Hong Kong, to get a mail-order 35mm Yashica camera and a brand-new BSA Bantam 175cc motorbike. By a quirk of economic aid, everything imported by western nations was brought in at a deflated rate, half the official rate. The black market rate was double the official rate, and there was a free-market rate just below that of the black. You could triple your money in minutes, legally. For those of us living there, it meant that consumer items like cars and motorcycles cost only half what they did at home. The Laotian economy, except for the leaders' pockets, did not benefit a cent. I got the Beezer for $175. It still defeats me why the economic-aid guy at the Foreign Office in London decided that we should export sports cars (three of them) to a country with only 35 kilometres of paved highway or ship large rocker bikes to a people whose stature was hobbitlike. When you went shopping for a major item you literally had to take a suitcase for the kip for payment because the country did not use cheques. Whenever they needed more, De La Rue, the company that prints notes for many countries, would ship out a Dakota's worth of hundreds and five hundreds and the finance ministry would revalue accordingly. Most foreigners, East and West bloc alike, changed their funds with Maurice, who charged a few kip handling charge.

The BSA came in Post Office red trim with leg shields, panniers and gloved handlebar grips. I stripped it down to a bare rig and took all the lights off when the electrics failed in the first monsoon rains. Often it would not start and the British had not thought to ship out any spares with the consignment. Martin's Japanese electric-everything quasi-scooter started first time every time. We rode out to the outlying wats and temples together, immersing ourselves into the spiritual world that Martin had studied and I pursued. Buddhism was introduced into Laos in the twelfth century by the king. The gentle philosophy of life had fit the Lao like a sarong and the country now followed the dharma to a person. The wat was the centre of community life, serving as a school, law court, meeting hall and holistic health centre as well as temple. They sit in walled gardens, planted with trees, always a sacred Bo under which the Buddha attained enlightenment. Their architecture is typical of Southeast Asia, steep, tiled roofs with gilded gables, tall, narrow, shuttered windows, porticoed entrance to the central shrine room. Inside in the still, incense-pervaded coolness, a giant image of the Buddha looks serenely down on the hall where people sit in meditation or pray in front of smaller images at the foot of the main statue. I found an inner tranquillity just being in these sanctums. I even started a scrap book filled with postcard-size black and white prints shot on the new Yashica, called *The Impressionable Buddha*. My first attempt to write the Lao language was the title of the journal and my name.

It was the summer of 1964 and I was about to be twenty. I was blissed out with no concept of what was happening to my gang of old mates 10,000 miles away. Even the Bangkok papers got to town a day late and my radio had been sold in Lahore. I was in fat city; a bike, a job, more dope than anyone in Amsterdam had even hinted at and no responsibilities whatsoever. It could not last.

That summer I got my first assignment as a cameraman. It was for Australian television. Gil Brearley, a mate of Neil Davis's, needed someone to go along to the traditional harvest festival after the Meo had got raw opium in. I was engaged as assistant silent cameraman, translator and senior gofer. I skived off from my latest gig counting seeds in a concrete warehouse. We flew upcountry to Luang Prabang for two days before we could get a milk run down to Sayaboury. Virtually uncharted jungle stretched 150 miles to Thailand from the Mekong; scattered ethnic hilltop villages scorched clearings for poppies. A battered long-wheelbase AID Willy's bumped us two hours deeper from the dirt strip that served Sayaboury's 3000 souls. An outpost manned by three armed Filipino R & D workers represented the limit of government influence. Here we would switch to hill ponies for the next 15 miles into the Meo village.

I had never been on horseback in my life. A bike I control, an animal does its own thing. I was assured it was no sweat. Prod with the right boot to make it go right, prod left to go left; both boots at once were a gas pedal, the rein was a sort of brake. I had the Bell & Howell 16mm Filmo, the tape recorder and a sack of groceries hung around myself and the saddle. The track was a tunnel through grabbing green thorns and bamboo. The beast beneath me was on another wavelength and took off down the tunnel, scattering the column, shedding bits of equipment. No command made any difference. It ended with me pitched headlong into a muddy, leech-filled, flooded river. I walked most of the way to Ban Houei Sim.

The village was in a glorious state, a bumper harvest in, jars of *choum* (fermented rice wine) and a stack of sway-backed pigs ritually slaughtered. Vast vats, made from abandoned fuel drums, cooked the opium, reducing out the impurities and dross. The pure stuff would be shipped out on a mule train, the crud would fuel workers' dreams. Every hut had a pipe going in the parlour. We were lodged on the reluctant head man, who just wanted to lie back with his buddies and sample the *nouveau* Beaujolais. Tomorrow would be the big feast; meanwhile we were invited to taste. Gil was reluctant, gagging until he learned the long suck. In the middle of this, an ancient European appeared, wearing a black cassock, solar topee and paratroop jungle boots. He was a drop-out Catholic monsignor who had served with the French forces, survived Viet Minh POW cages and gone native as a missionary in these hills for a decade. He had almost forgotten how to speak his native Italian or adopted French, and was as dirt-encrusted as the Meo, tinged red by the rusty mud. We filmed him, the village, the sticky refining business; we smoked more and chatted a lot. A good film. That night the floor was laid with heaps of steaming food, baskets of sticky rice and bowls of peppered fish sauce. With all the smoking we had had nothing but a few teas and coffees in thirty-six hours and now we dived into this mountain of fresh vegetables and freshly slaughtered, half-charred pork. The mountain folk don't wash their salad fixings and the pigs are prone to eat any old shit. They have bugs, worms and worse. Six weeks later I came down with the first signs of a massive sickness.

For some weeks I had been squatting in the deserted servants' quarters at the house of the British embassy radio operator. Our garden house had come to an abrupt end when its true spookiness had revealed itself. The bad *pis* or spirits had entered the house, the good ones departed, the servants with them, leaving us to hand-haul all the water and keep the charcoal-powered stove alight. It had been a carefree place to live, a tropical animal house for a fraternity of road runners, all of British origin. We held dinners, parties, rave-ups, smoke-ins, we became proficient leapers after shuttlecocks, but our Lao friends always felt uncomfortable there. At night doors would open, stairs creak, screens bang, something or someone was moving about in the house and yet the bikes, motorcycles and stereo downstairs were untouched. It was not burglars. I slept with a kukri under the bamboo bed. I seemed to come awake whenever the vibrations started. I could hear the thing's passage around the place. It was frightening though not threatening. It was totally spooky.

One night the sounds, the movements, the presence was so strong that after the apparent mounting of the stairs – the screen door at their base had opened and closed, and a few moments later so had the one at the top – we all six of us had got up and gathered in the central upstairs room. Pale, naked, sarong-clad spectators, all armed. Simon had his macho Luger, Ivan a kris, John the Welsh poet, another roadrunner, with a switchblade, even pacifist Martin had a nasty-looking kitchen knife. We had to admit it, the place was definitely haunted.

Within days, unripe papayas were falling unseasonally out of our trees, an ominous portent in superstitious Laos. I went down early one morning to collect the day's freshly laundered work clothes, habitually left on a low bamboo bed inside the saloon door. As I reached for the stack of linen, I spotted what appeared to be a length of black electrical cable under the slatted bamboo. I retrieved my clothes and started back upstairs. It dawned in a rush – no electricians, the imperceptible movement. The flex was a snake, a mamba or worse. I rushed out the back door hollering the servants' names, screaming, '*Na den, na den*,' – 'Black snake.' The whole family came at a run, the head boy with *coup-coup* and broom to hand. But the creature had slithered off. Locally the belief is that a black snake brings bad spirits. The serving crew upped and went the same day without a word said. We decamped after a week's struggle to cope and survive. Dave and Ivan went back to smuggling, down to the Malay penisula and maybe home.

Months later I passed the house and witnessed a group of bonzes exorcising the place for the new tenants.

In Bombay I had been naïvely ill, acutely ill. This time the onset of tropical malady was gradual. At the first visit to the OB Jaycee hospital they had told me to take it easy and consume a heap of pills against a possible malaria recurrence and to beef up my liver against the circulating dengue fever. The first doctor I saw took one look at me and ordered me into the nearest ward. I was boiling with viral infectious hepatitis. The ward was densely packed but they squeezed in another not too clean bed and ordered me into it. A smiling Lao nurse came in to stick an IV in my arm. She was still trying ten minutes later and I had five large puncture wounds in my arm. A squad of officials were finally successful.

The common, overcrowded ward was very sociable, more like a market than a hospital. Relatives stayed with the patients in and around their bed, occasionally hopping onto it for a nap. I got an unquenchable desire for condensed milk and, though advised against consuming it, guzzled four or five cans a day, punched open with a tap boy borrowed from one of my room mates. Full recovery took six months of pure lassitude, days when I would sleep for fifteen hours. I made a three-week excursion to Cambodia, staying downtown in Siem Riep, 10 kilometres from the Angkor complex, chronologically tracing the building of the ruined city.

I had shared the driving down through Thailand with a British embassy official. Unlike most dips, he turned on, and we had become friends during my recovery. We had converted his spare room into a *fumerie*, though our attempts to make pipes had resulted in the Foreign Office carpentry, wallpaper and divans getting as much of a coating of the treacly opium as our lungs did. The skill of making a pipe was one that few foreigners ever mastered; cheaper and easier to hit your local den.

Angkor was my first experience with sufficient film to wax photographic, the setting a natural for the worst hack. Groslier's guide in hand, we cycled slowly through the serene woods. They had an English cathedral-green feeling, belied by the exotic plants. Narrow lanes led between the Khmer sites spaced over 20 square kilometres. Bernard Groslier was the archaeologist in charge of gradually clearing the encroaching jungle off the ruins, and his guide is the definitive one. The temples were a bizarre sight, banyan trees sprouting from cloister roofs, roots draping down over Buddha sandstone faces twelve centuries old, lines of delicately carved maidens carved on 100-metre friezes, lost statues in partially cleared courtyards. The place had been discovered by a collector of butterflies who must have thought that he had found El Dorado. Butterflies the size of soup plates lazed on the stones, flocks of multicoloured flakes drifted in the forests. I spent a night on top of the Bayon, one of Angkor's ancient buildings. Here the spirits were wise and friendly, and there were often bats. But the shadows and jungle noises were unnerving.

Phnom Penh was a three-day flash of pleasure. French food at the floating restaurants, gilded temples and a nutty brown girl who crept into my hotel room in the middle of the night and who stayed for two nights without asking for a thing. Her French vocabulary was minimal, my Khmer nil. I spoke Lao and we both smiled a lot.

Back in Laos I was in puppy love with a French teacher, an

affair of the mind, never physically consummated, an older sister that never was.

Everyone over a certain age has been asked the stock question, 'Where were you when President Kennedy was killed?' I was sitting in one of the abominably uncomfortable chairs (made, it was said, by a White Russian count with a large tab owing) in the open foyer of the Constellation. I was now a temporarily accredited newsman. I was UPI's man in Vientiane, and I also held a *Daily Express* cable card. They were Martin's legacy to me while he went away for six weeks. Unlettered Simon was a full-time stringer repping for the *Daily Telegraph* and the *New York Times*. Laos had become news. As the conflict in Vietnam had heated up, American influence on its neighbour had dramatically increased. I was busy stuffing packages of seeds in with rice, cooking pots, carbine clips, grenades and blankets to be airdropped up-country to the Special Forces' trained guerrillas. Kennedy's infatuated policy of putting Green Beret teams in eighty-three countries was at its height in Indochina. A-Teams were scattered around the Plain of Jars, the Bolivens Plateau down south and along the Golden Triangle borders. They needed a heavy airlift and tactical air support to cover them. Wattay airport became a major terminal; the heavy stuff flew directly from USAF bases in northern Thailand – Udorn Korat, Nakhon Phanom.

The Pathet Lao with their Viet counterparts started to get very good at knocking the jets, transports and choppers out of the sky. This was an embarrassment, and the US embassy spokeman constantly denied these downings. The resident press corps had to field reports confirming the PL radio claims, transcribed thoughtfully by the Japanese embassy. The same report would then be taken to the Aussie military attaché, the most savvy in town, for an appraisal before going to talk to the US information lad in his freezing office. After making the rounds, the entire press corps, all six of us, usually gathered for cocktails *chez* Maurice to compare notes before filing. It was too small a town to try to scoop someone, we all smoked, drank and loved as an ensemble. Every secret in Laos was known to most people, every spook that walked in would be booed. The Americans got the transcript of the PL radio from their men in Saigon a day late. We knew more than we were supposed to. Anyone could be claimed as a usually reliable source in a cable.

USAID had fired Martin – a conflict of interests, they said.

With United Press needing a daily file, even a few cents a word made for a decent living. Tokyo had decided he was of promising material and would make a good full-time correspondent; all that was needed was a briefing course in Japan. During his training sabbatical I held the strings. He also left the keys to the staff car, the only black MGA in Indochina. Our headquarters was adjoining rooms in a stilted wooden house in the emerging red-light district of Dong Palan. UPI paid the petrol, the supplies for the communal kitchen and the shared maid. Next door lived the Reuters correspondent, a Scottish hippy, Tammy, and his Thai bar-girl wife.

My first reports were gibberish, prompting cabled queries longer than my original texts. It was fun being invited to all official functions. State dinners, national-day feasts at various diplomatic missions, cocktails at the French embassy, Lao ceremonies and, best of all, organized trips to the front. Traditional Meo New Year ceremonies were backed by unmarked HH-34 olive-drab helicopters ferrying in wounded, ammo boxes and fuel drums. I had days out in Luang Prabang to visit royalty, and examined displays of captured weapons at Seno airbase near Savannakhet. I cabled garbled impressionistic stories, put together packets with the odd roll of film hoping it would be used. My six-week stint earned me $100 and a Pentax camera. It got me asked to resign from USAID, too.

I had caught the media bug. Journalism in the Third World is a knot of intrigue and camaraderie. The handful of miscreants that made up Vientiane's corps were privy to front-line state councils of the kind novels are made of. We were sitting on the scene of *The Ugly American*, the philosophies of Malraux. I knew the whole cast of characters, had started to playact myself. I had let myself be persuaded to buy the first and last suit I have ever owned. I could pass with aplomb into a gathering *tenue de ville*, a foolish pretence in the sticky heat of the Mekong valley.

Laotians have periodic rituals when they discharge rockets, for fertility, across the river, and during an eclipse of the moon, they are likely to open up with anything to hand, mortars, machine guns, pistols and artillery as well as rockets – to kill the giant rat that is consuming the moon. One morning in January 1964 we were awoken not in celebration but in earnest anger. The town had become a battlefield. For days there had been rumours of manoeuvrings between different government factions led on one side by the right-wing army and air force, on the other by the even further right paramilitary police. It boiled down to which prince would get the biggest slice of the American pie, who would control the opium traffic, the gold concession.

I remember riding my new Cotton 250cc street scrambler at 50 miles per hour down the main, completely deserted Tat Luang boulevard. Occasional bursts of fire kicked out and spat past but I could not trace their origin nor tell whether they were of real threat to me on my bike. It didn't feel as though I was being shot at and I wasn't hit. It was a bit dodgier missing all the expended detritus left by the ebbing firefight. Cartridge casings, bricks, dead dogs and rubbish littered the Avenue Lang Xang. The only vehicles on the street had their windows shot out, their bodies punctured with holes. All the shops had shuttered up behind their steel grilles. The only traffic light in the land was still working happily away.

As a precaution, Martin had taken a room at the Constellation. That is where I was headed, doing my scrambler-to-the-front bit. I was in business. The hotel was overflowing with residents and refugees. No one had a clear picture of what was happening. Martin gave me his Nikon and a plastic bag of film and sent me to roam the streets. The local police station, four blocks away, had become a fire base for the rebels; loyalist armoured cars pumped 37-mm armour-piercing rounds at the smouldering post. The Lao, devout Buddhists, were not out to kill but to persuade the opposition to surrender. The danger was from stray rounds. The highest casualties that day had been among a family of Vietnamese noodle-shop owners who were pulverized by a direct hit from an indiscriminately fired 82-mm mortar.

The battle for Vientiane had isolated the city. No cables could go out, the road to the airport was blocked, and the ferries had stopped running. The beehive of journalistic output had no place to dump its hot story but down the pooled line from the American embassy. The five major agencies and the Coudoux Frères who strung for all the networks and French magazines were for the first time competing unsuccessfully for a scoop. The Indian tailor opposite the hotel, who had a sideline in passport photos, souped my film, and with Martin's hurriedly typed-up report I booted the Cotton into gear and set off for Tha Deua, the entry port on the Mekong 25 kilometres away. I felt like a dispatch rider roaring down the deserted streets. The soldiers who stepped into the road took one look at the mad longhair and stepped back, grinning. At the Chinaino army camp, a lot of shit was being thrown about, but again never felt destined for me: I had the bike, the *farang* face, my amulets of survival.

The returned headline clippings which came in the next week overplayed an exciting bike ride. 'Hand-carried through machine-gun fire, our exclusive report from Vientiane . . .' The politics of the events made a column on page 7.

Getting those few rolls of film to Bangkok had been a trip, the motorcycling the least of it. A lot of persuasion went into the hiring of a pirogue to be paddled across to the Thai side. The nearest secure telephone, where I could also ship the valuable frames, was at Udorn, 45 miles away. I presented myself at the gate guard post, to be immediately placed under arrest. They woke the base information officer, who grudgingly let me use a phone. It was three o'clock in the morning. As the base awakened I became the centre of attention, parked in a cafeteria with warm Coke from a vending machine and a stale sandwich. I was the only eyewitness from a closed country.

I was back at the Constellation for croissants and *café au lait*.

We stayed exclusive for three days. I nipped about snapping the dissipating mayhem, Martin churned out confused front-line stories, I got them out. Smuggled Bangkok papers bore our by-lines banner on the front page. We were the toast of the jealous bar, where our tab ran even higher, guaranteed by UPI.

No action in Laos could last longer than three days, and on the fourth, all went back to a relative normalcy. The grilles came up, more than one bar was open. The attempted coup had failed. The first incoming flight disgorged a gaggle of Asia's toughest newsmen on a post-mortem sweep-through, an excursion to the back garden of the beat. Martin and I were invited to an enormous Chinese feast, hosted by the Associated Press, where we were the star guests. The story got longer and better by the telling. The networks flew in to film long pieces. They ended up converging on the country's only golf course, which had two holes and crossed a dry paddy, with buffalo and dogs chasing the balls.

Ray Herndon came in for UPI from Saigon. Previously he had been a GI with MAAG Laos (the military assistance and advisory group). Now his task was to warm up the story for a magazine piece: *Life* also cabled an offer of $500 for use of my pictures and story, although in the event they did not run it. We celebrated at the Vieng Ratry, the town's hot spot – known as the Green Latrine. On the way home to our red-light-district condo, Martin asked me what I would think about a job as a photographer full time. In the euphoric post-conflict haze, the question passed me by. The *padiwat* – the coup – was over and so was Laos's three-yearly media exposure, leaving only the hardcore orientalists to their backwater bliss.

The next week Martin waited eagerly for my arrival at the Constellation bar. He was holding a blue PTT cable, which he thrust at me. It unfolded from a small square to a larger one of flimsy, recycled blue paper. From stringer paid by the word, through freelancer to staff member in a span of ten weeks, back on salary. My future was printed in seven lines, mistakes included:

PLEASE OFFER TIM PAGE FIRM DEAL FOR THREE MONTHS AS PHO-
TOGRAPHER IN VIETNAM AT NINETY REPEAT NINETY DOLLARS PER
WEEK STOP WE WILL PAY AIRFARE TO SAIGON STOP HE WILSL HAVE
NORMAL EXPENSE ACCOUNT BUT MUST PAY OWN LIVING EXPENSES
SAME AS OTHER STAFFER ASSIGNED SAITON STOP AT END OF THREE
MONTHS WILL REVIEW SITUATION AND HIS WORK AND DECIDED ON
FUTURE STOP CABLE IF HE ACCEPTS AND GET HIM STARTED SAIGON
SOONEST ADVISING WHEN HE WILL ARRIVE THERE. HOBERECHT

4

Bao chi

I arrived in Saigon from Laos on 2 February 1965, a green hippy kid with a borrowed Nikon and two lenses in a cardboard leatherette bag which was wont to fall apart in the monsoons, and a beat-up Pentax around my neck.

From the moment I landed, met by a rotund, grinning bandit photostringer and whisked to the Hotel Central, I felt as though I was stepping into a romantic novel. It got better as I started shaving in the twilit French bathroom; in glided a svelte form in silken *ao dai* tunic and descended upon my genitals with unabashed avidity, bringing Vietnam into an orgasmic focus. I still had not eaten my first meal or been to the office. I knew I was going to like Vietnam, the war was going to be a doddle.

My UPI photo chief, a métis Frenchman of fourteen years' photographic experience, was making ten bucks less a week than I. Henri Huet would tutor me for the next six months in how to see for the wire and how to shoot for yourself. He gave me a gentle introduction into an insane situation which at first seemed just like having a good time, making a largish wad of money and playing at dangerous big boys' games.

My first day was a crash induction course straight to the rank of captain in a war zone. I was briefed, accredited and kitted out with fatigues and French para boots from the black market. In appearance I was a pathetic sight in my stiff new gear. The first job was a press conference followed by a line-up, on the steps of the palace, of the new cabinet.

Nobody told me I was supposed to develop or print the film. I had never had to. I just dumped it in the back photo room of the

94

bureau and crept out the rear into the Melody bar next door to have a beer and hope to find the Viet lab lad. I got a bollocking after three beers when Henri rushed in with, '*Alors, Teem, le photo où?*' I took a crash course in black-and-white photo processing, though I never did get the knack of rolling the film onto the tank spool. I blame the left index finger, twisted to a gnarled root under the BSA in 1961. When in town all photographers were responsible for the developing, selection, printing, captioning and then transmission of their radio photos. Later, as the war escalated and a number of photographers worked the bureau, a full-time dark-room shift was employed.

Simon, lured south by Reuters, had already been in-country for four months. Both our agencies had thrown in a one-way ticket on a Royal Air Lao DC-6, our respective motorcycles strapped to the cockpit firewalls, cranks and gas tanks still primed. Initially we shared a pile of rooms tucked away in a back street behind the presidential palace and the Cercle Hippique; none of us could afford a decent crib. Simon had teamed up with a Batista Cuban émigré, Leonardo Michaelangelo Caparros, who called himself El Gatto. We called him the Cat. The Cat had gone to a military academy in Havana before getting out and let his fantasies trip him one way to Vietnam with a loose accreditation to an exiles' magazine, *Havana Libre*. He had come to play in the war zone complete with revolver and stripped-down Willy's jeep which was daubed a brilliant canary yellow. It went by the name of the Yellow Peril. Reuters actually paid Simon to rent it full time as a staff car for his bureau. Its vintage was early fifties lend-lease. It only had two seats and missed both top and windshield. Monsoon driving required a poncho or an umbrella. There had once been a winch on the front end, giving the rig an extended I-beam steel proboscis, ideal for nudging Saigon's traffic aside or assisting in tight parking. In the Peril we were invincible. It had probably originally been nicked but it never went missing again. It and we were a hazard, Simon and I both armed with Lao international *permits de conduire*.

We were prime meat out of the woods, still innocent about the magnitude of the issues, the chaos of emotions inside a war zone. The staff photographer for AP (the Roxy in coded messages on our wire) was Eddie Adams, a Marine veteran of Korea, who arrived two days after me. I already knew his name, he was formidable in his photojournalistic ability. I knew the picture he had shot at JFK's graveside in Arlington: JJ saluting, Jackie weeping behind the black veil, folded Stars and Stripes in gloved hands. He was to be my opposition, my inspiration. It would not be long before the two of us would find ourselves on the same mission together.

That early in the war, with only 17,600-odd Americans in-country, there were usually no more than a couple of operations going on simultaneously. The assets, the helicopters to carry the ARVN (South Vietnamese army) troops into combat, did not exist in sufficient numbers. The operations were usually reactions to Viet Cong attacks rather than the later, larger search and destroy missions where whole battalions were lifted in to hunt down enemy units, their base camps and supplies, and hopefully destroy the infrastructure which had built up.

On the first operation together, a sweep through once friendly villages to ambush the encroaching enemy, with the local regional forces south of Da Nang in late February, we were lucky to have an Australian adviser along whose map had all the strategic coordinates marked where beer was available way out in the boondocks.

It had been a long slog, with the typical boring perversity of a long, hot day at war. We were nearing the pick-up point and were in the last hamlet of the day. I stepped through a prickly hedge to gain the path out of a vegetable garden we had been traversing; the ruff puff troops plundered in passing what they wanted, causing some villagers to emerge from their hiding places in protest. The ARVN flushed a military-age lad with a defiant look.

As I put my foot through the other side of the thicket and down, it disappeared, my momentum carried me on and over, falling into the jungle detritus. A sharp stab of pain echoed out of the right boot, a *pungi*, a booby trap, had just punctured my instep, deflected by the nylon-and-steel mesh insole inside my French para boots. I had got the boot and sock off and swabbed out the cut; luckily there was no shit on the spike, human or buffalo.

I caught up with the hullabaloo going on down the track. The Viet Cong suspect they had turned up looked as though he knew more than he was claiming to. His bound hands were imploring, outstretched, while the company interrogator, a nasty rodentlike piece of work with honorific master sergeant's French pips, beat the living daylights out of him. A crowd of advisers and HQ folk, almost a dozen people, stood curiously watching, weapons on hips, relaxed, enjoying the scene. They'd got one of the little buggers dead to rights, there was just the nagging question of where his weapon was and how much he knew. The guy was being stubborn – brave or stupid, you could take your choice – and it was pissing the hell out of the ferret sergeant and his commanding officer. Eddie lurked, clicking away, staying out of sight but working. I hobbled down the path towards the action. Just as I got within decent shooting range with my mingy gear, the rodent proceeded to stick a bayonet in the suspect's skinny abdomen. I froze as the guy curled up dying on the bamboo-leaf-strewn dirt. I turned aside and dry-heaved a foul bile. The poor dude surrendered no more information and I made no more frames that day.

Back in Da Nang, Eddie and I shipped our films in separate packets down to our bureaus in Saigon on the regular courier milk run and went down to the bar at the hotel for a few cold, wet Buds. The next day, there was a cable in my box: it was a rocket, a public bollocking. It read: 'ROXY LEADING NATIONAL AMS. YOU SAME OP WHERE PIX. ENDIT.'

From that time on I never turned away again. The photo had to be shot, no matter what. The field was not a place to let the inner self take control, or you would never go out again. Much less freeze a frame.

My first real taste of combat came on Route 19, in the Mang Yang Pass, on the road between Qui Nhon on the coast and Pleiku in the Central Highlands. In exactly the same place that the Viet Minh in May 1954 had ambushed a Group Mobile 100, a French flying column escorting a surgical convoy, killing hundreds, their sons, now the Viet Cong, had decimated a Special Forces convoy reconnoitring westwards from the newly established A Team camp at An Khe. Beneath the French cemetery and the jungled, steep hills, the VC had sprung their trap at the same series of bends, where rusting carcasses of the 'Korean' legionnaires' jimmies and half-tracks rusted amid jungle plants.

The remaining Green Berets had their dander up, for the surviving indigenous mercenary troops had bugged out of the action, leaving two Americans hit, probably dead, along with their own killed and wounded. Very few of the survivors had even their weapons, they had been totally overwhelmed.

I had managed to hitch a lift in II Corps' Senior Advisers' B-model Huey as far as the still incomplete fort. The berms were still only waist-high, the team house under construction beside the HQ and communications bunker, there was a single coil of concertina barbed wire looped around the perimeter. Within an hour we were saddling up on a couple of jeeps, a three-quarter-ton ammo carrier and a larger sixby. Their floors and decks were heavily sandbagged, windshields folded flat, and perching on the vehicles were roughly forty, a platoon, of Montagnard strikers. Three Americans were along to run the show, including the weapons sergeant packing two machine guns, a .50 cal for his three-quarter-tonner and an M-60 for his lap. His Armalite was on the dash, his webbing held grenades and a holstered PPK. We ground out of the red laterite mud of the compound and crawled west along a narrow black-topped lane, screened on either side by a wall of elephant grass, bamboo and scrub trees. The only thing you could see beyond this screen was the upper regions of the old mahoganies and teaks. Charlie could pick the place where he wanted to hit you. It was more than a little spooky riding down this tropical country lane, not unlike those in the Terai of Nepal where I had been driving two years previously. This time, my first real in-country solo field trip, there was a more than fifty-fifty chance of a showdown.

We crept on, occasionally passing an abandoned hooch or once-tended gardens, now bush again, but still we weren't hit. We were being lured farther away from the camp, beyond mortar-support range. The tension mounted, the joking and chattering subsided. Everyone continually fidgeted with their weapons; I fiddled with the focus on my Pentax, my pucker factor went past f.22. My eyes tried to pierce the foliage, tried to pick out a weapon, a camouflaged shape, to react before it could. We made three or four kilometres in an hour and approached the ambush site with still no action. It was beyond the eerie now, it had become very frightening to me, a virgin, the tension was nine months pregnant. The road was littered with the debris of war: ammo casings, combat dressings, cartridge boxes, food tins, torn clothing, un-identifiable chunks of objects, once vehicles. Then the smell hit us, the stink of putrescent flesh. The ambush was eighteen hours old. A wound goes gangrenous in that neck of the woods in a matter of a few hours; a day in that broiling atmosphere makes a body bloat, burst and reek like nothing on earth. Birds, bugs, maggots get busy where AK rounds and shrapnel leave off, inseminating the air with a liquid, gagging fecundity that smells worse than any abattoir. It is the stink of your own death, the fear dripping down the inside of your leg. The odour was everywhere, thick enough to cut up into cubes with a machete.

Most of the bodies were alongside the road, clustered round the burned-out vehicles.

Everyone dismounted, save four lads manning the truck-mounted weapons. The Montagnards started to wrap up their brothers in ponchos and throw them in the back of the sixby. I stayed close to the lieutenant who was trying to find his buddies. We carefully pushed through the razor-sharp, saw-edged grass, coming on flattened areas where a break-out minibattle had taken place. A body left surrounded by spent casings lay frozen in tortured rigor mortis, skin greening, enormous bluebottle flies swarming up in clouds from the festering wounds, bust gut and popped eyes. Thirty metres back, we finally came on what was once one of America's elite. The crotch had been crudely amputated and stuffed in its mouth, the abdomen had burst, spilling purplish grey *boudin* on the dirt, a leg hung by a sinew, and the sun had burned the flesh third-degree black. The toughened looey span aside and threw up, I followed suit. I took no pictures but helped shovel the remains onto a poncho and drag it back to the three-quarter-tonner. During the whole exercise I shot no more than a half roll of black-and-white.

After we had collected the bodies, Charlie decided to have some fun and opened up on us with harassing sniper fire all the way back to base. Luckily no one got badly hit, or maybe Victor was just keeping us on our toes. Dusk descended as the last dust from the rearguard jeep settled inside the berm line. The concertina wire was pulled round, leaving us isolated, laagered up in a vulnerable, unprepared position. Night and the surrounding territory belonged to the enemy.

The next day I finally managed to get out to the relative security of the coastal town of Qui Nhon. The MACV (Military Assistance Command Vietnam) compound in Qui Nhon was in a frenzy. An overload of *bao chi*, members of the press, besides every unoccupied ranking staff officer in II Corps were around looking for a piece of the action, trying to get up to An Khe, awaiting a briefing or just attracted by the high that a nearby battle generates. I got lucky, the chopper belonging to the II Corps advisory mission picked me up at An Khe where Colonel Metaxis had stopped in for an update and to collect the oozing body bags. By the time I got off the dilapidated weapons carrier at MACV, it was late afternoon. I headed straight for the mess, where there was a guaranteed steak and eggs, salad, ice cream, plus a few stiff ones. I was starving, except for a couple of cans of C rations, miserable army coffee and a few shots of Jack Daniels, I had had nothing for forty-eight hours. War makes you fit but it does not necessarily keep you healthy. The speed pills we had been issued that night had left me jagged, on edge and very tired.

Filthy, hands begrimed with blood, laterite, grease and things I prefer to forget, reeking of sweat, dirt and death, I plunked myself down in the spotless mess at a table laid with an array fit for a banquet. Silverware gleamed on little rests, there were separate glasses for wine and water, small dishes with pats of butter in ice water, a roll and bread basket, and a folded, starched linen napkin, which looked sort of redundant on my soiled thighs. I had ordered, got a beer with chaser and was busily attacking the bread basket when two older correspondents came over to the table, asking to join me. They were Keyes Beech from the *Chicago Daily News* and Jack Foisie of the *Los Angeles Times*, both doyens of the press corps with many in-country years and vast experience beneath their web belts.

More drinks arrived as I poured out a discombobulated account of the last two days; my notes were stained and smudged and woefully confused. More bread was brought by a smiling Vietnamese waitress. I dived in and without hesitation started spearing the pats of butter out of their dishes. Keyes took great umbrage about his butter being abducted and said so; I, in my alcohol-numbed, shocked state, apologized, scraped the butter off my roll and stuck it back in his dish, but not before the first pat had been plunged into my mouth.

The incident was recounted whenever we came together again; the 'great butter theft' haunted me throughout my Southeast Asia days.

Number 47 Bui Thi Xuan, better known as Frankie's House, was the frat-rat dwelling for a hard core of residents, all *bao chi*. It took its name from the chief servant, whose real name nobody knew or bothered to find out and who had got stuck with the Frankie handle. He had come to us after we lost our first butler, a fastidious older Sino-Viet. Inviting Barry Zorthian, head of mission at JUSPAO, to our party had been a mistake for he had sneakily headhunted our original main man. He had protected us from the ire of our Tonkinese landlady, and could even be entrusted to hand over the 30,000 piastres of monthly rent. He was as honest as Frankie was unscrupulous. Frankie got us humming where before we had been borderline respectable. He arrived on a decrepit French bicycle but by the time I departed in the spring of 1967 he was cavorting around on a spanking new customized Honda 90. He used to have a wad of piastres in his hip pocket sufficient to set up an independent black-market enterprise. Needless to say, he was a draft dodger, habitually paying off the *canh sat* (white mice – Vietnamese military police) who called at the garage doors. Above the garage, Frankie slept with his growing family, getting fatter off our licentious tastes for living. He ran the dope, the kitchen, and the girls while his wife and mother-in-law worked in the kitchen and laundry and his nephew did the cleaning. Frankie was one of those enterprising servants who virtually become members of the household. A true guerrilla infiltrator.

The ferro-concrete villa had four floors. Bui Thi Xuan was a quiet cul-de-sac housing the Taiwanese embassy and ending at the side of the main USAID building, a massive twelve-storey complex boasting heavy defences. It was a nice, secure area a ten-minute cyclo ride from the hub of downtown, five minutes on the bike or in the Yellow Peril. Our garage backed onto a narrow through street cluttered with noodle shops and cottage industry, where life spilled out of the home onto the sidewalks and the open sewers.

Our food was cooked on a primitive combination of charcoal and kerosene and the uninitiated would take hours to get a cup of coffee hot. The old widow who ran this part of the shop made our table the talk of the Saigon lunch circuit. Our smoke – especially our opium – during Frankie's tenure became known to newsies before they even arrived in Vietnam. Frankie had an uncle, a long-time addict, who could be whipped up from his rooms in the Chinese quarter, Cholon, at any given hour and brought back to lie contentedly on the raffia matting in the air-conditioned front bedroom to make our nightly quotas. He was picked up and delivered by Frankie on a Peugeot moped purchased within weeks of taking over as *maître d'*.

Although the original three of us had not needed extra company, the growing ranks of the UPI bureau filled our two free rooms, both with a view of the stairwell and only a limping ceiling fan to stir the oven air. It made the bills easier to deal with. At one time, besides the five occupied rooms, a whole Special Forces A Team, hot out of the overrun Northern II Corps camp of Dak Sut, were squatting in the salon with the heavy-weapons section camped in hammocks and on cots in the garage.

There were also a dog, a cat, a rat, a squirrel, a parrot and a gay monkey called Balls, named after James Baldwin by the racist El Gatto.

The residents continually changed, one left and another one segued in. Initially the house was filled by the UPI connection Martin, who was shipped down to help cope with the escalation. Cat left, I got the only room with airconditioning, Simon stayed over the garage up front. Sean Flynn turned up, playing son of Captain Blood from the Riviera, as a photographer for *Paris-Match*, and moved in on his second day in town. The son of Errol had been assigned the story 'A playboy goes to war', swashbuckling in his father's image, chasing his own rites, another Gemini with handsome looks that stunned the bar girls who had seen his B-rate Franco/Italian movies. 'Seen Flin' they would call out when we weren't together. He came that time for a three-week trip and stayed a year.

So did David Stuart-Fox, better known as Minimus, to avoid the confusion of Foxes. He came from Australia after graduating. It was assumed that he would move in, camp on a couch or somewhere, when Martin announced his imminent arrival. Martin had the slightly dictatorial attitude of a father. He smoked his opium and dope with a feigned reluctance, as though he was saying, 'Take it away, I love it but I shouldn't.' Martin habitually carried a hip flask full of Courvoisier. Minimus was green bamboo when he arrived in Vietnam, travelled but not yet immersed in the overseas vices. That first night in town, he was roasted, toasted and popped. We got him, a gangly six foot three, rearranged in a sarong and then blew his mind apart with ten pipes fuelled by Frankie's uncle, interspersed with breathers of *chau doc* fresh from the Cambodian border, red supreme weed. Then he was called upon to select which of the ladies Frankie should import for his pleasure – Miss Trombone, Miss Trumpet, Miss Saxophone or Miss My. The poor boy surfaced for a couple of goodnight snorts two hours later.

Two days later we got him a job as chief gofer in the photo department at United Press, even though his glasses were as powerful as camera lenses. He became their Australian interests section.

He was as classically minded as Steve Northup. Steve was one of those photographers that remain calm, almost laid back, no matter what happens. UPI had almost inadvertently assigned him to the war out of the West Coast bureau. Steve had been getting high since he was a kid in New Mexico. He had the nagging habit of using my room when I was out on long assignments, leaving roach burn marks on my bedside cabinet, and I would find my objects and clutter stowed away in the cupboard, his own bits and pieces littered about. He was my most patient teacher of the photographic art, always playing around with bits of gear, showing me how to master the little tricks that once made me all thumbs. Above all he knew how to feel the light, the texture off the frame. He was a master in black-and-white.

Martin, Steve and I made a baroque country team. When we were caught in the crossfire of a hot landing zone on the side of the Chu Phong massif with the 1st Air Cavalry, Steve took a frame of Martin slumped behind a fallen log uncapping his flask, me beside him taking a smoke, while a GI puts out covering fire. Steve made an award-winning picture of a medic trying to save a buddy's eye using my lens chamois as a bandage. Members of the house and the honoraries often tended to go out on operations together, safety in a friendly number. It meant more than having someone to get your film back, it was someone who would try to get you back, should the worst happen.

Jack Lawrence of CBS was one of the few heads with any appreciation of rock 'n' roll in the TV corps. Generally the television crews, three to each – a soundman, cameraman and correspondent – trooped about, strung together by cables, demanding an inordinate amount of space on the limited-capacity early-model Hueys which plied about the combat zones like cabs. Jack was different. Back in those days of laborious 16-mm black-and-white film gathering, he carried the mike and tape deck. He had a room at the Caravelle Hotel but spent a lot of time at 47 Bui Thi Xuan, introduced by Steve whom he knew back in the world.

A sandalwood box, four by six inches, donated by Jack, made a fragrant stash for the best of Delta-grown green herb. It rests on my bookcase today, reinforced around the inch-high sides with green gaffer tape, the stuff the army used to keep its helicopters aloft. Sam Castan, another honorary member until his untimely death in 1966, pasted on the lid a clip from *Look*, the magazine he was writing for. It read: 'TWO SECONDS YOU'RE LOADED.' There were always ten ready rolls therein and a clean, sifted heap of fresh herb, one of Frankie's subduties.

The whole show – home, bureau, upcountry, downtown – moved to the sounds emanating from the in-country forces radio network. The war took its cue from the beat pulsing out of AFVN or Armed Forces Radio Station. Initially the military had relayed a TV signal from a couple of towers located in the major cities but this was found to be insufficient for the remoter mountainous regions. With the enterprising, practical logic that pushed Americans have, they boosted their transmissions into a relay of refurbished Super Constellation prop-driven planes which broadcast virtually round the clock, round the year. The zone favourites were topped by *Gunsmoke* and *Combat*. They passed the government angle and even had a weather girl who gave out stateside ski conditions as well as monsoon reports from the Highlands.

There was no television at Frankie's House, only a collection of a thousand records ranging from the ethnic to the ethereal and esoteric. Every member had their favourites from the others' collections. Anyone on R & R in Singapore or Hong Kong was duty bound to return with samples of the latest releases. I returned from a six-week binge in Hong Kong to astonish the elder educated peers of the house by putting on a haunting Gregorian chant. Minimus went for the New Seekers or Vivaldi, Simon was invariably drawn to Byrds and Beatles music, Flynn would want rock 'n' roll or Bach. Honorary members, folk who stashed gear at Frankie's but officially lived in a network-supplied hotel room, were unofficially expected to donate to the collection. Jack Lawrence contributed the latest Dylan and the tuner.

The stereo had been a problem, resolved by my paying for the deck and amp, Steve Northup and Jack boosting for the speakers. They, as Americans, had PX privileges, while the Brits were relegated once more to third-country-national status. Outside Saigon, out in the sticks, clad in the *tenue de jour* olive-drab jungle fatigues, I would wander the shelves of the minimarts, picking out cartons of Camels at a buck a throw, a bottle of Courvoisier for four. Essentials in the toothpaste category had to be bought hot off the street. The main store at the end of Plantation Road in Cho Lon was an aircraft-hangar-sized Sears-Roebuck complex. Their assigned mission was to guarantee that every American and their allies, excluding the Vietnamese, had a decent baggage train. Most hooches had a four-track reel-to-reel tape deck, most GIs a Seiko and a camera. The irony was that the allies took over the business; it was possible to order a refrigerator from a Korean, Thai or Filipino middleman even before the shipment hit the docks in Canh Hoi. Whole jeeps, crated-down helicopters or speedboats were available for a modest sum of trade goods. It was rumoured that one local commander in I Corps had got himself a personal HH-23 Observation chopper for twenty cases of Scotch and another two for the mechanics to assemble it.

In August 1965 I was fired by UPI. I felt cheated of the option of being able to resign and really pissed off when the official reason read: not going into the field enough, ruining cameras in the field and smoking dope in the office. With the lifting of my press card I felt adrift, lost and bitter towards the man who had done it. Dirck Halstead had come in-country after I had served my probationary period, to run a swollen photographic operation. The news media were arriving in proportion to the military. Our presence would reach battalion strength at the height of the conflict in 1969. Halstead brought his new wife, fresh from the New York head office, to the delicately balanced mayhem on Ngo Duc Khe Street. Betsy togged herself up in tiger-suit camouflage and went off to have a good time in the field. Dirck sat caesarlike in the back room, making sorties for junkets and beers, living in the dorm upstairs. My mates in the print department, Ray Herndon and Mike Malloy, who had hired me, were powerless. Henri left in a huff to go for a better-paying job at the AP with Horst Faas. I was let go and another, more malleable twenty-year-old replaced me. They had the gall to forward an account for 2340 piastres owed from my first in-country lodgings. A few weeks later their newsfilm division was screaming telexes at the bureau to rehire me after I had shot my first sensational newsclips which had aired network on ABC.

Harry Kaliski's franglais lessons in the Indian subcontinent paid off. *Paris-Match* could not afford a full-time team based in Saigon. Their man, Daniel, worked for other French papers and had served in the paras at Dien Bien Phu. The French were not popular with the US military hierarchy, who blamed their problems on France's downfall a decade earlier. I became their ears on the military circuit and back-up photographer. I got $150 retainer and a fresh accreditation.

I took Daniel to Pleiku. We got out to an ambushed convoy trying to relieve a besieged Du Co Special Forces camp on the Cambodian border at Du Co. I had swung a flight on a gunship which had touched down contrary to orders in the middle of the carnage. We dived for cover and when I turned around to photograph the next chopper, a dust-off, I was astonished to see Daniel hop aboard at the last second. He had the extra supplies of film, leaving me with a mere handful of rolls. I spent a night under a tank, being shelled, another night curled up in discarded flare parachutes, the third on a body plane back to Saigon. At the airport the *Life* limo awaited my arrival with 350 guaranteed green dollars for first look-see.

The 173rd Airborne had been committed to battle in the hills, the first US outfit to be so. Larry Burrows – *Life*'s top man – had gone with them. *Life* wanted to complete the story. It was my first freelance move, the first sale to the megamedia. Some other remote story bumped us out of the next edition of the magazine.

Da Nang became a second home. It was far enough north to make it isolated and independent from Saigon in the beginning, politically and militarily. It was a chunk of the country later to be dominated by the Marines Corps. Things were initially more professionally organized up north in I Corps and the life was relatively comfortable. The second city had rated the second-string new boy from the bureau; out of town all expenses were paid. The dozen *bao chi* shared a run-down hotel cum brothel with some helo pilots and Aussie advisers. UPI maintained a suite with three never made beds and intermittently working air conditioner. We careered around in Kim Chi's rented jeeps, whose front was a tailor's shop on Boulevard Doc Lap. He was a wily Viet hip to the wants of the press and also made leather replica medics' satchels to be used as camera bags.

The 8 March 1965 had seen the storming of Red Beach north of Da Nang city by the first combat echelons of a Marine regimental landing team. They were greeted by svelte, nationally costumed ladies who placed leis around their necks while a band struck up airs. I photographed the crack underwater-demolition lads building sandcastles at the water's edge. Behind them clanked tanks and ontoses, with their six mounted 106-mm recoilless rifles, splashing down ramps onto a perfect surfer's shore.

The Marines decided to try to police up and instil discipline into the press corps covering their flanks. They rented, and then bought outright, an old French-run *hôtel de passe* and bar fronting the Da Nang River at the end of the docks area. The Marines were smart enough to retain some of the girls to run the facilities. This dragged most of the semiresident newsies out of their various hideaways. An American-style coffee shop and diner was set up. Frozen T-bone steaks were jetted in, five different flavours of dairy ice cream, countless cases of beer and a bar that would have done the Rockefeller Center proud.

Living downtown on the cheap had been OK though the phones did not work, power failed and plumbing coughed. There had been an autonomy unregulated by the military. Advisers, pilots and spooks turned you on to what was happening and often gave you a ride out to the field. The Marines and organized all-out American commitment dealt a death blow to informality. We were to be watched over and shepherded whenever possible.

This was the dawning of the age of the press information officer, the PIO, and rule from the info shack. To tempt us to stay home at nights, they ran the latest stateside movies at the back of the compound projected on a giant outdoor screen, popcorn passed free of charge. Flynn and I would sit down on the little dock where the press dinghy bobbed, supplied by the Marines, and smoke a couple of big spliffs, giggling at the lapping wavelets, the starry sky and the backwards movie. Some nights the Marines were astonished to see half a dozen butt glows down on the dock of the bay. The Marines had a movie-culture attitude to the war, a John Wayne image of the conflict, and the press made them nervous. They could relate to Ernie Pyle – quintessential 'Stars and Stripes' reporter – but found it hard to deal with us when we filmed grunts firing hooches with their Zippos. That was unpatriotic. To get a good story with the Marines meant hard work. Eye Corps territory was hot and hilly with thick jungle. Along the coast were beautiful beaches and a populated agricultural plain. There were always tough photos to be made on a civic-action outing; their Gomer Pyles awkwardness contrasted starkly with the graceful Vietnamese. Mundane roadside snaps grabbed the human-interest side of the UPI wire. Their aviation units, stretched thin, guaranteed good action shots, a ride on a Marine medivac could grace a *Life* cover.

The drive to Hue is still one of the most spectacular I have made. Route Nationale 1 climbs over the misty Hai Van Col des Nuages and then across fertile coastal plain to the jewel of Vietnam, Hue. Two and a half hours in a Kim Chi jeep flat out to go lie in a sampan on the Perfume River.

Hue, besides being the cultural font, has the best food and prettiest women in Vietnam. In those idyllic years before the massive battle at Tet for the city, you could rent a boat for a night for a few hundred piastres and other sampans would come alongside to sell delicacies. Other craft purveyed girls or opium or both. There was no need to go anywhere near officialdom.

An hour and half further north lay the DMZ (demilitarized zone), beyond Dong Ha and La Rue Sans Joie, the Street without Joy, named from Bernard Fall's book of the same title. (He died on a mine late in 1967 just off Route 1 during a Marine search and destroy mission.) It was just possible to get to the Ben Hai border bridge and back to Da Nang in a day on a bike. The first trip I made was a pleasant outing, like riding on a Kentish lane in the summer; the second was fraught with a flat in no-man's land and I had to descend the col into Da Nang after dark, an unwise ride. After that the northern part of the country took on a hardened military stance, limiting travel to the air. Motorcycling became a southern number, relegated to the lower corps, the Delta flats.

The Cotton flown down from Laos was stolen from the Ton San Nhut airport, where it had been chained by both wheels to a Conex. Though it was the only one for thousands of miles, I never spotted it again. I was reduced to a 50cc Honda customized for cross-country work.

That whole era we were a little crazy. It seemed absolutely normal to climb in a jeep or on a motorcycle and drive anywhere. The VC had captured press before and released them with amazing stories a short time later. It was even possible to arrange to get taken, but not advisable when you were American. It was an axiom among the hardcore press not to carry a weapon because, should you need one, there would always be enough lying around for the taking at the height of the moment.

The fishhook – so named for its shape – was a jut of Cambodian territory into South Vietnam, 150 kilometres northwest of Saigon. Bo Dup was a Special Forces camp on its barbed fringe. *Paris-Match* assigned me the job after there had been probes on the camp and they were expecting a large ground assault. They had been getting probes on the perimeter, incoming mortar fire, sniping at work details, ambushed patrols and outposts for the past six months. The camp had been put at the strategic point virtually astride the Ho Chi Minh Trail in an area considered to be part of Central Office for Vietnam (COSVN) headquarters. Most SF camps were usually sited to frustrate and prevent the VC/NVA flow of men and material as well as to try to create islands of government stability in remote areas – often those having large ethnic minorities. Bo Dup was important enough to warrant a large A Team – fourteen men with three officers among them – and had 450 Sedang strikers as well as some Vietnamese

Civil Irregular Defence Group troops, all of whose loyalty was in doubtful balance since many were press-ganged or hoods.

It was typical in its construction, a bermed mud fort with various sheds and barracks with corrugated roofs inside its four walls. The hooches built for the strikers were of a flimsier bamboo and wattle, whereas the Americans had a pukka wooden team house, commo shack and a serious bunker in the centre of the compound, inside its own protective wire complex and minefield. Mortar pits dominated the corners of the camp and fighting bunkers lined the four walls. Outside, large fields of fire had been cleared back 300 metres to the rubber and jungle. Immediately beyond the walls was an intricate staked fencing laced with Claymores, anti-vehicle and anti-personnel mines, trip flares and booby traps – all the goodies that were in-country. The weather was late monsoon – muddy, miserable, damp and chilly – difficult for air support, but good for the viscous laterite mud to soak up incoming rounds and deaden the shrapnel. It helped, too, that the VC usually had lots of Chinese communist-made dud rounds. The whole base had a weary post-battle look to it: gaps in the wire, tattered sandbags, broken-up ammo cases, spent cartridges, unravelled, bloodied combat dressings. The occluded skies made it all the more depressing. Dirt and death made it smell bad.

I came in on a chopper with a squad of Nung mercenaries: Chinese riff-raff and criminals who had originally been with the remnants of the Kuomintang which had been thrown out of China after Mao's takeover in 1948. The unit was no longer purely Chinese but a hardcore reaction force, recruited off the streets and out of the jails. They proudly bore a skull-and-crossbones patch over an MF logo on their tiger-suit camouflage fatigues. Their advisers swore that MF stood for 'motherfucker', not 'Mike Force'. These troops were mean and hunted the VC for money – cash for heads, piastres for weapons captured. They had no regard for the Geneva Conventions. They were being brought in to Bo Dup to beef up the defences and to raid across the border. An expendable, nonpartisan force, owing allegiance only to its paymaster.

The Hueys had flown out of the B Team at Bien Hoa, high above the range of the 12.7-mm AA guns, then came scudding low to land on the mangled strip which precluded C-123s or even Caribous landing. Everyone bolted for the safety of the camp. I arrived at the team house and was quickly put in the picture and given the usual overbrewed army coffee laced with Jack Daniels and a couple of quick bennies. The layout of the camp was explained, a rack in the team hooch assigned to me, and then, with an air of gravity, an M-2 carbine and a clutch of M-26 frag grenades were issued. Intel had it we were to be hit hard.

The light was failing fast, the sun sank over the Fishhook, the rubber trees loomed. Shadows took on ominous overtones. Everyone was edgy, chilled with an expectant fear. The half-indigenous and half-American chow that night was tepid and school-dinner stodgy – mere fuel, a lining against a lengthening night. There was barely time to get acquainted with the A Team members. To this day all I remember is gaunt, sleepless faces, grubby tiger suits, orange mud-stained web gear and packs. Heavy raps about weapons and other bad times. A list of those who had got zapped recently, their names caressed over with feats of prowess; endless bitches about the command structure for its lack of support. Peeved resignation at their plight at the end of the line. I had been in several A Team camps before, including Du Co while that battle raged, but here it was touch and go. But since I'd just turned freelance I had a buck to earn. *Paris-Match* would only print what they thought was sensational, and my own personal intelligence net said that this was where it was going to happen.

Feeding over, people drifted off to check their mortar-pit perimeters and double-check their communication nets. I felt dirty and used already, and barely four hours on site. The rack I'd been assigned had a gritty poncho liner as the only bedding and I retreated to that. Bo Dup was a lifer camp and those still loose were killing a bottle in the team shack. You can sleep with your clothes on but, unless in total fatigue, it only comes in flashes, barely restful, never deep, fitful at best. Boots nag at the bottom of your bed, your mind is conscious of foreboding. The M-2, bandolier of clips and grenades, medic bag and cameras lay under the cot at hand grasp. Whatever dreams I had were continually punctured by the whoomp of outgoing mortars and illumination rounds. These you learn to live with and – with an inlearned sixth sense – to identify as friendly, almost comforting. You become highly tuned to the sounds of conflict; the first incoming round of whatever calibre pulses the adrenalin at high speed.

It must have been about 02.00 hours – the middle of the night, when the VC most often chose to launch probes or attacks – when the first salvo of 60- and 80-mm mortars bracketed the camp, a veritable sitting duck, plotted and sighted in now for weeks. I rolled from the cot – no mosquito net that night to ensnare my progress – and grabbed the weapon and gear as if I'd practised it for the Olympics. Scrambling from the hooch I was in my assigned position in a bunker in seconds. The mortars ranged on in, we could hear the team house hit and feel the spatter of shrapnel. The concussions shook the breath out of us. A frenzy of activity, a stench of ammo and cordite, flickering light, terror. Heavy MGs started cutting up the night. Our mortars responded spasmodically, jumpy strikers fired at the as yet unseen enemy. Louder explosions got closer, Bangalore torpedoes taking out the wire and mines, I hugged the damp corner.

The first waves of enemy troops came in, crawling, firing burp guns, covered by the 12.7s, whose blue-green tracers floated beautifully towards us. Our tracers burned orange-bright back. The defences were down, the wire blown, the mines used up. Charlie had even penetrated one corner of the perimeter and was fighting inside the base, grenading, fighting from behind. The Mikes raced across to plug the gap. Pandemonium reigned. We were about to be totally overrun. The 'Yards on one wall were proving to be disloyal and firing into the American inner compound. Now it was every last man to the walls. I lunged into a firing slit; gear spread on the sandbag of the aperture. Bodies littered the blown wire, strewn about like autumn debris. Livid flashes under the ghostly glare of the flickering parachute flares showed a clouded sky that precluded air support.

And they were still coming. Half crawling, they staggered against the hail of outgoing fire. A sapper, clad in black shorts and webbing, rose 30 yards away to hurl bamboo-handled Chi-com stick grenades. Time stood still. No thought focused. I raised the carbine and let the three prescribed rounds go. It was rehearsed Zen, like knowing you're about to hit the shutter-release button and a superb frame is about to be frozen. I knew I was on target, I had to hit to stop him. This was no time for photography, infrared flash or time exposure. It was a time to fight, every man for himself. No time to produce press card or passport.

He went down.

The next day I went out and assured myself that the awful thing had been done and flipped the body to check the almost neat chest wounds. It is a thing better forgotten; no pride, no regret, just a numb, drained, reality of survival.

Choosing a likely photo/story spot in the Nam was a haphazard operation, relying on sundry intelligence sources, contacts and, mostly, plain hunches. Working at UPI I had leaped all over getting to know the dispatching clerks, the sergeants at chopper outfits, and senior advisers, so that later, when I was without agency status, I still could count on acceptance and facilities.

Paul Dean was a fellow expatriate. We had the shorthand of common bonds and background. I never bothered to ask why Paul had left Britain, even in Chu Lai in September 1965. He had gone to the States, ending up working for Barry Goldwater's paper in Phoenix, the *Arizona Republic*, a chronicle of what was good about America, the last bastion of liberty, back at a time when Goldwater was as far right as Joe McCarthy. Paul, like myself, had drawn that wild card, the Vietnam assignment.

The two of us had been lured down with a swarm of correspondents and photographers three days previously from Da Nang by the Marines' PIO on the premise that the Marines had trapped the first VC regiment on the Batangan peninsula and were now, once and for all, going to annihilate it. As an added perk, the Anvil part of the force was going to stage an amphibious landing, theoretically good D-Day stuff. We would go in with the hammer part.

The operation was given the name Starlite and the press waited patiently for it to kick off. We all knew it had to be one where the landing zones promised a hot reception and the Marines would probably get in some heavy action. However, for reasons not revealed to the assembled media, their operation's kick-off was postponed by a day. Then by another and a third, by which time all the staffers had retreated back to Da Nang, where communications and stories were guaranteed.

They left just the two of us. I had the dubious *Paris-Match* accreditation with an as yet unpaid retainer; Paul was an in-country virgin, not yet baptized by fire, looking for solid Arizonians. The story blossomed and the Marines got the shit kicked out of them. A 60-mm mortar, which landed square on a Marine's head six metres away, drove three small bits of shrapnel into my right hip and buttocks. *Life* magazine picked up the pix, running them over six pages. I came home from the naval hospital on Hill 327. George MacArthur of the AP debriefed and guaranteed that the colour film would be processed, the wire having first pick of the pix. Paul got a scoop and dropped out of sight.

It had been the first major battle of the conflict between US and main-force Viet Cong units, destined to enter the annals of history.

It was a strange privilege to be able to fulfil all the Biggles fantasies from my boyhood reading. Soon after I was in the freelance lane with nothing but time on my hands, a dead spot after Starlite, I cast around for a fresh long-term story that had hardly been touched on. The Seventh Fleet sitting out in the Tonkin Gulf with a minimum of two aircraft carriers on station round the clock, round the year, were longing to be exposed. Granted, every time there was a MiG kill or significant raid they would drag the crews back for public exhibition at the five o'clock follies, the daily afternoon press briefing. Periodically the secretary of defence or some other ranking VIP would warrant a junket out to one of the flattops and the media would be expected to fill a pool press plane to cover the visit. I had never had the pleasure and was dying to experience landing on or taking off from the pencilbox-sized rolling ship, even in a lowly prop-powered courier plane, a twin-engined COD.

An American photo agency in New York had expressed interest in a story wherein I proposed to ship-hop from the northernmost station all the way around to the Cambodian border. A hitch-hiking ship cruise for over three weeks. That first on-deck landing reminded me of being in an auto wreck without the crash, just the breathtaking slam back into a rear-facing seat. A bustle of brightly jerseyed men hooked and unhooked us with cables visible through little thick Plexiglass windows as we jolted forward off the arrester wires. I stepped out into a machine-mad world, swept by high-velocity wind; the ship was steaming at 25 knots into a 20-knot breeze. The whole deck was awash with aircraft, prop and jet in various pre- and post-operation stages; crews swarmed over the wings and fuselages, dollies of bombs and rockets trundled around, giant hoses snaked out of deck recesses. And aircraft were still coming in to land. I loved it, the sheer exhilaration of being on the brink of being blown overboard or whirled into a propeller or jet turbine. Man-made mayhem functioning with clockwork precision. The noise was enough to pitch you overboard and you were ceremoniously given a pair of Mickey Mouse ears, antinoise fibreglass ear cans, and a deck officer's yellow sweatshirt. They even assigned an officer to escort me until I had a vague geography of the floating city.

It was an enormous cavern of steel passages with high-lintelled bulkheads where the lights became a dim red glow during combat stations. The hangar deck seemed like a railway terminus served by elevators the size of cricket pitches. The first time I was in it there was a ghostly air to the cavern space as a memorial service was conducted for half a dozen pilots downed over North Vietnam. Operation Rolling Thunder, the first phase of the almost continual bombing campaign to interdict the transportation infrastructure of the North, was keeping the carriers busy around the clock. Night launching, with strobes winking lights and vivid streaks of rushing afterburners, was a psychedelic routine.

The real kick was getting to fly in a jet off the USS *Midway* on the southern Dixie Station bombing in-country. I was bundled into the navigator's seat for a three-hour mission, starting by getting airborne in two seconds, 0–200 miles per hour in three. Thereafter it was a cramped bore, recovery an anticlimax, the arrester hook getting us first time. A hundred and forty to zero in another two seconds.

Getting between the different ships was more hair-raising, dangling on a rope between two steel monsters, sitting in a large styrofoam toilet seat. They called it a breeches buoy and insisted that no one got lost crossing, only wet. I made them send my gear across first, getting a little damp as uneven wave troughs dipped the lines horrifyingly for a few seconds. I made similar crossings five times in the next three weeks between tankers, destroyers firing support missions, ammunition freighters delivering bombs to the flattops, and an inshore escort which was caught from a DD Class Destroyer, the USS *Picking*. Back up the ladder to a carrier to cadge a flight home, a cod flip back to Ton San Nhut.

I walked off a launch-laden deck into a job. A diminutive blond Canadian lady, Beryl Fox of CBC, had flown out especially to hire me to replace Eric Derschmidt, the ace English cameraman struck down by infectious hepatitis in the middle of shooting an hour-long appraisal of the state of the war in mid-1965. She had seen my *Life oeuvre* on Chu Lai and liked my eye. I had to be converted to take up the moving image. At $175 a day the persuasion was easy. All she told me was to set the machine for eighteen frames per second and use the same exposure as for a still, think the same photographic idea. I started work the next hour, filming the next strike launch.

The next day found us south of Da Nang to finish the Marine segment with a CAG (combined action group) near Tam Ky. An M-48 tank slewed up at the unit's headquarters in a gutted school house and Marines threw three VC bodies off the engine deck, followed by a prisoner. The poor bruised black-pyjama clad peasant bounced heavily, his arms roped back by the elbows. The bodies lay grotesquely flopped at the top of the dyke. I tracked back round the other side of the ruined house, where the local ARVN liaison laddie and his policeman buddy were treating the VC to the sensation of drowning on dry land. The Marines gawked on.

They had the suspect half in the water of the adjoining paddy, bent back, a rag over his face. The interpreter hissed questions as he poured filthy water from a dented canteen cup into the mouth and nose of the struggling prisoner. They topped him up to bursting point, straightened him up, and zapped him in the gut. Vomit and blood spewed through the cloth, the rest he swallowed. They started again. My presence was unremarked and I crept closer to the tortured one's face, widening the lens, a mike virtually playing to the camera. It was almost too much, it was beyond control; I backed away, film still running. The man revealed no information.

A platoon patrol was to go out on a sweep, hopefully no more than a three-klick jaunt, perfect time for a 15-pound camera and sound-recording hump, exactly the fill-in stock that Beryl needed for her film. Another hot afternoon was spent slogging through drying rice paddies, menaced from every tree line in an area patchwork-quilted with small hamlets farming under the flight path of one of the world's busiest airfields. Not long after the Marine presence was established, sniper rounds had started puncturing lumbering incoming transports, and the leatherneck square had been extended into the cantankerous boonies. They set a slow, secure pace with flankers out, more, I suspect, to accommodate my filming than from diligence. As we closed on a small village surrounded by tall bamboos, a burst of light machine-gun and rifle fire cracked over from the hedge line 100 metres away. They were lousy shots and no one was hurt but it was too close. We had been on a dyke between two partly dried-up paddies when the firing started. We had dived for cover behind the 18-inch-high bank. I went the wrong way and ended up fully exposed to the VC, with the Marines opening up with their full stock feet away over an awfully exposed dirt hump. I stayed curled up tight around the Bolex, wishing that I had accepted the loan of a steel helmet; a flak jacket would have been comforting, too. Charlie fired a few more rounds and the Marines poured back over my head, a stream of tracer-laced fire interrupted by the occasional thump of a grenade launcher. From my prone position I focused on the protruding weapons and helmets a few metres away. The power

115

to control my fear returned as I squeezed the trigger on the camera, and the frames rolled. Within seconds, as though I was lying in a trench warfare movie of the First World War, the grunts rose up and charged over me towards the tree line, firing from the hip. All I could think of doing was to roll over and track the attack.

We went back to base soon afterwards, another day on the edge over. The grunts were happy to be alive and I got very drunk at the press centre. I handed Beryl a total of 850 feet; the final aired film used 450 of them, a still person's ratio. I saw my name finally on the silver screen in New York in the autumn of 1967 when they projected the George Polk Award-winning film, *Mills of the Gods*, at a festival. The Cat took me to see it before going down to the Caribbean, where he was to perish in a light plane that never gained enough power on take off from San Juan, Puerto Rico.

It was almost my last shoot as a film cameraman. It did not suit me. Every time I saw an image I wanted to freeze a frame, not run a continual sequence; the art was in the moment's selection. I wanted to hurl the cumbersome movie camera away and range the Leica. One picture is still worth a thousand words, a thousand words only a clip of film.

There was only one one-man film crew and that was Neil Davis of Visnews, my mate with the incurable I had fixed in Vientiane; he would go into the field and do on-camera reports which he taped and filmed of himself, always getting into the thickest shit possible. When he was wounded later in Cambodia and a coconut was used as an emergency IV drip, the operation was jerkily recorded. Neil was killed on my father's birthday, 9 September 1985. As he lay mortally wounded by insurrectionist Thai armoured troops, his abandoned Ikagumi had electrically pulsed his death throes. Twenty-one years of the deepest friendship blown away by an agitated tank commander.

That first big break in *Life*, six pages on 6 September 1965, set me on the road to a prospering freelanceship. I would be accredited by two separate agencies, *Time* and *Life*. My new press card read: 'Time/Life Freelance.' No one doubted the megacorporation's validity. From now on I would be getting regular gigs, featuring alongside greats of the magazine that television was slowly strangling. Bob Morse, the *Life* bureau chief, had a quiet word with Frank McCulloch at *Time* to ensure enough work was passed my way for an adequate survival, guaranteeing my being available.

ABOVE: The art of sneaking to the front at the Coronation, 1952 *(John Page)*

LEFT: Aged five

BELOW: Family holiday, Hastings, 1954

ABOVE: Mother and father on
BMW motorcycle during
shooting of BBC *Arena*
documentary, 1979 *(Tim Page)*

RIGHT: Before the Tour de
Scandinavia with Rex
Strickland, 1958 *(Orpington Times)*

BELOW: With Terry in
Amsterdam, 1962 *(Don Passman)*

RIGHT: Near Ysad, Iran, 1962. The bus, Therese, foreground *(Tim Page)*

LEFT: Peshawar, 1962, with dealers *(S. Mahoor)*

BELOW: Laos, 1964 *(Alain Le Mat)*

LEFT: Wounded in action for the first time at Chu Lai *(Unknown marine)*

BELOW: Driving the Yellow Peril in Saigon, 1965 *(Leonardo Caparros)*

OPPOSITE ABOVE: Near Chu Lai, 1965

OPPOSITE BELOW: Special Forces with a VC suspect, near Moc Hoa, 1965 *(Tim Page)*

ABOVE: Korean
marines after all-night
firefight in a cemetery.
Quang Ngai,1966
(Tim Page)

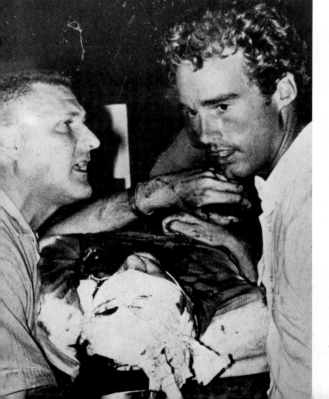

LEFT: Da Nang,
1966. Another little
accident. Major
'Mad' Mike Molloy,
me and Flynn
(Nguyen van Phuoc)

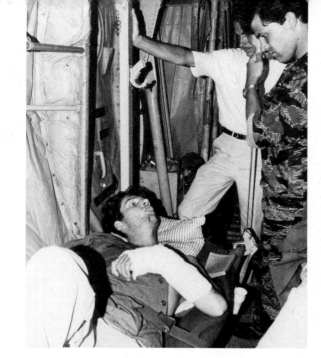

ABOVE: Demonstration in New York, 1967 *(Tim Page)*

LEFT: New York, 1967
(Steve Northup)

OPPOSITE ABOVE: Bedouin refugee during the Six Day War, Mafraq, Jordan, June 1967
(Tim Page)

OPPOSITE LEFT: With basic supplies in Phnom Penh, 1968
(Bob Kaylor)

OPPOSITE RIGHT: With Nik Wheeler, John Steinbeck Jr, Sean Flynn, Carl Robinson, Perry Deane Young at the ordination ceremony on Dao Island, 1968

LEFT: Fourth WIA. Train wreck near Phu Bai, 1968 *(Robin Pell)*

BELOW: Mini-Tet, near Y-bridge, 1968 *(John Olsen)*

ABOVE: Buddhist temple, Tokyo, 1968 *(Tim Page)*

RIGHT: Flynn in the Tu Do apartment, 1968 *(Tim Page)*

BELOW: My credentials, 1968

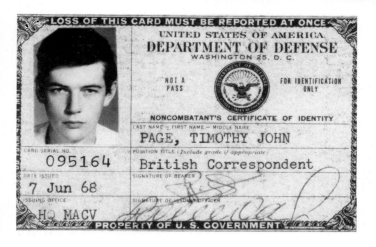

LEFT: L.R.R.P. Mission into Michelin plantation, 1969 *(Tim Page)*

BELOW: Last picture shot in Vietnam, after mine explosion

TOP: With Linda, being ordained at Dao Island, 1969 *(Dao Photo Service)*

ABOVE: Janice Ann Johnson Page, Los Angeles, 1973 *(Tim Page)*

LEFT: The unfurling of Christo's running fence, Petaluma Ridge, California, 1976 *(Tim Page)*

LEFT: In San Francisco, 1977, at the Media Burn *(Terry McDonnell)*

BELOW: Lecturing at Sunderland Polytechnic with touring ICA show, 1979

OPPOSITE ABOVE: In Da Nang, 1985 *(Tim Page)*

OPPOSITE BELOW: Tim and Lindsay Page, wedding party, Ulcombe, June 1987 *(Tim Hawkins)*

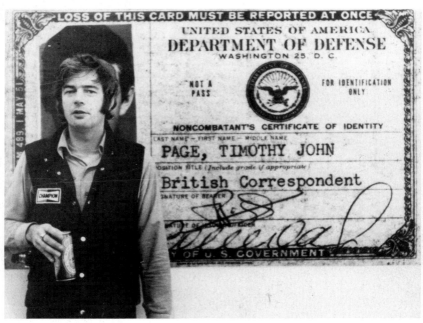

At home at Windmill Hill, 1987 *(Nick Didlick)*

A month after that first *Life* spread I enjoyed the glamour of walking around the bars with a carefully rolled-up copy. A simple 'Well done, mate!' from my mentors Eddie, Horst Faas, Northup and Henri gave me the assurance to decide that photography was something I would stay with.

Larry Burrows, the English *Life* staffer, took me under his wing, dined me with long raps about colour and texture. Bob Morse gave me an eight-day job with the 173rd Airborne on an operation into the infamous Iron Triangle; purportedly it was the first time chemical warfare was employed. Huge blowers would pump a mix of tear gas and smoke into the Viet Cong tunnel networks with the hope of flushing them out. The Airborne divided up a platoon of press over two battalions and for two days we ploughed through the rubber and scrub in the heartland of Victor Charles. The enemy had run this terrain since the Japanese occupation of Vichy Indochina. They let us pass with only the occasional sniper round reducing the pucker factor to beyond f.32. The airforce had tangled up the bush with defoliants and B-52 strikes; Mr Charles had faded away.

The press gang faded, too, leaving me alone with B Company of the 2nd 503rd. At least we were well looked after, hot chow choppered in the same night. Rain bucketed down and my hammock rig turned into a hip bath. The next day our own artillery got it wrong and brought in heat on the lead columns. The evening's placebo was half a ton of ice to supplement the cases of Welch's grape juice, and reconstituted chocolate milk. The next day, the day Charlie Company walked into the ambush, we were dealing with the purple chocolate runs.

The sign at the side of the road had read, according to the hastily summoned interpreter, 'ALL AMERICAN READ THIS DIE!' The VC had artfully rigged a dud-fused, American 105-mm howitzer shell behind the placard. As the troops bunched up on the derelict Michelin rubber road, machine guns opened up from concealed positions simultaneously with the detonation of a recycled Claymore mine. The results were devastating. Six dead and nineteen wounded in the time it takes to blink three times. We ran ducking towards the battle, entering a stage of mangled bodies and whipped survivors, a 50-yard stretch of road strewn in a Bosch still-life. My mind went blank. Memory serves up a jumble of crouching, dodging, snapping and dragging back wounded. Everyone and no one screamed orders. Four of us grabbed a GI with legs and arms virtually amputated, and as we ran out of the firing zone towards the rear, a leg detached in my hand. The camera was at my eye in the right hand as the dust-off bird clattered in towards the centre of the red marker smoke farther along the reddened road.

The irony of the war in Vietnam manifested itself immediately. I was back downtown in *Life*'s office, in Room 401 of the Caravelle, within two hours. The chopper got you into trouble and back out again, a taxi to the front on rank privilege tap. Bob Morse punched the shock out of me with three triple cognacs. I was incoherent, excited, a babbling survivor covered in gore, reeking from four fecund days in Agent Orange rain and shine. I upset the bureau's other occupant, a visiting senior lady correspondent, doing an indepth thing on the touring *Hello, Dolly* troupe; I must have grossed her out for she demanded I leave. Later it transpired that at the precise moment the ambush had sprung shut, the musical hit had opened at the Nha Trang air force base. Broadway, two pages and a cover; Airborne, four pages and one vertical double truck.

I put another two and a half grand in the account that Time Inc would open for me in New York. I had *laisser passer* to go on operations with the 173rd Airborne whenever I wanted. A pre-op tip-off would be relayed to me, a chopper laid on, an action assured. Adopted for the duration.

Since arriving in Vietnam and especially after Chu Lai, which had gained a few column inches even in the local Kentish rag, I had been more dutiful in keeping in touch with home. All the GIs and the *bao chis* did, and relished the incoming mail. Over the years, I had distanced myself, virtually creating a divorce of emotion between myself and my folks; it seemed the only way to have the freedom to live out whatever came round the next bend in the track. The first information they had received when I had headed out east in the autumn of 1962 was a postcard three or so weeks old, by-lined Tehran, shortly followed by a package from Greece, posted two months before that, containing a doll in national costume for the collection I had started for my mother with a wooden figure of an Alpine horn blower from my school skiing holdiay.

My father had, in one of the weekly letters that my mum has always dutifully written to me, wherever I have happened to be, asked me what my twenty-first birthday present should be. That summer I had finally reached adult age, although its liberating qualities had probably already been gained. Now in Singapore on my first R & R from Vietnam, I had the choice of any reasonable gift I desired. It seemed apropos to get something to last for ever, and the watch I had earned as a prize for passing my eleven plus had ceased to be an accurate chronological device.

It had been an expedition Saturday, buying that watch, my first, after my exam results arrived. We went into a shop in Hatton Garden in London and my father ordered trays of watches dragged out. We got one of the cheapest they had, with a leather strap, a few bob over twelve quid. The name upset me, sounding too much like brown sugar, a Damira, but it said 'Swiss made' on the face.

I saw my first Rolex Oyster perpetual that day. Now in Singapore, at Asia Watch & Camera, I was finally to get the symbol that every jet jock or Special Forces spook liked to boast. To this day I make it a principle to be on time, a little early, reinforced by knowing that missing the picture through tardiness is a crime. In the orient then and now, I spend my day chasing sunrises, the most benevolent time of the day, when the light is perfect. The only time the Rolex has been off my wrist is when it has been shot off (once), removed for surgery (twice) and lost (once) when I fell, drunk, into a fishpond in Marin County, California, in a rain storm in 1976. It was found in a drought two summers on and returned to me. It is still on my left wrist, set three minutes early.

In six weeks in Singapore and Hong Kong, I blew two grand, and came back loaded with new gear; two crates followed full of books and records. In Hong Kong I had holed up in the New Territories with Jim Wilde, a *Time* correspondent, trying to write a novel by dictation in one month. One of Indochina's true eccentrics, James had been in Vietnam on and off since the French fall. A hooknosed, bespectacled intellectual, forever rocking in his chair, addressing one and all as doctor, he was raving after a few too many glasses, but brilliant after too many pipes. He kept chambers at the Continental, where he would entertain naked in the bath, the tea service perched on the bidet, expounding his weird philosophies. His reasoning was Jesuit, his claimed ancestry Greek, Irish, Swiss, French, though he had Canadian nationality. He was born, he stated, in a Pullman car between Ottawa and Montreal.

James and I eventually cold-turkeyed the opium at the same time in the summer of 1966 after a series of heavy battles in War Zone D with the Aussies and the 173rd.

Time passed me a lot of work, time flew, I seemed to spend

119

weeks out in the field. I was working, flying, getting high, shooting, living so fast the moments blurred. Always broke, always flush, always film in the fridge.

Every time I was assigned by either of the magazines to get a new correspondent kitted out in the thieves' market and then baptized in the field, both of us usually came back with some outrageous stories that left the bureau gaping and wondering why I appeared to draw shrapnel like a magnet. I wasn't seeing it that way; I always carefully chose the same platoons and squads, although the faces were changing more rapidly. Safety in a known entity. It made both the grunts and the desk jockeys in the PR shack feel wanted and look good – at least photographically.

In fact, the more you went out, the better you got at surviving, and the better frame you could make. You understood the madness, you could slough off emotion and concentrate on the image and on staying alive. The problem was that the odds got stacked against you. The war was on an ever increasing tempo, the weapons and ordnance becoming more effective, more maiming, more deadly. A wounded man ties up at least two others in his care, besides having a demoralizing effect on his surviving buddies. A logistician's nightmare.

In 1965 the ripples of the biggest battle between NVA and American forces were still being felt and there were half a dozen of us hard core hanging out around Pleiku up in the misty Central Highlands. Jack Lawrence had a three-man crew in tow and Sean Flynn had been up in the hills for a couple of weeks, his bed sublet. We had got off a tank riding bush busting, dirty and boring with no contact all morning, and were idling off the chopper field for a cup of coffee when a big twin-rotor Chinook thundered in to pick up a group of assembling, fully loaded grunts. A flap was on. We ran in through the rear doors of an already overloaded bird as it was pulling pitch to lift out. We had landed in the middle of the heavy-weapons platoon of an Air Cavalry company that was going in to rescue the crews of three downed Hueys and then secure the wrecks. There were forty-four troops with their machine guns and mortars, a dog team and us three *bao chi*.

The Chinook made heavy air clearing the fogged-in peaks. Suddenly we were dropping in a combat spiral landing, elevator speed, everyone frantically slapping home clips and putting a live one up the spout of their weapons. The bird was raked by automatic fire as we plunged into a clearing of fallen logs and charred undergrowth. They had the doors open before we hit, lurching to a stop against a tree stump that impaled the front hold. We were in the din of a cone of incoming fire.

Our first darting rushes were only as far as the nearest anthills and tumbled tree trunks. The helicopter would never leave that ground under its own power. It had taken – we were later informed – sixty-five hits. Charlie had had the ingenuity to put machine guns up in the trees around the LZ at the edge of which smouldered the objects of our mission. I lay there, curled up, waiting for someone to shoot the buggers out of the trees before I moved.

The three of us were separated as conflicting screams ricocheted across the clearing. The only shots I got were jerked photos of the nearest troopers sprinting a few metres forwards. Seconds became hours. There were no pictures, only survival.

Survivors of a chopper crew were found curled in the roots of an upended tree, the pilot trying to reload a .38 pistrol from a loose cache of bullets in his upturned plastic flight helmet; the crew chief was struggling with the dismounted M-60 door gun. The rest of the crew were dead in the wreck, partially visible, 30 metres deep in the woods.

We never moved more than 150 metres away from where we had started, continually taking casualties who could not be reached, only heard crying for the 'doc'. I learned that anthills are the best bunkers, the best thing to lie behind, but become uncomfortable should you lie there more than a few seconds. For five minutes I lay in a colony of moving brown insects, a captain on my right, our CO, and next to him a platoon sergeant, as machine-gun fire grazed two feet either side of us. The North Vietnamese had sited their heavy weapons on the fighting holes chiselled out of abandoned termite hills, virtually impregnable to anything but a direct hit. The only move I could make was a retreat back to the trees, flapping at the fucking ants busy down my fatigues. The front end of my camera was wrecked after the compressing dive behind the nest. It was unbelievably comforting to find the other two cowering behind a felled tree trunk, and we did not venture away until the battle slacked down to sniper harassment. Helicopter gunships and fighter bombers zoomed overhead, making firing runs beyond our marker smokes.

They only just managed to get the first medivacs in before dusk. We scrambled aboard one of the last choppers with the lightly wounded and a couple of poncho-wrapped bodies. Sean and I got back into it the next morning. He stayed out there for a couple of days; I got out on a resupply mission after a short time. Back home on my floor, all Flynn could remember was stepping over a bank and sinking into a bed of dead leaves; when he pulled his leg up it was stuck in the rotting abdominal cavity of a napalmed North Vietnamese regular.

My pictures were pouched via Pan Am to Rockefeller Center, where, when I went through the files a year later, *Time* magazine had lost every single negative. I retrieved one print with the mislaid file number on the back and sealed the loss away with the fear of the moment. That was the last time I let unprocessed black-and-white film leave the republic. From then on, whenever I had an important magazine assignment, I would have one of the wires soup my stuff, select a couple of prints for the afternoon transmission – newspaper stuff, not magazine images – leaving me a few bob richer and the client with better detailed captions. It got to a point where I was scribbling out long briefing dispatches which would get translated into *Time* speak.

Da Nang was always a town of cheap thrills. To the north was the bay where the Marines had debarked, to the south was China Beach, a glorious strand corralled at one end for military use but public the other. We traded on our officer privileges to use the Lightning dinghies and surfboards provided at the in-country R & R centre. Beer was a dime a can, ice cold. Barbecue pits lined the dunes in pine groves. Vietnamese hookers patrolled the perimeter. German nurses from the Helgoland mercy-mission hospital ship moored below the press centre got shagged by black machine gunners in the surf. There was sex and drugs, rock 'n' roll and war, poured onto one strip of sand. Most days when we were not on operations we would work on our tans in the day and our minds downtown at nights. Walking into the press bar we would be shoulder-slapped by gung-ho young sergeants who were unable to understand our orders for chocolate milk or ginger ale. Only the younger ones were hip to our highs, and the waitresses were accustomed to our peculiar moods and orders. Bobbing in the dinghy off the dock we watched the perfect sunsets, long one to hand in a frosted glass.

One grotty opium den, behind a ruined pagoda, was a drop for the VC. Some nights you would find a mercenary *nung*, an ARVN NCO and an obvious VC, once even a Lao, and a Chinese from Hunan. Black packets were exchanged for envelopes. Our presence was grudgingly accepted and I swear that wherever I went in I Corps thereafter, the other side had its watchful eye on me.

The best place was behind a French bar run by an old Swiss legionnaire. His girls made the pipes and could be cajoled into accompanying you back to your room. They loved Flynn; his French B flicks had all made the provincial Vietnamese circuit. Seen Flynn, they would say; we took it up, teasing him. *Seven Thundering Colts*, *The Train for Stamboul*, *Le Fils de Captaine Blood*, they lapped up every faded one. In Saigon the bar girls would almost buy him a tea.

The Television, Writers' and Photographers' Society of Da Nang, permanent address at the Press Center, was an ad hoc fraternity of the hard core who had been based upcountry as early as the summer of 1965. It degenerated quickly to exclude the TV folks and became the Terrified Writers etc. The TWAPS arm patch featured crossed pens under a frontal silhouette of a Nikon F, the motto 'First to Know Last To Go' around the oval rim. It was mainly about drinking, rapping and getting the older, straighter members tuned to rock 'n' roll. The average age of the press in Da Nang was twenty-five, none of us ranking lower than captain on our MACV press card.

We were treated like royalty in a barracks. Each agency, net, magazine or paper had a permanent room at the press centre. The American TV lads had five racks crammed into theirs, UPI had three, *Time* a humble two. Should any of the rooms be full, one just took the next room with an empty one. Every afternoon there was an aggressive volleyball game in the courtyard. Across the street was the Da Nang museum, an old French stucco building stuffed with badly decaying Cham and Khmer pieces. The street was a rutted wallow home to Putzi the press pig and her shoats. She was our guardian mascot, the shoats our sweet and sour. During the Da Nang rebellion in July 1966, both Flynn and I turned museum robbers and hid our trophies in Putzi's home wallow by the fence. I almost got away with a really neat .50 cal tripod-mounted machine gun then, figuring I would put a sheet of armoured glass, say a jeep windshield, across the breech and barrel to create a chic coffee table.

I had almost not taken the assignment, I had been very tempted to go along with Sam Castan – the new *Look* Far East bureau chief – on an operation into Happy Valley, a notorious hot spot on the Air Cav circuit. Jack Lawrence had brought Sam, a fellow New Yorker, back to Frankie's and it had ended up with his giving me a run of minor assignments at top dollar. We had been together in the Hue, touring the troubled Buddhist universities and colleges on a political story. For some camera gear he brought down from Hong Kong, I had traded twenty bucks, and my back-up lucky Oz jungle hat. The soft-top had become a fetish, inherently blanketlike; I told myself I was safe with it on, although this had been proven untrue at Chu Lai in 1965. Sam went off in the floppy green to Bong Son; I got an open-ended job in Da Nang, where a collection of radical Buddhists, renegade local troops and auxiliaries had succeeded in taking over control of the city. The air base remained in American hands. The way to the press centre led through deserted streets littered with trash and abandoned vehicles, the only barricades manned by teenage boy scouts with a motley assortment of weapons.

For two days the dwindling number of diehard rebels were corralled into a shrinking area of downtown Da Nang as ARVN Marines and airborne units loyal to Saigon pressed ruthlessly in. It was actually exciting. You could stroll out the guarded gates of the centre and head for the sound of the nearest fighting, edging closer to the fighting positions. During a lull it was possible to cross between the lines or infiltrate round the back over walls. I soon learned the new art of street fighting. It took someone a second to spot you and another to raise and fire his weapon. In two seconds you could leap up the street to the shelter of another doorway, ditch or wrecked car. Photographically I was working in bursts of frames, looting refreshments to quench a dried-out adrenalin surge not found in the boondocks. In the middle of a city, civilians get in the way and tank fire incinerates buildings.

The closer the crack ARVN troops pressed on the Thinh Hoi pagoda, the rebel HQ, the heavier the resistance became. Fighting came, as usual in Vietnam, to a virtual standstill during the siesta 'park time' and after dark. Every time Flynn or I returned home, we passed through the museum, giving a few stiff tugs and pulls at a couple of cracked Cham heads on plinths. Putzi kept the secret until we brought airline tote bags.

By the third night the rebels' situation was desperate. A lightly wounded Buddhist boy-scout monk turned up at the press centre to request our presence for an important announcement. We walked the spooky twenty blocks to the fortress pagoda, odd rounds cracking overhead. Inside was bedlam; clusters of scared women and children, assorted uniformed troops in hastily dug firing pits and hysterical boy scouts apparently running the show. A wounded woman and her half-naked baby were brought in to be bathed in the floodlights of the TV crew. We had to shoot something, and she was their demonstration of the encroaching ARVN troops' brutality. There was no announcement. We had been conned, lured into the pagoda as possible hostages. It was time to leave, accomplished with a rapid backpedalling to the relative safety of a darker street, under their threatening gun muzzles. They had no officer prepared to order our execution.

We must have got a couple of hundred yards away when all hell broke loose. The entrenched rebels opened up at us with automatic weapons. Everyone dived for the cover of the shuttered homes. I ended up, with four others, kicking in the front door of the nearest house, revealing a terrified family of five squatting on the floor against a wall, the only light a shielded candle. Outside, the ARVN fired back, with bullets ricocheting haphazardly all over the block.

Two afternoons previously three of us – Flynn, myself and a Japanese lad, Shimamoto San of Pan Asia News – had been pinned down only a few blocks away. We had got caught up in the middle of a firefight and had leaped on the verandah of a house to cower behind a low wall. The fighting had ebbed and we had stuck our heads up slowly to suss out the situation. A brace of M-42 tanks were slowly clanking down the street, their turrets lazily swinging from side to side, like wild beasts about to charge. We watched hypnotized as the tanks crunched to a stop 100 feet away, the cannon barrel mercifully pointing down the street and not at our verandah. We made to get up as soon as the first following troops crept into sight, when a grenade arced over the top of the house, exploding between us and the tank. We felt the concussion brush over us; shrapnel and chunks of road slammed into the stucco. When we next peeked, the turret was traversing slowly our way, the 90-mm gun depressed to dead centre on the wall behind us. I produced a dirty white hanky and Simamoto raised first a hand, then an arm, his head and body, before we all slowly stood up, cameras in high-held hands.

This night there were no tanks to surrender to, no definitive lines. Besides, the rebel boy scouts had turned nasty, the street lamps were all shot out and the Airborne down the block trigger-itchy. A sensible lapse of time with no shots or explosions elapsed before three of us decided to edge out of a side door to try to make it back to the press centre over the back fences. Alain Taieb

125

of *Match*, Bob Poos of AP and I crept through the door and stood, sensing the night.

It is difficult to describe the impact of a grenade explosion three metres away from one's head. You notice not so much the noise as the light, blinding white hot, and a blast wave. The chunks of metal are almost an afterthought.

The force blew me against the wall of the building, into a sitting position. I could not see. I freaked, I screamed, my hand throbbed, my foot screamed, my face was numb, burned, stabbed, I kept screaming. I could hear a chatter of voices and a heavier exchange of automatic gunfire in the street before being dragged back inside. I was blinded and the upper part of my face was sticky wet to the touch of my uninjured right hand. The left hand felt soggy, heavy, mangled. I could hear people working on Bob and Alain. Steve Van Meter, a young VPI photo stringer and former 101st Para, had taken charge. He was holding me up a bit, trying to wrap a long cloth around my head. The concussion had left everything with a curious ringing sound, very muffled.

The eventual evacuation made history, splashed as double page spread across *Paris-Match*, beamed on both major US wires and segued into network news. The Marines came to the rescue. Flynn had doubled-timed it back to the centre and dragged the chief PIO, mad Major Mike Malloy, out in a jeep which they had driven, lights on, up the street to the house. Frontally ballsy. The star photo had Flynn and Mike carrying me, head bloodily swathed in a mosquito net, on the front door. I rode that way, balanced across the back of the jeep, to the airbase infirmary. It was straight out of a World War II movie, another retreat from the Chosin.

An M-79, affectionately known as a thumper, is a 40-mm grenade launcher. It is a giant shotgun capable of lobbing an assortment of ordnance up to 400 yards away. You can get illumination rounds, rubber bullets, gas canisters, fleshettes comprising 500 little steel darts on one shell, or – what had landed in that kapok tree – high explosive. An HE shell is a shell made of wire wound around an explosive core, serrated to create little fish hooks on explosion. It was designed to maim and inflict maximum enemy wounded rather than to just kill. None of us had been further than three metres from the epicentre of the blast. We were not supposed to have lived.

Only Alain was not discharged that night. I almost fainted in relief when the aftershave-scented air-force surgeon pronounced me not blind. My eyes were just flooded with blood from a puncture wound in front of my right ear, and a chink of the grenade base cap had neatly sliced the bridge of my nose. The ecstasy of seeing again through the wash of morphine numbed the suturing job. My left hand was done up in a boxing glove of gauze. The air-force was kind enough to throw in a jar of really strong pain pills for 'just in case'.

Motto: Whenever you visit a medical establishment, leave with a known drug.

Shock set in on the Sunday. The same day we were ambushed, Sam Castan was gunned down in Happy Valley. The platoon he was with had been overrun, with only one survivor to tell the tale. Twice wounded, Sam had finally gone down, firing the top sergeant's loaned magnum. A week later his camera was retrieved from an ambush of North Vietnamese regulars by another Air Cav unit. I got back to Saigon a day late for his memorial service, but just in time to get completely smashed on my twenty-second birthday.

The ensuing article in the press section had me saying, in that week's *Time* speak with Brit overtones, 'All you can do is drink vodka collins. Besides, they're perfect buggers, those Buddhist rebels. It's my birthday, mate; let's order some champagne. I never thought I'd live to see it.' A picture was captioned the 'unbowed Brit'.

R & R took place in Singapore. When I got back, I needed a short field-trip to get into shape.

The coast guard, the minority force in the war zone, with a dozen cutters, had never taken a casualty. Theirs was the safest duty. They ran patrol patterns just offshore between the Vietnamese naval junk force and the larger destroyer and DERs, a destroyer escort, lying 12 miles out. It was all part of Operation Market Time, designed to prevent the North Vietnamese from gun-running sampans, junks and trawlers down the coast. Since the South Vietnamese and the Americans enjoyed total air supremacy south of the seventeenth parallel, the North Vietnamese only risked the odd boat to run the gauntlet of patrols backed up by the Seventh Fleet aircraft carriers in deep water out in the Tonkin Gulf. American and South Vietnamese vessels screened the coast from the mouth of the Ben Hai River to the Cambodian border at Phu Quoc Island, and the naval press information office was always keen to get someone interested in their aspect of the war. I was the first photographer or correspondent ever to take the coast guard up on their offer of a three-day patrol cruise from their

Da Nang base, and it was a speculative shoot, not a paying assignment. Hopefully a few frames would be flogged to the wire services. They guaranteed decent food and sunshine with a lot of bouncing around on an 80-foot aluminium cutter.

The *Point Welcome* was a military version of a shrimp boat with virtually no armour plate for protection. Its mascot, painted on the flying bridge side, was the cartoon road runner doing 'beep beep'. It packed a heavy machine gun on the back, another piggy back on the front mounted over a 81-mm mortar, plus assorted automatic weapons of the twelve-man crew's personal choice. A Vietnamese naval ensign was aboard as interpreter to question any suspects. He bunked down with the crew, I got to share a rack in the two-bed officer's cabin beneath the bridge.

The swimming calls were uneventful. Half the crew toted sundry weapons to discourage sharks, the rest of us lolled in the tepid Tonkin Gulf. I worked on my tan and made the odd snap when we made a short shore raid, coordinating with the junks out of Cua Viet on the Ben Hai estuary. The patrol pattern overlapped with a sister boat that hardly ever left the sight of land.

A sun-and-sea deep sleep was brutally sliced open by the sound of a series of explosions six feet from the end of the bed, followed by a gush of fire stinking of amanol and burning metal. Something had hit us, and hard. Probably a plane. I fell out of bed, clad in shorts, and grabbed a camera. Through the Leica's viewfinder was an inferno of blazing gas cans on the shattered fantail; some crew hopped about playing extinguishers at the blaze. I must have got off half a dozen frames in the eerie flare-lit light before the next jet came in. It was death winking you directly in the eye. The F-4 US Air Force Phantom was skimming the waves at sonic speed, its 20-mm Vulcan guns pouring 6000 rounds per minute towards us. I couldn't actually see the plane, just the fast blinking guns stabbing yellow shafts at the lens. The cannon shells exploded inches away in the hollow end of the flying bridge, blowing out the electrical cabling and hydraulic lines in nasty, quilled shards. I stood in the way of a hot shower of shrapnel designed to create wounds difficult to operate on. The shells are composed of tightly wound steel wire serrated to create minute penetrating barbs as they explode. I collected untold hundreds of fragments of shrapnel and boat plumbing ranging in size from specks to half-crown-sized slabs. The heat generated a sear of burns.

There hadn't even been time to move, duck, shoot or think. It all happened in microseconds, with a noise beyond decibels; the aircraft's jets boomed after it passed, a giant ripping clouds of silk sheeting.

There never was a satisfactory explanation. The US Air Force had just goofed again, at a time when friendly casualties were becoming an altogether unpleasant statistic. The air force in Da Nang tried to claim we transmitted the wrong automatic-code identity signal. The facts spoke for themselves. A B-57 Canberra on a regular patrol pattern had spotted the cutter, circled and dropped a flare. The Junior Lt on bridge duty had thrown on our riding lights and the floods that illuminated the stern for searching fishing vessels at night. A Stars and Stripes drooped from the transom and a coast-guard pennant from the masthead. Our silhouette, even at that ghostly dogwatch hour, could never have been a North Vietnamese mission or Chinese-built craft. The 57 had radioed up a pair of Phantoms running migcap, anti MIG patrol, detouring them from their high-altitude enemy-fighter protection patrol, and then stood off to watch the attack.

The first run raked the deck, cooking off the gas and ammo, triggering an SOS. On the second pass from the second bird, everyone on deck fighting the blaze had been hit. Before the next pass the skipper had gone up to the burning bridge and started signalling the planes with an Aldis lamp. The third run decapitated him and razed the superstructure with a five-inch Zuni rocket. The F-4s made eight attacking runs, leaving the *coup de grâce* to the 57, which dropped a string of cluster bombs across us before peeling off to go hunt our sister vessel answering the mayday. They left us burning, listing, sinking, dead in the water.

Pain never hurts at first. The first sensation is a numbing, searing, white heat, an uncomfortable suffused glow. Then come the stabs, the agony as the flesh, muscle and bone are exposed in all their rawness. Luckily I had my trusty Leica to my right eye at the time the burst hit, the viewfinder full of the swabbie with truncated arms who now lay beside me below decks. A shell had blown up the extinguisher in his hands. Where there been hands and wrists there were shredded, bleeding, blackened stumps. Horrible third-degree burns disfigured his front, plastered with a chalky froth of fire-fighting foam. All the wounded and dead were piled on the mess-deck floor. People were groping for first-aid kits, screaming, and slicking everything with a gloop of blood. The Vietnamese employed to clean the boats at the Monkey Mountain base facility had stolen all the bandages and morphine from the emergency packs stowed on the bulkheads. We lay there in shocked fear, feeling the drumming concussion as the successive passes raked us stern to stem. The cramped quarters were full of choking smoke. The chief bosun and another man scrambled up the forward ladder to douse the fire on the forward deck, terrified that the heat would cook off the mortar-ammunition locker. They were blown back on top of us moments later. One more dead, one armless.

It seemed like an eternity. Time had stopped. My Rolex had been sheared off my wrist by a chunk of shrapnel that had gone clean through my forearm, leaving the bone exposed. A porcupine quill of steel electrical cable had penetrated my left eye, cheek and nose; the Leica saved the right side of my face. A similar quill stuck in my left side. Somewhere near balls level a warm seep of blood flooded down, both feet felt razor slashed and I sensed a dart sticking in the small of my back. I still had the camera round my neck, the frames I punched off all out of focus. By the time the silence left by the departing Canberra had sunk in, we were too numbed to react.

'Abandon ship,' 'Pass the word.' I got my waterproof medic-cum-camera bag from the cabin wreckage and retrieved my sneakers, aware that should we reach the kilometre-distant shore, I would have to walk. I wrapped a discarded towel around the gaping arm wound. The hurt was all over but I was still functioning and, thankfully, never seemed to have gone into shock. Strange how shock kills. Some men hit in the finger flip out and fade in minutes, others, with horrendous sucking chest wounds, guts exposed and traumatic amputations, sit there nonchalantly puffing a smoke, quipping bullshit with their buddies.

The previous day I had hauled myself happily up the side onto the deck after the swimming call. Now, looking down at the water only a few feet below, I refused to believe I could jump, much less swim. Nobody had found a lifebelt, though an inflatable rescue dinghy in a bundle had been heaved overboard to inflate automatically, in theory.

Sliding into the water, bag held high, felt like slipping into a bath of acid as the salt permeated the shrapnel wounds and the burns shrieked. What felt like hours but must have been minutes, thus does agony distort time. I floated on my back, barely keeping my sack above water. Later I claimed it was twenty minutes, but I now suspect only a few had passed when I reluctantly let the bundle slip to the bottom of the Tonkin Gulf. The Leica went with it, and the exposed film – the gear or me.

130

It got worse. The Viet Cong and North Vietnamese based on the Cua Viet peninsula started lobbing mortars our way while the valiant South Vietnamese junk force motoring to the scene plied 50-calibre fire in our direction, believing the burning, silhouetted wreck to be a northerner. As we bobbed on the swell the red tracers from the machine guns plucked at the sea; as we sank into the troughs, the mortars plopped fairly harmlessly into the ocean around us.

I found myself drifting towards a Carley survival float. Draped half across it was the Vietnamese interpreter, badly torn up, whimpering, with a nasty head and chest wound. He must have known he was dying for he kept trying to keep his head under but his instinct to live dragged it back up again. I clutched the plastic float and held his collar with the less wounded right hand, murmuring sweet nothings of attempted consolation. I could feel myself ebbing, the salt eroding the wounds, cauterizing them but pushing the pain to a raw nerve ending. This was no time to think of the sharks which I suspected must be closing.

Twenty metres away, partially illuminated by the burning cutter, I made out a group of men struggling with the half-inflated life raft. I paddled our craft their way, beholden to the life-saving classes at Warren Road primary school, in the longest length I will ever swim.

We flopped over the limp rubber tube into a half-flooded interior, half water, half blood. The life-saving device was punctured through and through with shrapnel. It was like trying to put to sea in a leaking kid's paddling pool. One guy, a Chief Petty Officer, was hardly wounded but had lost his mind. He had abandoned ship clad in a helmet, boots, shorts and flak vest, clutching a Thompson submachine gun. He was frantically trying to find the collapsible baler, rummaging through the raft's survival-gear pockets. As he found an item he would jettison it overboard; we lost the water, food, emergency radio and a bunch of rations before I calmed him down. It lasted minutes before he started shooting at what he thought were passing shark fins. He hit nothing but water, and drilled a couple more holes in our flexible float. Then he threw the Thompson away and plunged overboard, saying he would take his chances on the burning hulk. We let him go, all five of us too fucked up to do anything.

Although help was on its way, lying there in that leaking dinghy I believed that this was the end and swore that I would quit the game and return to the world. By the time I reached Phu Bai, a

Marine base south of Hue city, I was positive it was over. We had sloshed in the sinking rubber for an eternity before our sister cutter had hoved up to us. They had to lower a thing like a giant shrimping net to get me aboard, to rudimentary bandaging and merciful sister morphine. Daybreak saw our transferral to a shallow-draft naval junk for the slow ride back to Cua Viet.

The story unfolded as the survivors were grouped in a corrugated iron shack, reeking of fish, beside the helipad. The executive officer, stumps for arms and a foot gone, had been picked up just before he reached the beach, where one other lightly wounded guy awaited rescue. Three more were in between ship and shore, floundering along. Everyone had initially believed it had to have been a South Vietnamese plane and were still too shocked to accept the total fuck-up that the US Air Force had perpetrated.

Yet again, I was lucky, arriving at a major medical facility, Charlie Med at Phu Bai, when there was no other heavy action going on in its catchment area. The triage room and all the surgeries were empty, awaiting the full attention of a breakfasted, rested medical team. I was on the operating table, conscious, for over a hour while they worked on me from different directions. Six sutures here, fifteen there, ten under there. I felt trussed and clotted, vomiting all over their work when the anaesthetist hit me with a bit of a boost, the only thing to which I am allergic, Demerol.

Within hours I had a visitor, Martin Stuart-Fox. He had flown up on the milk run on hearing the news at the Press Centre in Da Nang.

He sat on the edge of that starched white bed in the air-conditioned post-op Nissen hut, taking down my choked-out story. At one point he stopped and looked down, saying that I had wet the bed. He felt under the sheet and pulled back his hand, slick with blood. Treating the 200 or so puncture wounds, the surgeons had overlooked a gash at the base of my spine, and a vein was dribbling onto the rubber sheet. Back to the theatre, with the consolation that Martin had retrieved two of my cameras and my Rolex from the coast guard when the craft was towed into its Monkey Mountain base. The film was already on its way, awaiting his dictated story. A small salvage from a wrecked assignment cum orientation trip.

My wounds were swabbed out with giant Q-tips. The wooden sticks disappeared four inches up the slit in my arms and an inch and a half into my thighs. I screamed the house down.

Ceremoniously I was transported south to the hospital of my choice, the army-run 17th Evac on the main Saigon/Cho Lon boulevard, Trung Hung Dao. I could have been evacced anywhere in the free world, but I chose the hospital closest to home. That was now Frankie's House.

I was expected to be out and home in three weeks. They passed in a constant flow of journalists and girlfriends bringing monster opiated joints and iced vodka collins in thermos jugs. I got so smashed the first night out that I insisted on a victory parade downtown, arm in a sling, raw scars reaping an extra round as the story was rehashed to an alcholol blurred audience.

The army had the audacity to send me a bill for medical treatment amounting to nearly $400, which I stapled to the *Time* clipping about the incident and remailed to: The General commanding 7th Air Force, Ton San Nhut Air Base, Saigon, Republic of Vietnam. I heard no more. Rolex in Hong Kong fixed my watch for nothing and *Time* picked up a couple of cameras for me.

I hardly worked for the rest of the year. A delicate spring in my inner mechanism had snapped.

Frankie's House was changing. Simon left to go back to the UK, Flynn went back to Paris for a bit. Tom Corpora of UPI slid in, then Joe Galloway, Steve went to *Newsweek* in Washington DC. The ratty English hippy on the roof, Jim, drifted off to Malaya. The pets were allowed to escape, all except the black dog and Balls the baby monkey. Joe, the dog named after Galloway, was thrice taken to the extremities of the city and dumped by Frankie, but it always came home. I am sure he came back later to haunt us, on a dinner plate. Balls had to go; he had a dirty temperament, prone to sitting on the bookcase and masturbating, spurting usually over female guests. He was given to my girlfriend at the British Embassy. Her compound had another pet simian which proceeded to bugger Balls, causing his final escape.

Through my French connection I had got involved with a buxom, aristocratic lady. Roberte de Tichy was the consul and doubled as Deuxième Bureau drop. Everyone was madly jealous of my round-eyed lady. I was bowled over in my first affair with an older woman. I would return from the field a mess, draped in my gear, sour and sweaty, reeking of the worst shit. Roberte would virtually rape me as I entered her balconied third-floor flat, hot from the field. Or I had to go home, clean up, shave, shower and *parfumé* before biking over to the diplomatic compound. Then a superb candlelit four-course meal would be served by her maid on a damask cloth with family silver. The *commissariat's* amazing wines, Roberte voluptous in raw silk, the warm evening, the relief of survival, the large bed with ironed linen – the dream was complete. The highs and ecstasies erased the realities faced hours before.

Flynn and I received invitations to the French embassy's New Year's Eve 1966 party. The embossed card requested our pleasure in '*tenue de soir*'. I asked Roberte what that implied, neither of us possessing a tie. I said we would come as the VC would. She laughed. We arrived punctually in black pyjamas, sneakers and pistol belts. Flynn was surrounded by the ambassadorial nymphets, passing ready-rolled joints out of an ammo pouch clipped to his webbing.

The French were trying to walk a middle line in Vietnam, protecting their plantations and business interests while pleasing the Americans. After an action where I had been out on our side, I would get the VC figures from one of Roberte's spooks fresh from the rubber and tea tracts. Being with Roberte really gave status in a male-run society, hung up on sex and war. Somehow we kept it relatively private, steering clear of the haunts where the military hung out. Water skiing from the Club Nautique I tried once, having horrors of falling into the snakes and corpses floating in the Saigon River, though not of being shot at in an area basically controlled by the VC, twenty minutes from downtown.

R & R is supposed to get you healthy. The one I took after the coast guard workout left me back at square minus one. I hobbled off the Bangkok plane, my broken collar bone supported in a sling, two left toes fractured and a few more stitches up top. In the vernacular of the time, expressed so well by the underground press, 'speed kills'. Both sorts had got me.

We were riding out to Don Maung airport in Bangkok, Martin on the pillion of the 250cc Honda motocross, to pick up his fiancée Elizabeth, daughter of Maurice, the owner of the Constellation Hotel. I had slipped back to the pep pills and Klosters beer, the grass was Lao, the road a disaster. Stuck behind a bus in swirling cement dust, I did not see, until too late, the pile of concrete beneath the front wheel. It was a slowmotion cartwheel into irregular lumps of construction debris. Fortunately the bike stayed where it had impacted. I was rudely stitched up in the corridor of the Christian hospital, condemned to a hallway by the overflowing charity wards. Martin managed to meet Elizabeth, hobbling, scratched though basically unscathed.

I had been in Singapore, sitting by a round pool in the round grounds of the Round House off the Bukit Timor road, picking bits of shrapnel, electrical conduiting and rubber insulation out of every cardinal point of my body. The house was a high-ranking diplomatic residence where my status was one of an adopted son and lover, star from the strange planet, visitor from the war zone that was on everyone's top-ten talk list. The parties were legendary. The young English damsels in bored distress were empathetically entertaining. And then Flynn turned up with a crew in tow, or vice versa, to shoot a bomb B flick, *Cinq Gars pour Singapur*.

The gay French director had in tow his boyfriend and the boyfriend's best friend; Terry Downes, a former Marine and world middleweight boxing champ, was cast as a gunny sergeant on R & R; most of the crew were French hipsters and the starlet a sultry Paris-based American model. Flynn was their leader and the star of the production. A thin plot of dagger derring-do had five grunts out of Eye Corps painting the town, being kidnapped by Red Chinese based on a freighter in the harbour, where they were put into cryogenics and reprogrammed to return to Da Nang and win the war. 'Seen Fleen', as the bar girls chimed, naturally had to save the day. I got paid to sit around the various sets as an extra.

With a cassette player strapped to the tank of my shiny new bike I had plunged north into the monsoons of the Malay peninsula, the Stones trembling in my mind, soaked to the skin, peeling round the rubberized road bends. Penang was a beach with sea snakes and a temple with kraits, deadly snakes, dripping from the rafters and offering tables.

My wildest fantasies of the primal modern explorer cum moto-cross champion were fulfilled as I hit southern Thailand, where the road was unrecognizable in the mud of the jungle. I needed the Judy Collins tapes on the bleak Thai village inn beds where I had to hole up between storms. The electrics of the Honda packed up; riding after sunset, on an unlit jungle track, through thick forest, the suspension welds unfroze. Bogged down to the saddle I had to wait two hours in bandit country before two local lads puttered up on a scooter. After hauling my overloaded beast out I trailed them at five miles per hour, dodging round the deep ruts, slipping between lakes on any little firm bits, like tramping across a bog. It took four days to get to Bangkok. The benevolent manufacturers had taken a week to remount me for the rest of the trip home; the ride to the concrete slab was a test run.

The bike went back to Honda; I was put up for a week by the doyen of the resident journalist set, the *Observer* correspondent John Stirling. The lovely restored Honda never got beyond the corrupt Vietnamese officials and I was too damaged and broke to go and retrieve it.

I had just recovered when Mad George, an Irish contract worker with Decca radar, put his Austin Healey Sprite, Indochina's only one, through a concertina barbed-wire fence. It was Boxing Day 1966, passing by mistake the presidential palace, George was drunk, doing forty, I was perched up on the dickey. The black NCO medic on reluctant Christmas duty did not even bother to administer a local before he slapped seventeen sutures in a T on the top of my head. The concussion gave me something to think about. The message was getting through. I needed to get out.

Still, a bit like getting back on after my first bicycle accident when I was five, I had to go and test it a bit more. The third time, in the new year of 1967, the Year of the Horse, I went north to Dong Ha, right to the edge of the DMZ where the ARVN airborne had got chewed up probing the encroaching NVA. Sean came along, back from finishing an affair and the movie in Paris. We went in with the relief battalion to bring back the disoriented survivors of an overnight long-range North Vietnamese 130-mm artillery barrage. At one point, Phantoms were putting down bombs and napalm 150 metres away, too close for comfort. Sean and I hit a house bunker, found next to every residence. We lay there, curled up foetally in a Vietnamese-sized space, hugging each other in real terror. In cold sweat and fear trembles, we put our heads back out for a few minutes before the NVA got the range again and we dived once more. Under fire the unit had lost much of the day; we had to retreat under incoming harassing fire in a night so pitch dark that every man picked up a piece of phosphorescent jungle litter and put it on the back pack of his buddy in front. As the column jerked through dense underbrush it fell apart, panicked voices calling out until the snake contracted in. At the defensive line further south I slept coldly in a foxhole screefed from the turf under an APC. Rode the chopper out that had come to pick up the night's dead on the morning's mist.

I came to feel that there would be no more pushing the edge, facing the vertical plunge at 450 knots in a dive-bombing Sky Raider, no more bike rides to the rubber, no more monkey bridges to balance across. The times with Sean had been the best I had had. There were too many dead, too many of the hard core had gone home, a new crop of young dudes, many opting to take their military discharge in-country, joining the blossoming ranks of the *bao chi*. I was tired and jaded, traumatized without really understanding why. Frank McCulloch at *Time* and Don Mosler at *Life* concluded the same.

Passing through Da Nang on the way south from cringing in the DMZ with the Airborne, I had gone out to the Monkey Mountain naval facility to check out the *Point Welcome*, back in commission again. The road runner mascot on the flying bridge now had a crossed Band-Aid painted on its arse, the 'beep beep' changed to 'Ouch!' The new crew laid a commemorative Zippo on me.

With 500 in green I went down from the Caravelle Hotel to the Pan Am office on the corner of Ngo Duc Khe next to UPI to reserve and pay for a one-way ticket to London. Back in Room 401, I was doled out another five bills. It was surprising to pack the amount of stuff I had accumulated over the past two and some years. Of the thousands of dollars I had made there were only a few hundred in the Manufacturers Hanover account and a few hundred in Hong Kong, the rest was in a thousand books and the same count of records. I owned all my own photographic gear, which looked as if it had been through hell and high water. A large heavy-duty plastic battery bag contained a jumble of trashed equipment. My wardrobe was entirely olive drab or navy blue, bright colours were sand and brown. At the bottom of the foot lockers, neatly packed around with books, I packed the spanking new M-2 carbine I had been given by the Special Forces and an expended LAW, a disposable antitank bazooka, which I believed would look fine hanging in the downstairs toilet of my dream house. My tape decks went into the lockers; the stereos became common property. There was an awful lot of military and battlefield bric-à-brac which I just could not part with, virtually security-blanket material. The traditional going-away party, normally a joyous and sad event, was forsaken, I was leaving too soon to print the invitations.

Only Roberte came to the airport, hanging back at the check-in, hiding my cornucopia of carry-on pieces. I sweltered in my black-market cold-weather pilot's jacket, limping under the strapped-on cameras. The Zippo, the Cambodian tiger claw worn on the peace dog tags chain around my neck, the Rolex and my floppy Oz hat were the true talismans of the *bao chi* trip.

Going back to the world I felt the gnawing of anticipation and fear that the prospect of a hot LZ had brought.

5

Interlude
Back in the World

As the 707 laboured towards Heathrow, the weather became increasingly depressing, grey cold rain, snow. Pan Am 1 took almost 40 hours on its milk run to New York from Bangkok. Deplaning at Heathrow I went for broke and hired my first rent-a-wreck. The Vietnamese international licence performed perfectly. I would surprise the parents, who assumed I was still precariously thriving in the tropics, while they braved the rigours of a Kentish winter and my gran's ails. Their weekly letters, written by mum and signed by dad, were the only bridge I had to the old world, I had not kept in touch with anyone else. The tax-free hangover lagged my cattle-class cramped body, and I prayed for a toasty fire as I skirted the drab suburbs, vaguely trying to compose opening lines for my bemused parents. It would be tea time when I got there. I had been up for forty-eight hours.

I knew every last turn into the top of the estate and pulled up outside 47 North Drive. No lights, no answer. I had no key. I went next door to the neighbours. My mother, Ken Powell told me, was in Orpington Hospital. My dad knocked as I was digesting a second large Scotch.

In a common ward, my mother looked like death propped up, crying on the pillows. They had taken a tumour the size of an orange out of her liver. She would live. We left an almost embarrassing ten minutes later, leaving her behind the screened-in bed, clutching the doll in national costume I had bought for her collection in the Karachi transit lounge. Dad was camping in the house. We had greasy bacon and eggs, beer and Jack Daniels, and slept in damp, chilly beds. I moved out the next day without telling anyone.

I would not see them again for another three years.

The anticipated feeling of being a returned hero was dismally missing. The light was grey and everything as glum as when I had left. Trucks passed me going uphill.

I went on to Paris, where there was promised Time Inc employ and a room at Jim Wilde's Passage de Désire apartment. The back seat of the '52 Austin black cab, a £60 steal from an East End garage, was adorned with Arianne, bundled into a fur coat. She was one of Flynn's camp followers working for *Elle* in Vietnam while Jon, her husband-to-be, worked for the *Washington Post*. She had jumped out of a chopper over the Delta with Sean, clad in skintight, leopard-spotted camouflage fatigues.

Tommy Thompson, *Life*'s Paris bureau chief, expressed his anxiety about having me courier the film of Chancellor Adenauer's funeral, but I was the only one out of the crew of twelve who had never been either to the head office or the US. It was decided reluctantly that after all I had earned it. As the deadline for the magazine was tight, I would have to hand-carry my film and that of five other photographers straight to the New York office from Bad Godesberg and Cologne.

It was a cold, slushy day in April and I spent twelve hours on a freezing steel bridge across the Rhine for a photo that got used as a quarter page. After three rounds of schnapps with the other photographers the transit through Heathrow was a blur, but I dimly recall being steered by a friendly Pan Am stew to the New York-bound 707, deluxe, up front, clutching the big red 'Life/ Urgent' envelope, then powered through immigration and customs into a *Life* limo to be whisked to the twenty-ninth floor of Rockefeller Center.

I was introduced to George Hunt, the editor, and various other luminaries, all of whom were aware of my work in Vietnam and who plied me with more bourbon and branch water in styrofoam cups than I could handle, whilst laying out the next issue. When I had been up for forty-five hours I pleaded out, pleased with seeing my quarter page and another half put to bed. I had earned my freelancer's weekly due. Dick Pollard, who was chief of photography, told me, 'I guess that now your day rates should be $150,' – an extra $50 a day from what they had been for almost two years. No longer the debutant.

*

When the Six Day War broke out, the bureau was nearly empty. Teams had been slipping into the area for some weeks, waiting for the story to break. A radio appeal for volunteers to be parachuted from El Al jets prompted Flynn back in his gran's ex flat in the 15th Arrondissement to persuade me to join him at the Israeli embassy. There was a throng trying to get in, and we went away. The next day I got a posting: proceed to Amman via Athens and Beirut. The ticket wad had Amman, Nicosia, Athens, Istanbul, Amman, Beirut, Nicosia ad infinitum returns, so I could keep going in and out. First class to boot.

We got marooned at the King George Hotel overlooking Beirut's corniche, the only action was being buzzed by the Lebanese and once an Israeli jet. Nasser threatened to resign in Cairo on the third day of the war, when Egypt was already beaten, the Suez virtually reached. Arab sympathies caused the streets of Beirut to erupt into a frenzied beehive. Angry mobs stormed through the streets, destroying anything with an English or American sign on it. They believed their propaganda that it was British planes from Cyprus and carrier-based American ones that had knocked the Arab air forces out of the skies. The army withdrew to protect the diplomatic missions, leaving the mob to run amok over half the city.

I posed as a *Paris-Match* photographer, using my Indochinese Franglais as a passport. Swirled along by the mob, I was boosted onto PLO shoulders to get a perspective on their 40-foot flag being paraded. Suddenly the mood changed and an ugly surge went through the crowd. I was summarily dismounted as the leaders torched cars and improvised battering rams as we swept into a place fronting the US Information Service library. I worked in the crowd, framing, shooting, watched over by a Palestinian journalism student from the American university, and a dock labourer. Part of the mob turned on me, more than my bodyguards could handle. My sunglasses starred on my face, the old gash bled on my nose: I went down, was buoyed up by the bodyguards, went down again and was running, to be jerked up over a stone wall. I was in the back end of a coffee shop. Nobody seemed surprised as I walked through and sat down, trying to blend in, rapidly placing fresh rolls in the cameras. No one had followed me. I gulped a Coke and dodged down back alleys to the bureau. Getting cut and bruised made good copy and earned a few free rounds on the George Terrace.

With Israeli victory imminent, we were cleared for the drive, nonstop, to Amman. I was crammed into the back seat of an old

141

Chevrolet with two Arab Press lads and an incongruous figure in a dark pinstripe suit. He was the *Svenska Dagbladet* staff court photographer who had been posted straight from the palace to the Middle East with two bulky boxes of Hasselblads. The tough Hashemite guards at the Jordanian border post unbelievably let us pass, with a cursory stamp.

The four-day-old dead horses and camels, the stream of dispirited refugees being hustled by harassing quad fifty fire from the Israeli side, never made the magazine. The vomiting, the flies, the heat, the wading in the mythical Jordan River were to no avail. The same shots by a fellow *Lifer* from Jerusalem got back to New York nonstop from Tel Aviv on El Al. Mine had been hand-couriered back to Beirut overland, then to Paris and then on to the 28th floor in the Rockefeller Center. Amman was a bad case of the runs, flyblown and hostile, and the first PLO camps out on the Iraqi border near Mafraq were worse. I went back to Beirut after ten days, via Nicosia.

Then there was Katya. Her father was about the seventh richest man in Lebanon. She offered the use of a range of cars, Jag through Mini, to be delivered by the chauffeur to the hotel. We spent idyllic days in her daddy's hash fields in the Ba'albeck, or lunching beneath the Crusader Castle at Byblos, and I was tempted to take the offered Beirut posting, but I itched for a non-Arab world. They were driving me crazy; the hash was not enough to blunt the oppressive discourteousness outside the hotel. Beirut was not my scene. The war was over, and the world was losing interest in the losers' story. I calculated I had enough cash for a long vacation.

Flynn came back from Israel, where he had returned from the front with Don Wise dragging a recoilless rifle behind their rented Volkswagen, to decorate Mandy Rice-Davis's discotheque in Tel Aviv. It was confiscated. He gave me a Russian helmet from the Sinai, I gave him a tablecloth type headdress from Amman inspired by a photo session with King Hussein. We cruised off to Chez Castels Disco, he as outrider for the black cab on his Triumph Trophy. We would pull over when hailed by an attractive woman.

Flynn came back from San Francisco and visiting his mother in Palm Beach with the latest sounds, The Grateful Dead, the Jefferson Airplane, Canned Heat, the Doors. We were on the Riviera and so were the Living Theatre, the Soft Machine and the dad of French hip, Jean-Jacques Lebel. Everyone was walking around with fluted, glass-stoppered bottles full of Sandoz 25, the purest LSD on the tightening market. Traditionally you were given a drop on a lump of sugar; I got mine as a splash on my hand, behind the left thumb. I just licked it up. Endlessly.

St Tropez was the setting for the play *Désire atrappé par la queue*, Picasso's only theatrical work, *Desire Caught by the Tail*. It had been performed only once before, on underground liberation radio during the occupation of Paris, when it had co-starred Malraux and Camus. Jean-Jacques was directing its revival under a circus top at a campsite four kilometres from chic downtown. The cast had strippers, New York gays, fats and freaks. The Living Theatre lurked as understudies. The Soft Machine performed in a beer garden down the road. Somehow we were included in Lebel's entourage; myself, Susan, my current American affair, Alain, a con man, and Priscilla, Flynn's girl, a model. We were packed into the Lebel holiday villa along with half the cast and more entourage. It was hot, we were naked, the kitchen was an ever open snack bar of country-fresh food, a bottle of acid stood in the living room, everyone boosting their trips periodically, couples slipping off for tranquillity. A haze of kif and incense hovered in the house, the sun shone on the terraces outside. No one guided me on the first trips, those first uncontrollable spurts and wobbles of emotion and experience. The place was idyllic, the vibrations relaxed, no one freaked out in any of half a dozen different tongues.

We took it further, tripping downtown, bursting into giggles in bourgeois harbourfront cafés. The cast performed wrecked; I joined in the happening, shooting film like one possessed. Shapes and colours dissolved in the most fantastic creations. A lava lamp effect in time unreal. I came unglued driving the first time. The road became a four-dimensional holographic back projection with lights rushing at me below and above screen to right and left. I abandoned the wheel for the passenger seat, but the oncoming lights still threatened. I passed the rest of the journey, to a Luxembourg contessa's *palazzo*, cowering under the glove compartment. Too terrified to ride in another car, I tramped home across the Midi, draped in cameras from the previous night's performance, not a sou in my pockets. For 25 kilometres I photographed dead dragonflies, trash dumps and flowers. Looking back at the slides I shot then I cannot imagine what I was really seeing. Never had I felt such an inward rush, such lifting of barriers, of thought constraint. Though I had to conquer driving on it.

143

The six-week orgy of sex, drugs and fantasy helped let go the tension the war had bolted down; tripping had nearly the same edge as combat. The fear and fun rolled along one very sharp line where life and death were separate blinks. The central meaning of it all was still fuzzy, but the corners of the frame were pulling a sharper overall focus.

Jim Wilde had come back from an overseas gig to find the whole of the Living Theatre occupying his *objet*-filled Paris home, with myself heading a squad cooking up nasi goreng for thirty-eight in the designer kitchen. I lived four walk-up floors in a fourteenth-century box with balcony and bidet, subletting the apartment of a fallen aristocratic lady. Alain moved into the one room, sleeping in the corner behind the television set. My sex life was heavily disturbed as, unemployed and broke, too lethargic to take long walks, he would retreat only to the toilet or balcony to read. He overcame the sexual problems by seducing Susan. I slapped her around and threw them both out. We all made up but the true magic of those friendships had gone.

Paris had become a hassle. I wanted just to get high and fuck around all day, and the summer's money had dried up. I converted the leftover first-class *Life* tickets to a round trip to New York, telling myself that Time Inc would throw me a lifebelt, a mere change was as good as a holiday. I was convincing myself that I was in love with Yvonne, a *Life* reporter I had met in May. I returned to her prestigious Beekman Place condo, *Life* started handing out nice round-town jobs, the doorman got to know my name and I found the Cat living with his filmmaker father five blocks away.

The mood in New York started to turn nasty in the late fall, a harbinger of the revolution coming in 1968. The East Village was flooded with runaway kids searching out the hip, beautiful existence. The Diggers and the underground *Other* screamed for sanity, but too much speed tipped the balance when a hippy black kid and a runaway white girl had their heads smashed to a pulp during an amphetamine strike. An insight team was sent down from the Rockefeller Center to root out the truth of what had become known as the Linda and Groovy double murder. We gained entrance to the crash pads with pure crystal meth bought on expense account. We commuted to the front lines twice daily, feeding interviewees at corner doughnut shops. The story made the cover, we made the op ed page, posing with the hustling kids on St Mark's Square with the Electric Circus, the psychedelic disco, as the backdrop.

The protest started downstairs, right outside the Time-Life building on the Avenue of the Americas at 47th. Dean Rusk was staying next door at the Hilton for his daughter's wedding. A mass of peace-in-Vietnam protesters pressed against the police barriers, mounted cops panicked bystanders, while the young radical element sat down in front of the traffic, skirmishing with the cops. Surprisingly it was a mixed black and white, old and young crowd. The demonstrators were well behaved. After the first heavy confrontations outside the Battery Draft Induction Center, there were demonstrations all over lower Manhattan for the next three days. I was caught in the middle, emotionally and physically, fluorescent NYPD police press tag around my neck. The police thought I looked like a demonstrator in my bush hat and the crowd thought me a police spy. My only protest was, 'Hey man, I've been there, I know and anyway, I'm British and, hey, don't . . .' The whole dormant emotional bank was being questioned. Dove or hawk? Hawk or dove? Love and hatred. Of course peace is always logical and that the war was groovy is impossible to explain to those back in the world. There lay the dilemma of having been there.

The story boiled but was spiked as insignificant. The big Inc was still being cautious in its commitments, the legacy of a Luce doctrine embedded with spooks. I have a black-and-white image of a winter-wrapped mother bearing a placard: NOT OUR SONS, NOT YOUR SONS, NOT THEIR SONS.

I was unable to sell a projected book on the war, tired of trudging round book art directors with an oversize heavy folio. The time was not ripe to open America's mind, the idea was laughed at; the whole attitude to the contentiousness of patriotism was just now simmering. My relationship with Yvonne had gone off the boil; my outspoken comments about the draft, the war and America at her folks' Christmas do up in Hartford had not helped the tension. It was time to head west.

Had to get out of the Apple, turning rotten post my projection to the front lines and subsequent arrest for a string of offences allegedly committed as the Doors crescendoed out to 'The End' in a New Haven ice hockey rink. *Life*'s Fred Powledge was 'insighting' the current psychedelically edged Haight Ashbury-inspired music through the eyes of his pre-teen daughters, replicating a pre-pubescent look up at the gyrating leather-clad erection thrusting at a packed stadium. Morrison lit their fires and a ring of teenyboppers' instamatics winked back at the strobes as they encroached the stage's apron. The reality was that it was – like many of those sixties busts – a police-induced riot, in an over-reaction to the youthful genre. Another attempt to nip protest in the bud. Morrison peaked, 'C'mon touch me . . . get together, right now, the whole thing together baby, we want the fucking world, we want it now . . .'

That did it. Reacting to a previous complaint when the singer was supposedly caught by a fan's jealous boyfriend getting blown in the privacy of his dressing room, the police surged on-stage as the power was cut. Morrison had enough left to parry the mike at Lt Kelly's face with a 'Say your thing, man' before the whole hot moment was stunned briefly into ill-lit silence. As the cops dragged the protesting performer off-stage, a riot errupted on the boarded rink floor.

Yvonne, my *Life* researcher friend, Mike Zwerin of the *Voice* and myself all seated advantageously in the front row made through the flying folding chairs and bottles for the foyer. Outside plain clothes pigs lammed into hapless teenagers. I danced about shooting the punch out. An officer grabbed and began beating me, telling me to move on. I protested to the Lieutenant in charge and went back to work. Instant arrest, squad car back seat. Yvonne, perturbed, drifted over and was thrown in beside me. Mike followed suit. A complete conspiracy. We sat crammed in the grilled rear of the blue and white until a convenient paddy wagon came along. An hour of cruising, copping knife-flicking drunks, before we hit the New Haven central tank. We arrived in time to share central holding with the star himself. We presented a motley spectrum for the night's catch, the three of us flying on the hastily swallowed evidence hoarded for post-concert turnpike descent back home. Only then did they want my cameras, shoelaces and all the other good stuff to prevent you from suiciding. I am still a wanted man in Connecticut having skipped the $350 bail *Life* deducted from my fees, being back in the Nam by the time the case actually came to court. The others got suspended sentences and $50 fines. The magazine ran the story with five pages of black and white photos, promptly losing the negatives.

LBJ's wife, Lady Bird, had a whole PR campaign going, 'See America first', 'Vacationland is homeland'. *Life* magazine was reflecting the trend, sending their top staffers to do down-on-the-farm stories. Wonderland USA ad nauseam. I conned them into

146

giving me a loose letter of accreditation and six bricks of film. My self-assigned angle was the US coast to coast in the winter in black and white, a homage to Robert Frank. The Volvo with its green and white, neutral Arizona plates was only 400 bucks, bought off a *Lifer* going out to man the Saigon bureau with whom I had covered the runaways. $128 in cash my total reserve, though the route would link the friends from those first days at the front. Steve Northup was working on the *Post* in DC. Fayetteville, Arkansas, was the unlikely locale for a Frankie's House temporary, Jim Tucker, back at law school in his late twenties, preparing for a political career. A year before, we had humped around Northern II Corps on a Special Forces patrol in the monsoon and leeches, he on an ABC radio gig and researching for a book on Arkansasians at war.

We went good-ol'-boying, moonshining, to the legislature and to my first horse race in the snow at Arkadelphia. My photo essay started to focus on cemeteries: the overgrown tombstones of Pea Ridge, the battle fought the farthest west in the Civil War; automobile graveyards in Tennessee; Nam headstones in Arlington. I finally sussed that 'Y'all come back' was not referring to the U-Haul Trailer rental firm. I was slowly absorbing the culture behind the names of the home towns of the GIs I had photographed for the wire services.

The last time I had seen Larry and Alice Travis was on their honeymoon in Saigon. He as a cameraman and bike nut, working for NBC. Larry had been trying to negotiate Jim Wilde's black-and-white-tiled floor, believing it to be vertical, using only every other black tile. Now they were living above the smog on Mulholland Drive. Belatedly I was accepting their invitation to some R & R. Los Angeles drew me like a moth to the perfidious bright lights, the endless concrete, the freeways. The speed of life was intoxicating, the celibacy of the road forgotten.

The Cronkite show on TV showed the new American embassy in Saigon under siege, a fire fight in the grounds; NBC carried the execution of the Viet Cong that won Eddie Adams his Pulitzer. The battles for Khe Sanh and Hue were digested daily on the breakfast show and I got a queasy feeling in my gut. Photography, Disneyland, surfing, Bobby Kennedy and Topanga Canyon happenings did not seem to fill the void that the news had created. I wanted to go back, but I could not make up my mind.

The reality warp that the entire planet went through in 1967–8 was the most exciting I ever walked. It was the Chinese Year of the Monkey, just as it had been when I was born. There was too much to do in too many places, there was a linking rock 'n' roll beat, the common language of youth on the move. I was fortunate in having Time-Life back my escapades. I had become their stoned fireman, on a civilian parole.

I spent Lunar New Year 1968 on acid at the Fillmore. The Jefferson Airplane played. The truce for the ushering in of the year of the Monkey had been punctured not by traditional fire-crackers but by the Viet Cong's largest ever offensive, the Tet Offensive. They occupied over fifty provincial and district capitals. There were thousands of casualties, the enemy losing dispro-portionately, the highest casualty figures since the Marines landed. The Viets' cause etched into the collateral of a newly emerging consciousness amongst America's young and enlightened. For the next week I went on a fast of fruit juice and marijuana. The decision gelled to take the flight back home to Saigon.

At the veterans' cemetery in Westwood, hard by the San Diego freeway, the serried ranks of graves grew at an appalling rate.

6

Dead on arrival

Returning to Vietnam in the late spring of 1968 was to instant
arrest at Ton San Nhut. Having no visa had become a crime since
the Tet Offensive, not – as once – easily adjusted with a $10 bill
tucked into one's passport. There were only fifty cents in my
pocket anyway. On hearing of my detention in the immigration
office Sean Flynn, Jack Lawrence of CBS, his brother Art and a
dozen other old mates stormed out to the airport. I had been
stuck there for nearly a day, strung out after flying out from the
West Coast (with a short visit to former Frankie's residents in
Tokyo, Minimus and Joe Galloway of UPI). Piastreless, buckless
and unwelcome, I had consumed nothing but some lukewarm tea
out of the communal immigration pot and a bowl of *pho*, the
traditional Vietnamese noodle soup.

The press rescue party blew officialdom away. They brought a
complete bar with sandwich counter. Soon we had something like
a hogmanay revel going on in the senior immigration officer's
spartan room. A cassette tape jived out the Stones and Hendrix,
the Doors screamed for the lighting of fire. Curious airport officials
clustered round, even the odd incoming passenger bypassed the
nearly empty check lines and dropped by for refreshment. All
this kind of won the hearts and minds of immigration, much loss
of face was in the making, and, on the promise that I would leave
the country within three months to get a proper visa, I was released
into the custody of the press corps.

Digs had been arranged by the old boys for me: Flynn and
I were crashing in Room C2, the CBS overflow room at the
Continental. On a camp bed under the window was the field gear
of Perry Deane Young, a camp, charming UPI reporter from

149

North Carolina. Other people's clutter spilled out of the wardrobe and draped over the three chairs in the bed-filled room. A ferocious, dirty white kitten lurked near a pile of fishheads and a bowl of rice inside the bathroom door. Jack had found Mao orphaned in a monsoon ditch during the battle for Hue at Tet. He had snuck the mewling beast out in his combat jacket, buttoned down in the top pocket. His brother Art, Garspon, was the designated kitty keeper. C11 were the chambers next door of CBS cameraman Keith Kay. Room service was a bureau affair; we took care of the room boy for services over and above the call of duty. He would make emergency dope runs to the corner for a carton of ready-rolled Marlboro, Salem or Park Lane packeted joints, box seals intact, at a buck a pack. The music and the dope identified our clique, our alternative outlook. We spoke in a lingo coined from obscurer album tracks and smatterings of foreign tongues, military jargon – Namspeak.

The music still echoes today, in a shot-up hallway at the back of my mind: 'I Had Too Much To Dream' by the Electric Prunes, 'Going Home' by the Stones, and the haunting cry of Morrison's 'Light My Fire'. 'The end, my only friend . . .' It could blow your head off just being in the sound cone in an armchair with tight friends and a head full of the finest weed, a cold beer to hand. It was the best time anyone could want to have. The density of camaraderie reflected the happening of the Haight. Outside was the greatest news story taking place daily on the planet. Up north the battle for Khe Sanh and the strategic routes it controlled was still waging, witnessed by a handful of hard-core press on day trips. We almost became invincible, and then it was the merry month of May.

Mini-Tet, as it grew to be, slammed into downtown. The VC kicked it off by exploding a 500-pound bomb packed into a little Renault 4 blue and cream taxi outside the AFVN TV-transmitting station and studio. They didn't get it quite right and collapsed the Viet-American Student Association building next door. The station went off the air temporarily. They were only just pulling the young bodies out when I rolled up. A lot of us did, you could jog it from the Place de l'Opéra and the Shelf in ten minutes. Most people drifted off, having missed the first ambulances. I knew there was going to be a picture. The frame was a circle of French-style firemen's helmets and the dead crooked, trapped, white-sleeved girl's arm, the fingers paled grey in pain on the brick.

For five days we all lived beyond the edge. A fully fledged, no-holds-barred, living-colour war raged no further than a 200-piastre ride away. We indulged in security, sortieing in fire teams after the first heavy rush of casualties in Phu Tho and then the old French cemetery out by the airbase. Five guys in a Mini-Moke took a wrong turn to be confronted by a VC fire team. They were riddled with AKs though one escaped unscathed to tell a shocked tale to a numbed press corps. It would get worse. The US Army 9th Division armour flattened three southern arrondissements with a Stalingrad effect. Photographically it was a turkey shoot. Refugees, civilian casualties of their and our fire, pandemonium. An abattoir heap of offal rotting, a thirteen-year-old worker's daughter accidentally gunned by a burst across the chest, her screaming brother. That day I cadged a ride with my *Life* mentor Larry Burrows and Philip Jones Griffiths shooting for the *Sunday Times*. For two hours we shadowed each other, terrified, with no safety net, just a brother *bao chi* to catch your fall. That was the week that the Paris peace talks commenced so *Life* ran the stuff over ten pages, five of them mine, against stark black-and-whites of Kissinger and Le Duc Tho.

Garspon was another victim of Mini-Tet. He collected the central steel core of an AK round. The copper jacket shed itself all over the inside of *Life* photographer Co Rentmeester's Nikon and 200-mm lens, then diagonally through his hand, exiting at his elbow. The NVA sniper in the battle for the old French graveyard next to Ton San Nhut had obviously beaded in on Co, who later would require fifteen major operations to be able to use his left arm for photography. Art got the hot metal slug square between the eyes, and it dropped into the area just above the roof of his mouth. A nasty piece of dental work was necessary to dig it out complete; it also gave him a couple of super shiners, shocked black eyes. Getting zapped between the eyes by an AK-47 must seem like a very direct message, and Garspon left Southeast Asia shortly afterwards.

I was offered a room at the *Life* villa, a beautiful colonial building three blocks behind the US embassy. After six weeks I was evicted because the English staff reporter had been indiscreet in his telexes. I did not mention the antics of cub reporter Colin taking to the roof to discharge his .38 at whim.

I automatically drifted down to the Tu Do crib where Flynn was now installed. It was reputedly the apartment where Graham

Greene had written *The Quiet American* and the film of the same title had been shot years ago. I took over the southern front quarter of the two giant rooms with en suite baths plus kitchen and two toilets, the latter isolated at the ends of long corridors at the back, overlooking a square mouldering stucco yard. The other half of the room, partitioned with a giant mahogany wardrobe, bookcase and unopenable 1920s vault safe, was occupied by Perry Deane. To get next door to the other residents you had to go through the tiled kitchen and hallway, past the bowling-alley toilets, first into Flynn's quarters, entirely surrounded by tall bookcases, then into Nik Wheeler's almost palatial bedroom where the phone was kept. Nik, a suave, francophilian Brit and UPI staff photographer, ex-overlander and Bangkok graduate, had originally rented the flat with another expat, Derek Maitland, who had had enough of Vietnam. The two adjoining bathrooms usually had hot and cold running, rusty and unpotable water; the kitchen was home to a sect of cockroaches that we occasionally ignited with a squirt from a Zippo fuel tin, laying long trails towards the *cafard*. A devout Buddhist lady did for us, often bringing her two svelte teenage daughters to help, keeping them off the street. Below us, a newly opened bar, the Blue Bird, was staffed by second-rate girls, half a dozen of whom shared cribs on the floor above us, accessed from a scuzzy passage where touts proffered dirty pictures and did black-market money deals. At night the passage was barred by an iron grille guarded by our concierge, a bloated Chinese Viet we christened Toad. On a slow night the Blue Bird staffers could be induced upstairs at a below-par rate, sometimes even a free ride.

On Tu Do there was no Frankie to procure for us, but our opium man could be summoned on his moped by phone, one of Saigon's few working numbers. Nik had found him. Monsieur Long had been a blender for the Société Anonyme d'Opium d'Indochine, the French government concession in the days when the yearly stipend guaranteeing their loyalty had been paid to the princes of Tonkin, Annam and Cochin: 500 kilo blocks of opium each. Long had been the man responsible for determining the melange of raw stuffs that was the Annamese bankroll. Our sources became renowned in hip Saigon. A thousand piastres could secure the best night out off in town. Long introduced us to an antiques dealer who sold us classical pipes: a slim bamboo-lined silver one with an ivory mouthpiece and bowl for the ladies, a solid amber one which purportedly had belonged to a Tonkinese prince for the men. I was back on my standard sixteen pipes a day, and getting out into the field the day after was getting more difficult, the thought of combat harder to handle. The opium made me more conscious of the madness, but helped the hard sleep.

John Steinbeck IV – the writer's son – was to say of the Dao Island, 'If all religions were rivers, this is the lake into which they would flow.' John had got out of the army after he was busted, and wrote a book about it called *Out of Touch*, a condemnation of the military, its role and drug abuse. He was back in Vietnam loosely working for a new, hip agency, Dispatches, which later went on to break the My Lai massacre story. He had stumbled on the island while investigating Buddhism and peace movements in the country. He and Flynn were tight buddies, sharing the burden of being sons of famous fathers. The Tu Do apartment gravitated down to the Delta for peaceful, macrobiotic periods.

The Neo-Catholic-Buddhist Church of Dao – Dao being the Vietnamese for the Tao – were a sect led by a French-trained former chemical engineer, the Dao Dua, who had dropped out to start his own cult some twenty years before. When he had taken his vow of celibacy, he had retreated to live without lying down, in a coconut tree on the southern Mekong banks, north of the town of Ben Tre. He had become known as the coconut monk and consumed nothing but the flesh and milk of the fruit, the only one that provides everything essential for survival.

As the strange cult had gathered a following of disenchanted, war-torn folk, including many wealthy Saigon businessmen, the temple had moved offshore to the Isle of Phoung in the mile-wide Mekong stream between My Tho and Ben Tre. A sand bar covered in coconuts and mangroves. The faithful had set about constructing an oriental Disneyland with overtones of the garish Tiger Balm gardens in Singapore. The end of the island was completely covered in a circular concrete prayer platform surrounded by walkways on piles driven into the viscous mud. Beyond the prayer dais was a cement mountain representing the holy range of Cochin. In the base was a meditation chamber, on the first floor, facing downstream, the Dao Dua's open receiving room from where he could gaze at a 50-foot relief map of the country on which had been built model houses, bridges and tanks. He retired to one of the two 70-foot towers, linked by a spindly catwalk, where he squatted the night away. The towers were linked by a mind-boggling spider-work rainbow welded out of rods and old pipes.

The whole place had been gaudily painted in primary colours, reds, yellows and blues, the colours of the Buddhist standard, predominant; garish dragons – the *phoungs* or phoenixes – writhed up the columns supporting the covered walkways, on which yellow barrels were tied down to enable the whole island to float away, ark-like, when the next cataclysmic flood arrived as predicted by the guru. After the Tet Offensive of 1968, the population of Phoung had swollen to over 5000 from all sides of the conflict, though many still commuted to their jobs on the mainland on one of the Dao-owned watercraft. Their families were secure on the island, where no weapons were permitted, where there was no curfew, where choppers flew around rather than over, and napalm strikes regularly splashed 300 metres away on the Ben Tre shore. Nothing that grew on the ground or in the water was consumed; they all lived on fruit and nuts. Everyone prayed for peace round the clock, accompanied by the chimes of bells and gongs fashioned out of shell casings from the various Indochinese wars. They prayed in silence, reading from treatises prepared from the Dao Dua's writings and thoughts, in turn lifted from the learned works of Asian and occidental philosophies.

We were accepted as apostles to be turned around to spread the light to the west. Working for the media made us important in their eyes, and they were only too pleased to have us stay as long as we wanted. They accepted our dope smoking as being part of our philosophy; after all, it had been part of the lore of their ancients. They even built a press room and dormitory for us, next to the conference room overlooking the prayer platform. Johnny and his girl, Crystal, were installed on a moored yellow rice barge. We were required to go barefoot and to eat their diet. It was like being in a retreat, the pure food and healthy vibes spacing you out after a couple of days. After a military operation, coming here was taking the brain for a bath. All of us regulars – the Tu Do flat plus Carl Robinson from the AP – were absorbed into the sect and presented with robes made of four pieces of brown material symbolizing the paddy and given ceremonial begging bowls in accordance with Buddhist principles. In return we started to bring down other foreigners to spread the word.

The Dao Dua had a bold plan for peace. He was going to invite the superpower leaders, the NLF, Ho Chi Minh, Sihanouk and the Saigon government to a conference at his purpose-built hall with his custom-built peace table with eight sides. The centre of the table had a pacifying yin and yang in black and white marble. The invitations stipulated that the leaders should arrive a week in advance of the conference date to live on a macrobiotic diet on ships moored off the island, to clear their minds out before getting down to the talks. Not a single head of state had the courtesy to send a reply.

This was at the time when the various factions were squabbling in Paris over what shape table they should sit around, and the war in Vietnam had drifted to an accommodating lull after the May VC offensive. They were licking their wounds, regrouping, and we were taking a breather. To prove that all creatures could live in harmony the Dao Dua had Johnny Steinbeck release a cat and mouse from the same basket in the foyer of the American embassy. It made a few inches of column locally and on the wire. Selling tranquillity in Vietnam was exasperating work, though John Sheppard's *World In Action* TV documentary broke the mould, focusing on the Dao Island in 'An Outbreak of Peace'. We all had unpaid starring roles.

Weeks later an incoming British ITN crew brought out an enormous Fortnum's hamper and a stack of the latest sounds for our renowned, hip collection, which could usually be heard wafting out of the windows onto Tu Do. At night strobes blinked through the shutters, for we were the cutting edge of the media psychedelia, our lifestyle provoking the envy and anger of the straighter, older hacks and TV personalities with their trailing crews. By mid 1968 there were over 600 foreign press folks, of every race and creed, officially accredited to the war. Only a small minority, a hard core as we liked to think of ourselves, actually went out into the field to see and report what was happening. The others spent most of their time mooching around Saigon or Da Nang, or hanging around corps headquarters echoing the computerized pabulum officialdom churned out to convince the public back home that the war was being won. More and more journalists were dropping in for short visits, including a sponsored whisk around the country, a packaged interview and a whiff of danger. The war was becoming a hip event to be seen at. Even Walter Cronkite, the veteran US newsreader, had turned up to report live from the Battle of Hue, emblazoned with the honorary rank of brigadier general. We lowly freelancers were lucky to be majors, our bureau chiefs ranking privilege at full colonel.

I had my old slot back with Time/Life, inducting new correspondents to the field, teaching them the difference between an AK and an M16 and an RPG and a LAW, what C rats tasted like, how to colour their middle-of-the-road *Time* speak. I was getting enough work to be able to laugh when four more bikes were stolen in quick succession. All were locked in the steering and chained through the wheel. The last went from the front steps inside the compound walls of the *Time* villa near the palace, the engine still cooling. Finally we had our revenge, Steinbeck and Carl, coming round after dark, found a Viet naval petty officer bending over one of my machines, dripping acid carefully onto the chain around the back wheel. Each day they would return, drip another drip, and pull the protective plastic back over the eroded metal. After four days the bike was theirs to be smuggled out of the adjacent naval yards up and down country on a landing craft. A flourishing quasi-government-sponsored business. During my first tour three machines had gone M.I.A, this time so far it was four.

When they dragged the naval officer upstairs I was ensconced on the mat with Long, head on a porcelain headrest, amber pipe to lips, a million miles away. Flynn was on the other side of the lamp. They burst in with the terrified prisoner and we all adjourned to the kitchen to examine the catch. We emptied his pockets; a plastic-wrapped slab of opium, a megawad of piastres – twenty years' salary – and a military ID card. I gave the opium to Long for examination; he rated it as dross for GIs. Johnny was cajoling the thief to reveal his fence in a street-fluent, menacing Vietnamese. Mad at being disturbed, and finally confronted with a genuine baddy the week after the last theft, I slapped the poor guy around the side of his head. We stood him against the white tiles and stuffed the matchbox-size chunk of opium in his mouth, had him hold his ID card next to his chest and popped off a set of black-and-white Polaroids. He still would not talk. Flynn went to his room, returning with his 9-mm Browning, into which he jacked a magazine and let it snick off safety. No reaction, no fence's name. Flynn brought out his LURP-awarded CAR-15 assault rifle, a souvenir of three weeks' goofing, playing recon with the 4th Division in the Central Highlands. He locked and loaded. Steinbeck played the soft inquisitor. I hovered. He spoke; Gia Dinh, the name of a suburb. He clammed up again. This time Flynn came back with a grenade, the pin removed, the spoon secured with rubber bands, a Special Forces-learned quick-release trick. The guy's eyes lit up with heightened tension. Flynn, speak-

156

ing monosyllabically with slow motion gestures, said that 'no info the guy might get home to find no home, no wife, no kids'. Sinister Steinbeck inked the details. He blubbered the whole story. The whole scam, his drop, the works.

We let him go without the ID card, not good for him in days when ruthless ARVN MPs were pressganging the streets for Vietnamization. The others aborted their plan to raid, in tiger suits, the fence's warehouse to reclaim our bikes. We divvied up the money. I got fifteen grand and we smoked the opium, to Long's chagrin, feeling shitty about the way we had behaved, though solaced by the inferior black. Some sort of justice had been done. The next one from the *Time* compound was to be the last. Switched to one of their vehicles, usually getting the fateful Mini-Moke.

The vehicle should not have been alive, for twice it had been patched up after serving as a death trap to successive journalist owners. During the Tet Offensive the previous year, a despondent freelancer, Bill Hall, had taken the then UPI-owned Moke and driven it straight into an ARVN guard post, committing hara-kiri on the hail of 30-cal machine-gun rounds. UPI had sold it on to *Time*, the holes camouflaged in a new red paint job. Mini-Tet had washed over Saigon with somewhat less violence though this time more *bao chi* were caught in the crossfire. The Moke had ended up in a blind alley near the Phu Tho racetrack with five guys aboard who were not aware of the enemy's proximity. Four of the five were gunned down trying to escape the vehicle, the fifth survived to tell a tale which had us all freaked for weeks. We took a dozen casualties that week, my first back in-country. Time-Life had the luckless vehicle replugged and on the road again, and I had the free use of the blood rust coloured truggy.

I still got the work that nobody else wanted and covered whenever no staffer was in town. I got accredited. I went look-see, got shelled, pissed myself and got out of Khe Sanh in six hours too long. I remember standing in the sandbagged door of the C-med aid bunker at the edge of the chopper pad with a grunt screaming at me over the roar of incoming shells and birds to run when he hit my helmet, which I'd borrowed from a dead man in Dong Ha. He would time the shells' arrival, listening to them leaving the tubes, and the lowered tailgate of the twin-rotored Sea Knight would serve as my green light. I was too old for this; only terror, fear and adrenalin got me across those 50 metres and I slumped, drained, on the aluminium-plated floor of the chopper.

We took off as more shells landed – big stuff, 130-mm, fired from the security of caves over the Lao border – then landed again to pick up more grunts. I urged us away from there, screaming at the wind, the pilot, my own frustration. We took off, circled and spiralled in again for three more outgoing Marines. Bleak Dong Ha, the Marines' forward base, felt like heaven.

I thought of quitting late that summer and said so, toying with the idea of a posting to Africa with its turmoil in Biafra – small peanuts, I thought, after here. I considered putting in a formal request until Priya Rimraka, an Indian freelance working for Time-Life, was killed in an ambush, and I did not want to appear to be trespassing on his grave.

Going out took more ergs, danger seemed more apparent, odds shorter. I did fat long shoots of visiting Australian prime ministers, Westmoreland going-away parties, GIs rotating in the field, the first election ballot taken. I got myself a new visa on a Hong Kong shopping trip. I went to Cambodia, having defaced my passport, changing 'occupation: photographer' to 'agronomy student' for their benefit. Missed the plane to Singapore with Flynn, so caught independence day in Phnom Penh's Asian Games stadium, Prince Sihanouk presiding. Paid for the R & R with a job photographing the International Control Commission, the ICC, investigating an alleged US gunship attack on a Cambodian border village. A delicious affair with the French military mission commander's daughter, Armelle, ended when she gave me a lift out to Pechtong to catch the Singapore flight a week later, and she passed straight into Flynn's incoming arms.

The Time Inc businessmen's tour required almost as many security measures as a presidential visit; these were the lads who owned America, owned the war. Once a year *Time* magazine leases a reconfigured jet and invites aboard the chairmen of the megacorporations that rate consistently in *Fortune*'s top hundred. They are whisked somewhere on the planet in the company of the chief Time Incers and fashionable editors to see their products ticking. In 1968 they chose to whirl them around Southeast Asia; Vietnam for five days was the highlight of the expedition. The richest men in the world would visit the sandbox that the politicians they had bought and installed were playing mayhem in.

John Wilhelm, a new *Time* correspondent, and I had been working a week on a dangerous essay on the Muddy Water Navy, the in-country naval forces operating on the Delta waterways. We had been riding the little waterjet-powered PBRs, the fibreglass boating equivalent of a superfortress later featured in *Apocalypse Now*. The units riding them on the narrow canals and meandering rivers were taking as many casualties as platoon lieutenants in the First World War trenches. We had lived top drawer as guests of the force commanded by Elmo Zumwalt; we had been choppered, planed and shipped from one end of IV Corps to the other, getting to spend three nights on forbidden Phu Quoc island right in the far southwest on the Cambodian border. Half the island was VC-owned and the other half contained an enormous POW camp. At the naval airstrip a lot of unmarked craft came and went. Going into the Ca Mau peninsula, John and I had worn armoured vests and miniskirts, pumping out repressive M-16 fire into the hostile mangrove-lined banks.

After a week of adrenalin, landing on mini-helipads on landing craft, riding through ambushes, we had been deposited at a small Delta strip outside Kien Giang to catch a Saigon-bound shuttle. It was deserted save for one worried crew chief guarding a broken-down navy Seawolf Huey B-model gunship. The machine guns had been taken off and he was left with his personnel weapon and boxes of smoke grenades, alone; even the Vietnamese at the tower had gone downtown after the morning's departed flight. We helped ourselves to a selection of different-coloured smokes – purple, green, white, red – and popped them into our rucksacks, which were already bulging with bartered gear and bottles of Phu Quoc's one-off *nuoc mam* (prawn-based fish sauce). The forced delay had us feeling even raunchier that we had been, champing to get back at the office wallahs on their fats at 7 Han Thuyen, the *Time* villa/bureau, 100 metres from the presidential palace and the cathedral. We would stage a mock assault on its portals using up part of the smoke stash, a purple attack.

Nobody paid us any attention as we slipped off our rucksacks. I got out two smokes, pulled the pins and popped them over the spike-topped wall surrounding the French villa. The contained concussion of the bursting purples was horrific, and the massive air-conditioning unit greedily sucked the eddying screen inside. As the staff and Americans poured out, we stepped into view, making ta-a-tat-tat sounds and grinning like demented fools. The last out were the advance team from New York planning the security for the Time Incers' swing. It was with trepidation that they approved my inclusion in the Vietnam segment of the official scrapbook to be given to each participant. My gig to make compromising *verité* shots of the few that owned the lot for their visitors' albums.

On the first day out to Ton San Nhut for a C-130 flight up to Cam Ranh and the Highlands, only one of the two army schoolbuses with grenade-proof window screens turned up at the Caravelle Hotel, where the VIPs occupied an entire floor with replaced security room boys. This bus broke down near the bridge where the Viet Cong had almost blown Defence Secretary MacNamara away. The caught saboteur had featured in the first public execution in the market place in 1965. The military security police closed the highway, isolating the sixty strap-hanging billionaires while transport could be found. I was filming a farce. All these out-of-shape corporate executives in brand-new name-tagged GI jungle fatigues, peaked army baseball hats and pistol belts complete with canteens, were clambering in and out of fighter bombers, transports and choppers asking inane questions of the crack crew drawn up for inspections. We all went for boy-scout rides and I made pretty souvenir snaps.

We had four days of gallivanting and official din-dins in combat tuxedoes. It was a gas to infiltrate the ranks of power to shoot the privileged, but I never kept the film or the contacts. I was paid cash and given a chrome-plated 105-mm Howitzer shell turned into an ashtray, engraved commemoratively for the tour with my name. Everyone got one, the bureau gofer had had sixty-five made up. The fatigues, jungle boots, helmet and kit were packed up with the ashtrays and shipped back to their offices courtesy of the US Air Force.

At Christmas 1968, stumped for a gift idea for the bureau chief and foreign staff, I took a grenade container, filled it with corner-bought spliffs and decorated it with O.D. gaffer tape. The whole bureau was stoned for a day. The truce outside held for most folks and Bob Hope came and went one more time with the same cornball jokes and a bevy of busty blondes pussy-pushing the heated crowd.

A large group of us had assembled on a hot sultry afternoon, just after Christmas 1968, for drinks on the Continental Shelf, the terrace bar of the Continental Hotel overlooking the square in front of the old French opera house, now the Senate building.

Apart from transvestite hookers cruising for traffic, the Shelf was a respectable though somewhat seedy watering hole famed among travellers. The place in Saigon to watch and be seen, immune since French times from terrorist attack, thanks to the devious machinations of its métis Corsican mafia owner, though the VC had blown up the Brinks bachelor officers' quarters next door before Christmas 1964. The only protection the terrace offered was the butt-strewn, flowering windowboxes, and any of the phalanx of bicycles and mopeds parked on the sidewalk below could have contained an explosive device. Upstairs there were three floors of colonial-style hotel rooms. Many correspondents maintained quarters here and *Life* magazine had moved its bureau to the end of one wing. It was a preferable accommodation to the ferro-concrete, prudish, Catholic-owned Caravelle towering across the square. At the Continental room service would deliver anything and turned a blind eye to its occupants' activities.

The number swelled as friendly passers-by noticed the attractive young round-eye females. We were a macho society; the married ones were lucky to see their wives every couple of months in Singapore or Hong Kong, the rest of us were thrown upon the extensive bar-girl network of the city. To be seen accompanied by a white woman was a status trip. There were not a few sleazes capitalizing on this: it was a known fact that some of the USO artistes, Red Cross, Donut Dollies and the base-camp nurses were putting out for a profit. Some smart call girl would have cleaned up and probably did.

It was even rarer to meet an intelligent, good-looking blond traveller who turned on. Linda and I hit it off from the first round of drinks. Linda was staying with Robin, a hip Kiwi lass, and her brother, who had a fibreglass-boat repair yard, fixing the shot-up PBRs for the navy and servicing the few remaining ski-boats belonging to the Club Nautique on the city's outskirts at Than Da. She accepted the invitation to retreat down the street to our flat above the Blue Bird on Tu Do for a quiet smoke. She moved into my side of the double apartment two days later.

Linda slipped right in that first evening. Both Nik, who could pull any passing round-eye with his cherubic good looks and English manner, and Flynn presumed she was my girl, and left us alone. Zonked on the music from the speakers, which had survived from Frankie's, we collapsed on my bed and curled up, but there was no sex. It was a strange vibration which was to be respected for nearly three weeks. Our unspoken love was distilled further by weekend visits down to the Dao Island.

Early in 1969 *Life* made me bureau chief for a week, with the same trepidation they had had about dispatching me, unaccompanied, to New York with the Adenauer take. There was simply no one else around who knew the scene, the *Time* folk were up to their ears in memos. All staff reporters were on their R & R break (they got one every six weeks) and none of the heavies from the photo brigade wanted to sit and hold the fort in Room 12 at the Continental. I was able to hire Linda for $100 as my secretary and telephonist. For six days I drew a day rate and enjoyed the facilities and prestige of a resident head of station. Nothing happened, though we entertained regally with room service. Then an Englishman, John Saar, took over to run the shop, hot from crime reporting in New Orleans.

The North Vietnamese sent a crack battalion to try to bust open a heavy POW compound which lay right under the flight path of the sprawling air base at Bien Hoa. They were unsuccessful and were caught in the open by the bare wire in flare-light. They took heavy casualties before the survivors retreated to make a last stand in an adjacent built-up village. A company had centred their defence on the white stuccoed church that catered for the community of Catholics, most of whom had come south as part of the resettlement promises made during partition in 1954. Their refuge, a well-tended brick-and-mortar hamlet, was erased from the map. First light enabled the helicopter gunships from the five surrounding bases to minigun, rocket and automatic-grenade fire the entrenched NVA into a final circle in the chancel of St Waswhere. The first rushed reaction force comprised a can-do collection of gung-ho colonels, cooks, civilians, and a sprinkling of serious Special Forces types. The ramshackle force ran head on into the desperate NVA. In the ensuing slaughter, two army photogs got wiped and two more wounded.

Spooked awake with the dawn I had gone across the street to Bo Da, the Franco-Viet coffee shop, for an early breakfast. The rumour mill of civilian construction workers and military going on/off duty buzzed Bien Hoa. By late morning I had half a dozen rolls in the can. Theirs had been a surreal death with a macabre white mask dusted on after rigor mortis, quicklime against putrefaction, which attracted huge bluebottle flies. After three or four hours the smell was already gagging. The bodies were stretched out in a crescent of frozen upside-down insect forms at the base of the church steps. Nuns retched prayers discreetly into their hankies. I floored it back to Saigon to drag Saar out for a quick look-see. His first glowing piece of coverage accompanied my two-page spread, an auspicious beginning to a new year and bureau chief. It was his baptism job in-country although he had hard core qualifications from editing *Soldier*, the British army mag, and a couple of hundred parachute jumps, half free fall.

I managed to sell John on an operation about to kick off, the first ever sweep through the French-owned Michelin rubber plantation, north of Dau Tieng. The newsworthy angle was linked to the payment of $200 the military had agreed to make to Michelin for every tree damaged or destroyed. The plantation had long been a haven for NVA forces in transit. Now the US 1st and 25th Divisions plus the eleventh armoured cavalry regiment were to put 200 armoured vehicles in a line while forces from the air cavalry and ARVN blocked from the other quadrants.

I spent a day alone with a bridging unit playing Tonka toys over a creek once spanned by a concrete French job, and then cruising around with George Patton Jr, son of the general complete with his daddy's pearlhandled .38s. Obviously, with so much warning, Mr Charles had gone, leaving only a few diehard rear guards to cause some ugly moments. The principal casualties were the two-bill trees. I decided to take Linda out in the field the next day. Saar provided a covering note, and the PIOs were blown away by the sight of a lithe, blonde-haired female. They cranked up a chopper to take us to the action with a second lieutenant, a real dufus, as our chaperon.

Either they forgot to brief the bird's crew or the second looey was too chicken to tell them where to go, or maybe they were new in-country or totally stoned; we will never know. The rig was short of a door gunner though the pig was on its mount with a can of links ready to load. We plopped off northwest over some spectacular pieces of destroyed and burning plantation; we went right on by the action, the advancing line of tracks and tanks. We flew on at an alarmingly low height, no more than 1000 feet up. Suddenly there were large whip cracks as heavy machine-gun fire zipped past. I peered out of the open doors to watch several streams of fluorescent blue-green tracer coming our way. Blue-green is their colour, we use orange-red. By the amount of incoming we were over a major base camp, over Cambodia, over the Fishhook, the promontory of land jutting into Vietnam north of Loc Ninh near the Special Forces Camp where I had been almost overrun. We were basically over COSVN headquarters. We were lost and in danger of getting shot down. In '65 I had had to kill to survive a few km south of this same spot. Bo Dup was below us.

As the surprised pilot pulled for height I clambered over into the empty door gunner's seat, belted in and locked and loaded up the M-60, the slipstream billowing my jungle jacket like a balloon and forcing my mouth open. I cranked off a belt at the jungle-carpeted hostile turf, aiming for the flash marks in the canopy. It felt better than sitting idly by as a practice target. Our chaperon became quite flustered and tried to communicate with the crew chief or the other gun, only to lose his bush hat to the void almost following it. We made a U-turn at a safe altitude, up around 3000 feet where the tracers no longer scratched their message, and flew back towards the action.

We were dumped in a clearing where a mixed bunch of grunts were busily tearing up a cache of rice stored in sandbags. Reputedly a couple of sacks full of primo grass had disappeared into an APC which had a peace sign and MR CLEAN painted in white on the side armour. The platoon sergeant said they had 'stumbled on all this tea, ya know, not the kind ya drink, Lars saw it in that a vehicle'. We sauntered over, the cameras doing the introduction. Linda got to pick her favourite ration out of a new case of Cs. When we got back on line, advancing under a continual outpour of automatic weapons fire, she mounted up and loosed off the pig and the fifty. The crew of Mr Clean were enchanted. The PIO relaxed and lent her his .45 automatic, someone else volunteered his .16. The US Army at its zaniest best was eager to please by letting off a few rounds without too much competition from the enemy. Delighted to crush $200 Froggie trees for the camera with their spanking new experimental Sheridan light tanks.

The corpulent PIO, anxious to expose other units in his charge, and in need of lunch, radioed a passing helicopter to get us back to a mess hall. We diverted, as usually happened with a free bird, landing on a criss-crossed tangle of downed rubber in a clearing only twice the size of the Huey, where two APCs guarded a disabled tank, its cannon still hand-transversable. Another tank, blackened and detracked, slumped 100 yards down a line of trees. Livid scorch marks showed where the RPGs had torched through. A gaggle of contorted NVA dead lay strewn towards the depressed tank gun. Just as we had said hi to the bewildered survivors, the NVA opened up with a machine gun from a couple of hundred metres down in the trees. Rubber trees are not good cover, they are soft and heavy rounds go through – a lesson learned with the 1st RAR, the Aussie regiment. The platoon sergeant passed our 16s and told us to get on line. We propped the rifles against the less exposed side of the command truck and huddled behind them.

There was a din of American fire from another outfit on the other side of the hostile gunner, then calm. An eerie calm with the sounds of war now far away. The dry leaves ticked, flies buzzed over a man with the top of his head sliced off like a soggy boiled egg. We wandered over, careful of an unexploded 500-pound bomb.

In full perspective here was the conflict: two teenage peasants wasted and one half-million-dollar vehicle plus crew also wasted. A hundred-yard ideological dash between them. A dusty green lane linked their fate, all of them had come farther than they had ever gone in their short lives. We had too. We went home a little later to downtown Saigon and got very drunk.

Linda and I left for My Tho in the Moke early the next morning and blissed out for four long peaceful days with the Daoists. We got back to Saigon and called Long. We must have smoked twenty pipes apiece when climbing into my narrow double bed. We did not emerge for forty-eight hours. We consummated a magic. I touched another part in myself and knew that I was getting short to the war. We planned a trip to Indonesia after three more cash-winning assignments. Flynn had established a house on the beach in Bali, at Denpasar. There were bikes and a good sound system and it was still way off the regular track, barely surfed. We hoped to spend six months there.

For the first time I was living with a woman who meant some-thing more than casual affair. In Linda there was the magic that the bandied love words of rock 'n' roll had not erased.

The Parrot's Beak is a large neck of Cambodian territory jutting out towards Saigon's jugular barely 25 miles away. The Tropic Lightning lads had been set down on its northern fringes to interdict the routes back to neutral Cambodia, operating out of fire bases and small company-sized forts. A pattern of helicopter flights kept a regular flow of material and men resupplied to these forward posts, the VC and NVA effectively controlling the surrounding lands and roads. For as long as there had been a maquis, a liberation or resistance movement, this had been bandit country. Government flags hung in the villages in the daytime, at nights its presence locked itself up behind rolls of concertina studded with Claymore mines. The US forces tried every which way to neutralize the enemy base area. It was bombed by B-52s, burned with napalm, the tunnels flooded, gassed and blasted, it was defoliated with dioxin and finally 'Rome' ploughed, whereby the topsoil and vegetation were turned deeply over and the populace turned into refugees. The 25th Division base camp at Cu Chi sat atop a labyrinth of a 200 km underground network, all hand-dug. The VC moved right back in after the 50,000 allied troops finished their massive operation code-named Junction City. The war never went very well out there, almost within sight of the bright capital lights. It was a commute to combat, within bike or Moke range, though a little on the hairy side.

On the northern flank lay Tay Ninh, home of the mysterious Cao Dai sect which had featured as the third force in Graham Greene's *The Quiet American*. They were a virtually autonomous group with a communal pope whose garish Vatican housed their most sacred icon, a globe of the world surmounted by the all-seeing magic eye. They took their beliefs from the sayings of the famous they canonized: Buddha, Jesus, Jeanne d'Arc, Victor Hugo and Churchill among them. They ran a lucrative cross-border operation, courting respect from all sides, in no-man's land, along a border badly demarcated. By April 1969, the free-trade zone they ran at Go Da Ha had bloomed into a regular market with stalls, coffee stands and semipermanent shops, fabricated out of palm thatch and war detritus. The Cambodians and Vietnamese of all persuasions could indulge in a bowl of *pho* and *café au lait* while poring over the latest in military hardware and consumer items. It was a horizontal department store in the dry paddies, the war raging on in a 360-degree perimeter, peace at the cash register. The area was not secure for round-eyed foreigners, though it warranted a column in that week's *Time* magazine, also requiring an illustration of the place. I was assigned to photograph it from the air, the 25th Division only too happy to lay on a Huey for the possible resulting PR. The army habitually bent to our whims, courting a favourable press. It was not often they looked good.

The bird would leave from Cu Chi at 0700. I would have to make my own way the 30 klicks out there, along metalled route 1 and then north along the dodgy laterite road to the Tropic Lightning's camp. The road-clearing teams probably would not have finished their sweeps for mines, having started at daybreak. I relied on speed and a cautious enquiry at the bus terminal on the edge of town. It was a heart-in-mouth bouncing Moke ride, the spectre of being blown sky high was sitting right behind the front seats waiting to tear my back off or maybe punch me straight through the canvas capote. With every pothole a crater, every patch of fresh dirt a possible explosive implant, I drove like an insane amateur downhill skier. It was an anticlimax to see the suprised guards as I pulled the filthy vehicle up to the main gate of the base.

The 25th was not known as a good outfit to go out with, big on PR and big on body count – the computer game to prove that our side was winning – but short of spirit, loaded with disgruntled GIs always drawing a bad neck of the woods for their TAOR (Tactical Area of Operations). They were not a popular unit with the press although they courted even the lowliest freelancer to come see them operate. I had spent effectively three years in the war zone and they still insisted on my having an accompanying escort officer, supposedly to smooth the ride, in reality an encumbrance likely to wander into frame. The D-model Huey was down at the pad awaiting our command, my taxi to the front, a cab to the shops.

We flapped north and west for fifteen minutes and the pilot put us into a nice low photo orbit over the surprised marketeers. I am sure they were expecting a stream of 7.62 rounds any second. Mission accomplished, film in the can, all I had to do was to get back to the bureau as soon as possible, to ship in time for the mid-week deadline.

Over the spare headphones I could hear interunit chatter requesting a bird to pick up documents and intelligence from a fire base that had been hit hard the same night: we were to divert. We circled low, around the perimeter, waiting for a marking smoke, getting in a couple of rolls of the failed attack. VC dead were strewn right round the base's coiled razor-wire defences, already bloating in the 100-degree late-morning heat. At the pad a sack was heaved aboard and we thumped off back towards Cu Chi, an apology for the delay crackled over the intercom. I had an extra shot or two for *Time*. Almost carefree, we rode within ground-fire range, a couple of hundred feet up, the itchy crew lobbing out smoke grenades and letting loose the odd burst from their door guns. Home for lunch. For no apparent reason, two black-pyjama-clad farmers bicycling in the direction of Cu Chi caught the co-pilot's eye and we went in to look-see. A door gunner put a few rounds across their bows, causing them to topple into the dry paddies, terrified. We flared in beside the wreckage and menaced them to come aboard; we flapped off again, two petrified suspects without documents adding to my photo list.

We diverted once more to drop off the poor civilians at an ARVN police post where they might be released when their relatives came up with a bribe should they survive questioning. Off again and another divert to a FOB, a forward operating base, where our intelligence documents were to be used to mount a counterattack. By now I was feeling more and more like an unwanted passenger, not the paying fare, but it was the only ride I had, and eventually it had to go back to base.

This time, we landed in the small compound of an old French fort where two companies were patrolling the border north of the Parrot's Beak. We shut down and everyone climbed out and headed for the corrugated shed optimistically labelled the mess for a coffee. It was a bleak post surrounded by a head-high berm of white sand, no trees for shade, only a few scraggy, furze-like bushes for decor around the dusty tents and three decaying buildings. Two disconsolate men of military age squatted, blindfolded, their wrists bound behind their backs, in a circle of hot sand, surrounded by a concertina of wire, just outside the radio shack. I got another couple of file snaps. A worthwhile stopover.

The crew reappeared with a gritty top sergeant and a radio man. We were going back up to act as a command and control ship (C & C) for an eagle flight that was about to launch. An eagle operation was the American vernacular for a quick-reaction strike force that was used to insert a unit of platoon size or smaller when required. This one was reacting to the intelligence we had brought in, hoping to catch the surviving, retreating VC, and, though I was not told at the time, there was a possibility that we might liberate two American POWs. I had to stay with the ride or sit, possibly for days, at this godforsaken post in the middle of nowhere, the film staling.

We lifted out and spiralled up while the three slicks went in to pick up the platoon. While we were on the ground the crew chief had strapped a large cylinder inside one side of our bird – a new weapon. Another one to be framed. We were to swoop over an offending area saturated with bunkers and drop this canister which, at a predesignated height, would split and shed thousands of tiny bomblets filled with tear gas. Theoretically this would infuse itself into whatever funnels and bunkers were there and force anybody who was there out of hiding, to be picked off by the low circulating brace of gunships. The top kicked out the canister, a small wire uncoiling to explode it; a curl of choking gas seeped across the target as the slicks hove in to put down the grunts. We circled lazily, coordinating the scenario.

It was only minutes later that the ominous call for a dust-off echoed through the command-net radio channel. Some hapless soldier had tripped a booby trap, a bouncing Betty, the sort that pop up from the ground before exploding between groin and head height, the max killing zone. At least two of the guys downed needed immediate evacuation but there were no choppers flying the Red Cross in the area, a larger operation to the north claiming their priority. Against operating policy the C & C ship, my cab, was to divert once more in another role, as dust-off bird.

We began that sickening combat landing spiral which drops mouth, heart and arse into one bottom line, the wind rushing in through the open doors, the gunners coiled tight behind their M-60s. The last words I heard before we touched down were: 'Should there be too many wounded, kid, you stay on the ground.' I jumped out to help, to shoot the evacuation, and ran towards the knots of GIs gathered round the fallen, ever mindful to step where the sergeant was stepping because the area was probably seeded with more mines. The chopper had set down 50 metres from the wounded and was still kicking up squalls of dust and debris. We ran bent double to avoid the rotor tips.

The next thing I remember is sitting stunned on my backside, feeling very wet around the midriff and top of my head. I was changing lenses from a 24-mm to a 105-mm on the Nikon round my neck. The sergeant had disappeared and I was having trouble focusing on the not too distant GIs. Something was wrong. I felt I had been hit but was more disorientated than hurt, just awfully groggy and weak, every action requiring supreme effort. The lens changed, I made two more frames and drunkenly staggered towards the chopper a mere 30 metres away. I felt the pain of the skid on my knees when I collapsed, arms thrown over the door sill, acutely aware I was missing my lucky hat, and unable to pull myself aboard. I might have been screaming for help, though I was insisting that my Aussie cover be retrieved.

The next light was bright, and directly above me. I could hear a serious doctor's voice. I could not move and throbbed all over. The light went out. The doc murmured, 'He's only got twenty minutes left.'

Another light, that of the bright sun, hit me as the stretcher was hoisted out of the C med beside the pad at Cu Chi. I could distantly hear the bird still turning over. I tried to sit up and ask what was happening. There seemed to be a crowd of people around me. It was a *déjà vu* of the flight back to Phu Bai after the cutter incident. All I wanted to know was how much longer till it would be better, how many minutes more to reaching help. I passed out again. At that point I'm told I died.

I died three times. Three times the accompanying nurse had to thump my heart back to the go mode. The brain, though I was blissfully unaware of it, was doing a massive haemorrhage. We were en route to the large field hospital of Long Binh. I was DOA.

Another light went on. I was on a gurney in a cool corridor. Blurred voices hovered out of vision. They were familiar; the bureau chief of *Time*, Marsh Clark, and my friend John Wilhelm, who had helped me attack the villa with smoke grenades. In a gush of consciousness I was simultaneously trying to find out what had happened and trying to tell them my version, plus captions, for the film, and as an addendum where I had left the Moke and that the keys were in my fatigues. A surgeon was telling an aide to start shaving off my hair. I tried to protest, asking them to leave it long at the back. Marsh's voice insisted I be told the truth. A grenade had gone off and they were going to have to open up my head to get the shrapnel out. I was told to count to two thousand in thousands as a needle went into a vein somewhere. I never made it past a grand. The sodium pentothal did its merciful work for the duration of the cutting.

It was a deep spiral, an endless twist towards infinity, a perception of clarity, of a light not bright but dark, of no colour, of no vibration, it was a still glow, I was dead. I could not be, I refused to be dead. I would go no further down the spiral; that door could shut since I had seen the other side. Now was not the time. I would pull back. I was nowhere, I was everywhere, I was not.

A beam painfully probed my unblind right eye; my bent, catheted cock screamed in agony; I could not see and I felt swollen up all over. Voices were far away in a lost space, a television white-noise backdrop. I was not dead by my reckoning, but not aware of what was going down. Above all, it was confusing and very frightening. I feared I might be blind, or paralyzed. I could not move and I was dying for a drink and a cigarette, unable to express it. I could only concentrate on trying to live.

Linda says she passed out once, the others say a dozen times. She and Nik had run out of gas trying to get out to Long Binh to catch me post-op. They made it the next morning, or whenever

170

it was. She tells me what the doctors have done, and that what hit me was a booby-trapped 105-mm US-made shell, not a grenade. A graver reality. But I will live. She fades. She tells me that after the initial opening of my cranium I was awake through the removal of the enormous haemorrhage, plus an assortment of imploded bone splinter. I was even mumbling incoherent words, throughout my two and a half hour neurosurgery. She goes away. Nik is unable to take a picture. I can sense his form at the end of the bed. Rosemarie, his lady, smells of her French toilet water. I think I am screaming. I know I am only whispering. I am trying to ask for a cigarette, or water, or am I just communicating, life-proving.

The next time they come I am being moved into a middle ward via a wheelchair lift contraption, a medical forklift. They give me a lit smoke and I puff distractedly, in the effort dropping it. I glare with one lidded, swollen eye, bloodshot and sutured. They bring presents and messages including cables to and from my parents and more attention than any of the other poor motherfuckers in this neurosurgical block get. It is good to feel I am going to make it, though the pain is now dawning and they let no post-brain-opper get to sleep. Awake to monitor, awake to test. The TV screams off the wall opposite the bed, *Combat* and *Gunsmoke*, the in-country hit shows, full volume, no sleep; the ward station shines fluorescent bright. During the graveyard shift, the bloody box finally off, I am dozing, then nightmare awake as the Aussie with tree-crushed skull two beds away begins his ritual screaming for water, water, water and God. This awakens some other poor soul who moans over and over for his mother. The station comes alive with carts bristling with medical implements, off to deal with the fires. Experts arrive, gowns over pyjamas. Screens arrive though I don't see why. The aluminium morgue box comes and goes. Dawn brings a nurse sticking a thermometer up my bum. I am back in the land of the living and vaguely expect a solid breakfast.

I am pleased now to introduce my saviours, my surgeon, Major Dr Jacob Mathis. He will reemerge but at this time his character is undefined, his very presence a consolation. His firm, pliantly strong fingers probe and touch. He peers in my eyes with fibre-optic lanterns. He humphs and grunts, smelling fresh and together but not antiseptic. He is not old enough to be my father, though he is already, like everyone in-country, going prematurely shocked grey. His eyes twinkle, professional blue, steadily into my own.

He is honest and explains what is done and to be done. I am so drugged with all kinds of interesting pain killers that I barely take it in.

Prognosis: I will live. We all laugh at that one, it hurts too. Great metal skewers are looped across my abdomen like a stuffed chicken, an interesting sideline to the shells make-up. They will come out in a week or so. We smile. At the moment I am not able to move anywhere along my left side. I am hemiplegic. Some movement, some usage of the limbs may return; how much, when, *que sera*. No mention is made of divine anything. It is one pro to another. Dr Jake has done his homework. He says he had to open my head up and go in to get out a bit of shrapnel, a bent nail, yay big – finger and thumb two inches apart. And pointing at his own head he explains where it had lodged up in the back upper section of my skull, having gone in above the eye. I don't find out right now how close it really is or was or is going to be. I am better spared in this macabre neuropsycho ward. My left eye will gradually open; how much I will see is unpredictable. Already my right one is periscoping the immediate area at a very reduced aperture. I start calculating how many days off sick I will be at full day rate, just as after Da Nang. I figure fat city and daydream villas and boats and motors and fun, and I wake up again unable to move, aching all over the right side, hot stabs where the IVs go into my arm. Why not put it in the paralyzed one? I lie watching it drip.

Sean Flynn was on a bike trip up-country to Laos with Carl Robinson from the AP photo ward. He got a cable from Marsh Clark (probably in the same pigeon-hole that my hiringgram had been stuck into) saying I had been hit. Our room mate Perry Deane, who had just got into Vientiane, found him in a state of shock, sitting on his bed in the Constellation, cluching the telegram, which read: 'VOTRE AMI ETE GRAVEMENT BLESSE ET PEUT ETRE MOURIR'. He said, 'Page got hit, maybe gonna die. Let's go for a walk.' On the stairs down he turned to Perry Deane and said, in the way he had of making things seem vaguely theatrical and solemn, 'Well, you just have to make new friends.' Tough words, meant in place of crying. We all held too much back in order to survive moment by moment. They both went to an opium den until curfew put them on the street. Sean sat outside an all-night café mumbling *'Peut-être mourir'* over and over with Perry consoling him, 'Listen, man, its all right to cry.' Sean sobbed on.

'But a man shouldn't . . .' stuff passed down from Dad and falsely held onto.

They were beside my bed a couple of days later. Sean brought me a beautiful wooden Lao Buddha for the bedside cabinet, creating an instant shrine with the flowers and fruit. He was impeccable in a white linen Pakistani wedding shirt. He brought me strength, his energy ebbed across from his strong hands into mine, a jolt of life.

The revelations of Sean's emotions did not emerge until Perry Deane published his book *Two of the Missing*. Perry Deane had almost fainted, stunned by the way my 'head was shaved off and there was a pie-shaped outline where his head had been sewed back after the surgeon had sawed out a chunk of skull and stuffed the brains back in'. He flashed on seeing the family calf in North Carolina going through the abattoir as a kid.

That was the last time I saw my brother. I was evacuated a few days later, and Sean had been so shocked that he left for Indonesia to seek a separate peace, joining Minimus and Galloway, now with the Djakarta bureau, Frankie's removed. One last trip took him back to Indochina, to pack up his things and see old friends. Then, on 6 April 1970, he and Dana Stone, who was shooting news for CBS, were captured in the Parrot's Beak area off Cambodia near Chi Phou, believed to be taken by the VC before being handed to their NVA controllers. He is still listed as MIA, missing in action, known to have been taken alive, reported in captivity for several months, then nothing.

Linda had the last word in the hospital to Perry Deane, 'You people, you come here when you don't have to and this is the chance you take . . .' with an elegant swish of long hair ' . . . but I just look at all those young men around him. They're just out of high school and they didn't even want to be here. Now their lives are ruined.'

My getting hit pointed up the fragility of our existence and caused many friends to decide to leave.

I had not seen a lot of Larry Burrows just before I stepped on the mine. Back in 1965 when I went freelance he had let me tag along, the learning puppy. Then I was junior understudy and had been invited out to his Repulse Bay home for lunch and met Vicky, his wife, and the children. Their daughter had a severe leg deformity. After the Michelin plantation madness there was a slap-up bureau dinner at a French restaurant, L'Arc en Ciel. Larry was in town for a few days, honing his story on Tron, a little

Vietnamese girl with no legs, and her rehabilitation. It was an evening of subdued war stories over too much wine for my taut mind. Without the least thought, I had turned to Larry and accused him of being 'hung up with cripples'. For the first time ever I saw anger in this quiet, compassionate man as he deliberately got up and strode out without a word. He avoided me from then on.

I did not really see Larry again, except as a blurred form at my bedside. He had come alone, of his own volition, out to the 6th Evac at Long Binh to wish me the best. I felt his presence and calm as he took my hand in his. All I could think of was to blurt my apologies for that faux pas months before, saying I understood what crippled was now. There was a silence, it seemed, in the turmoil of the post-op ward and I could feel a tear fall on the back of my good right hand. He brought me hope then, a reassurance that I would make it and be shooting again, he would always be there. He left as quietly as he had come. I savoured the visit, not knowing what the future would bring.

The chopper Larry was riding in over Laos two years later, during Lam Son 39, the definitive ARVN expedition to sever the Ho Chi Minh Trail at Tchepone, was shot down by a North Vietnamese radar-controlled 37-mm flak gun.

Ironically, although this massive attack had been to prove that Vietnamization would work, it was the US that had had to provide most of the airborne logistics and fire-support missions, reopening the oid Marine base at Khe Sanh as a forward staging post. The American-crewed bird had been flying four photographers out to the armoured spearhead. That day, 10 February 1971, saw four friends go MIA, for no trace of the wreck was found in the triple-canopied ravines and mountains. Another Huey had watched the shell blow into the chopper and its descent in a fireball. Besides Larry there were Henri Huet, my old UPI bureau chief, head-hunted by Faas to the AP, Shimamoto, the Japanese lad who had waved the white hanky at the tank in Da Nang in 1966, and Kent Potter of UPI, a young head with whom I had spent a lot of cold 33 beers in the Melody.

The turning point came for me when I was lying quietly sobbing, bemoaning my own fate, feeling helpless, alone, nowhere. I felt as though I was dropping and panicked. I must have screamed for something. All of a sudden beside the bed was the large black male ward sister, a senior NCO who had seen it all in a lifer's service. He chewed me out, hushed me down and flatly accused me of feeling sorry for myself. I had no need of that there moaning. I was gonna make it. I was gonna live an' I knew it. So hush up. 'Too many of these other dudes won't even see mo'nin' so shut up. But now hear. You need something, you call me. You got pain, I fix it. No sweat. You gonna make it, my man.'

7

Dissolving Recovery

Hemiplegia was a weird number. I could think of what I wanted to do but was unable to make it physically happen, however hard I concentrated on it. Not even a little finger would move on the left side of my body, much less the leg. A slight sensation of touch on the afflicted side was a hopeful sign, but the doctors had little idea what would happen. No one refused to make a prognosis in my presence, and once I left the care of my original neurosurgeon, Dr Jake, the medical profession's speculations ranged from depressing to ecstatic.

For the first three weeks I was a vegetable in a patch of assorted varieties, all of us totally dependent on the military's tender, loving care machine. Then I became the proud owner of a brand-new set of wheels, small front ones which swivelled like castors and big balloon-tyred rear ones. A top-of-the-line Crest wheelchair. Once I had learned to make the initial transfer from bed to wheels, life took on a rosier glow.

As a civilian inside the system I was a rogue card and caused a confusion of paper work. Getting me out and to where was a problem and since there was a distinct possibility I might expire or have mental problems I would require a nonmedical accompanying attendant. The bureau assigned Linda the task, with reluctance.

The air force did not deem the army fit to get me prepped for the evac. That was to be done at a special unit next to Ton San Nhut airbase. Riding down there I was strapped horizontal in a chopper. It was boring lying down now that I had figured out how to sit up, painfully, the wires holding my stomach together pulling taut.

Twelve hours in a stretcher rack sandwiched under another patient, from whom sundry body fluids are constantly dripping, the wet red patch over your middle widening, is barely conducive to relaxation. The in-flight medics were constantly busy. Only the worst hit warranted stateside processing; we were an extremely fragile cargo, triaged statistics. All I saw of Japan on that trip was from the sky above Tachikawa AFB en route to Yokuska Naval Air Station on the top rack of three in an air-force Huey.

In the base hospital in Yokohama, I could just make out from my bed the chants of anti-war demonstrators at the main gates. Linda visited daily to pick up another list of shopping for the bureau to buy for me tax-free. I had started to calculate my sick pay, figuring six months, a couple of hundred days, at day rates, enough to get a place in the South of France and relax. No one had talked money so far, no one really thought I was going to make it. I still had not seen my gear, but it had survived. Later in New York I used to sit and scratch off my own blood and brains from the interstices of the Leicas; though they never looked really clean again.

The 105th Medical in Yokohama was constantly full, an assembly line of disaster. It was dull and military. In twelve days I got to the gym twice and I was itching to go, I could vaguely feel things stirring without being able to pinpoint exactly where. The left side of my face had gone slack and did not pick up for a smile or occasional, painful laugh. The plastic food came airline style on plastic trays. You were expected to complete a week's worth of menus, ticking off boxes labelled Wheaties, oatmeal, eggs – sunny, poached, boiled, easy over – ham, sausage, juices and so on. The only difference was the colour and consistency. I continued to lose weight. The last night in Japan was a delight of air-force hospitality. A steak, a wheelchair to the toilet – bye-bye bed pan and screen – and a black aide who handed me a jay. Looking back I guess they were joying me up for the bummer of twenty-four hours strapped down in the C141 to the US. The air force lashed out on pills too, gave me a stash of the ones that were dosed every four hours. It was a junkie's cocktail of striped capsules and morphia tablets. The Dilaudids, a kind of synthetic morphine akin to heroin, were numbingly delicious, the phenobarb and anti-epilepsy just felt like hydraulic fluid in the brake lines. They made things bearable and there was a noticeable buzz ten minutes after popping.

Our plane landed in the dawn of an early Alaska summer

outside Anchorage. My berth was at the back, and I got blasted by the icy Arctic air straight from the lowering ramp, a slap of revival. Anybody not woken up by that got aroused by Donut Dollies, Red Cross girls, thrusting scalding cups of horrid military mashed coffee or tepid sodas at us. For the hungry, and those permitted, there were cookies and stale boloney on Wonder Bread.

Frank McCulloch – my old *Time* bureau chief – had pulled some of his spooky Pentagon contacts, and I was the first foreigner to be admitted to Walter Reed Hospital in Washington DC. It was obvious from the start that I was not going to blend in harmoniously with the officers and their relatives making use of the splendid facility. The room I shared with a retired colonel was decorated like a hotel suite with attached cripple-facilitated bathroom. The beds had powered gear shifts to move, tilt and angle themselves, a control panel of jack sockets and toggle switches was recessed into the wall at pillow height.

There was a reception committee already gathered when I arrived, led by Steve Northup, formerly of Frankie's, now a staffer with the *Post*. There were a ring of Saigon faces, all bearing goodies or spirit offerings. My roomie never ceased to be surprised, or courteous, when my outrageous visitors turned up. Luckily there was a balcony where we could lurk. We made the zealous, regimental staff nervous.

They took the wire brackets out of my guts and I took my first free-swinging crap, my first warm bath, I was able to feel more. Steve leaned over the bed, handed me a lit roll and said, 'Brother, when you can roll a three-paper number again, ride a bike and hump on top, then, my man, you will be well.'

Sam Castan would have loved to be at my twenty-fifth birthday party. I thought of him when I woke up that morning in the sublet Linda had found. They had let me out for the weekend to celebrate. I think Sam would have willingly paid up the $500 bet that I wouldn't make it to be there. His loss is still heavy.

Steve was on the downstairs doorstep at just after nine. I cannot remember how many people crammed into the two-room apartment. I eventually passed out, spun out of the wheelchair by a circle of sitting, squatting and standing friends, who appeared to be making a carousel of my head. I was never so deliriously happy.

Time had Linda and me shovelled into a Cadillac limo to New York for the last leg of rebuilding. There was a certain karma in that the institute I was now in was endowed by one of the

178

perpetrators of Indochina insanity, Dean Rusk, a former foreign secretary. It was the most expensive rehabilitative medicine unit in the world. Some cheapo at Time Inc admin had decided that I did not warrant a single room. The other beds were full of strokes and back cases for my whole sojourn. The Italian in the bed next to me had worked in the subways; he had backed out of a cubby hole and there he was. There was a Haitian ton-ton macoute whose Cadillac had been rammed when it was standing, hood up, on the upstate turnpike, he peering at the engine innards. He was visited by a strange fraternity of black guys and their molls. Another inmate was a once famous criminal defence attorney who had lost the use of his left leg and arm and voice in a stroke. He was speechless except for a dah, dah, de haah, a start that the therapists were working on. Most days he sat playing cards to gain dexterity or squeezing a rubber ball. He wandered through the corridors, looking twitchy. I would catch him on my rolling expeditions in my wheels, in strange wings lurking by the vending machines. He could come and go as he pleased, hampered only by the inability to voice his communications. The bar round the corner had instructions to set 'em up when he plonked a ten-spot on the counter. They kicked him out after four. His wife would come visit, sit chattering abstractedly as he got more worked up and frustrated. Usually he would signal her departure with a loud 'baaa' and slap her across the breasts with her handbag.

One night there was a traditional going-home party in the dining room. All the aides and patients there were getting bombed on illegal booze. The lawyer was leading the pack in consumption. He described a perfect arc to the floor from the plastic chair and lay unmoving. Two big black aides rushed over and lifted him up. 'How ya feel, John? How are ya?' His eyes opened, he looked around and got to get up. 'I, er, I, er, er, er, feel fine,' long and drawn out. Everyone froze; he looked surprised and slipped back into the arms of the aides. A week later he was in regular speech classes and left about when I did.

Most institutions are the same, depressing. This one had, as New Yorkers were wont to say, 'a bettah attitude'. They had a good track record for recovery. They put you to work from the word go, thinking about getting out of there. New York was also full of friends and Linda soon found a place to live. The Big Inc in the Rockefeller Center finally decided I was entitled to $200 per week sick pay, all their insurance allowed. My bubble burst.

But a much delayed bank statement announced I was six G clear. Time to spend; a stereo, 120 records, then cash for a new Saab wagon I could not yet drive. The more incentive I showed the more freedom I was allowed. I graduated to toothbrushing, bum wiping, taking showers and getting dressed. Then I could go home for weekends. I took Wednesdays off to go to the cinema by cab with Linda. (I remember seeing *Easy Rider* limping and slinged, going to the head of the queue, leaving the others to proffer explanations.) Lunch times Tom Corpora, a latter-day Frankier who was working on 42nd Street, would stroll over. We used to sit on the unused fifteenth-floor roof terrace, which offered a panorama of the East River and the chopper traffic, with a little terracotta Moroccan *kif* toker to ward off the therapy blues. We were both on parole up there. Tom got a freebie car for wounded vets out of Avis and we cruised upstate to Woodstock where I got to bed Linda in a wooden cabin and afterwards went to the White Elephant and heard part of the Band and Tim Hardin. Getting well was turned into fun by a group of indulgent, sympathetic friends who always had time to come by.

At about that time my body showed remarkable leaps forward. I discovered that, should I sneeze or orgasm, my otherwise inert left arm and leg would shoot up to 45 degrees in a *Sieg Heil*. It evidently boded much for recovery.

None of us returned *bao chi* were coping with being back in the big world terribly well. We were all a little unfocused, reminiscing a lot. Mike Herr was struggling to write it down and understand why he had gone. Garspon was blown away by the wound and still could not talk about it, burying it in the bottle. Robin Mannock was a Third Worlder and was trying to deal with a desk at *Time* and stay sane in an unpiped world. At Frankie's poor Robin had had acute appendicitis and been convinced by fellow householders to try to forget with opium, before getting emergency surgery. He kept a 'gentleman's' cellar and is the finest round-eye Chinese cook.

I got cheekier, cabbing over to Time-Life to run up a bit of sympathy and plop my flipper about. I limped horribly then, my left deltoid had atrophied so much you could put a fist in the gap so it now hung suspended in a reconstructive Velcro harness. On top my skull had a distinctive dent where the scalp and a trace of hair were refoliating the crater. The ladies on the twenty-eighth floor at the *Life* photo headquarters helped me while away the afternoon. I was trying to convince Time-Life that I could be entrusted with a retainer, capable of going back on the job, even getting a half-dayer shooting a federal judge. Nothing I took was used.

Our star outing was an away visit to Washington DC, weighed down with a surplus 8-mm cine camera and tape recorders. Got to fly over Quantico Marine Corps Base and throw firecrackers out of Tom Meyer's bird-dog L-19 spotter plane. Tom had been temporary at Frankie's House, coming through on Steve's intro as a fellow New Mexican he had grown up mushrooming with. He had come out to Nam on a fat *Playboy* gig to write about flying in the war; flying being his passion. The piece that had surfaced in print, entitled 'Anson's Last Assignment', had spooked me rigid. He had written up an adventure we had gone out on with the ROKs Blue Dragons, the rather nasty Korean marines, on a routine patrol, but in his story I get greased by a machine gun crossing a paddy. He sent me the galleys when I was still in-country. It jibed with the image of staying alive to be blown away fictionally. Tom had a slick job working for a radical New Mexican congressman and kept his toy plane out on a Maryland field.

Looping over Quantico's war-game practice fields I could literally feel my brains plopping against the retaining scalp. The hospital thereafter monitored my activities with greater care. Aerobatics *verboten*.

That weekend we went to retrieve the Lao grass that we had mailed ourselves from Japan. Linda had bought four beautiful caddies of fragrant Japanese green tea at an upmarket department store. Back at the Yokohama hotel she had dumped all but the top inch of tea leaves and stashed in plastic our means of survival in the Big Apple. The department store was happy to mail the packages to us at the DC American Express office.

Later on, GIs were running a lucrative smuggle back from smack-laden Indochina straight to mainline America. One of my last stories in-country had been on animals at war for *Time*; we had photographed geese guarding bridges and dogs searching for mines or explosives. In Da Nang at the aerial port for outgoing I Corps personnel was stationed a bona fide dope-sniffing Alsatian called Taddy. His job was to snuffle around the baggage being processed, but to his superiors' chagrin he was more interested in the half-eaten stale burgers and boloney sandwiches in the trash bins. Down south at Bien Hoa and Ton San Nhut the handlers were known heads who had detoxed their charges. The geese guarding the Y-bridge honked anyway at friend or foe, and any

181

elephants left out in the bush were fair game for any frustrated door gunners.

Looking back it was crazy to drive 6000 miles to have a plastic manhole cover fitted into the top of my brain drain. I had insisted on the best, in a warm place, and the Inc medical board came up with an appointment in downtown Los Angeles.

The first plastic surgeon I went to see turned out to be a repressed gay who appeared more concerned with making a photo study of the minute scars from the Starlite shrapnel on my arse than with the large hole to be filled on the top of my head. His gig was mainly face lifts, cosmetic breast, hip and thigh nips and tucks. I stormed out, retreating to our temporary refuge with the Travises high on Mulholland Drive. The next doctor was of Georgian clarity. Herbert Cuneo had beautiful rock-steady hands, clear blue eyes, a severe, fatherly attitude. I knew instantly he could do the job. Later I discovered that he was in charge of the team that had a last stab at trying to save Bobby Kennedy after Sirhan put a .22 round in his brain. He had been DOA. I had a brain scan, one of the worst tests around. Nuclear gunge is dripped through your system as an X-ray slowly clunks back and forth over your clamped skull. It took two hours. Dr Cuneo had me scheduled on the table for ten days later.

David Travis, whom I knew from birth in 1968, had horrific allergies; Linda and I had brought out west the sublet Apple kittens. Alice backed over one of the kittens. We moved to a plasterboard ferro-concrete block 150 yards up the hill from the Whisky a-Go-Go on Sunset Strip, right in the middle of Hollywood's finest madness. There was a handkerchief-sized pool flanked by half a dozen palms. The flat was full of tacky furniture and Formica surfaces. We were constantly giving shepherd's-pie parties, feeding masses on little money – lots of therapeutic peeling and chopping. I took up building model airplanes with miniature ethyl-powered 12,000-rpm engines. Larry and I flew them until they crashed, then he flew them soaked in fuel hoping for a burning, I unable to spin around with the control lines.

Larry brought Alice's flu to me on a hospital visit after H. Cuneo and team had finished trowelling a perfectly moulded piece of epoxy resin, the colour of pink icing sugar, in the palm-shaped manhole. Instant pneumonia. My temperature took off to 104, I was delirious, watching squads of sterile-clad folk hustle my room full of cold. A barrage of fans, cold, wet blankets, icy air-con units. Frightening cold. Saving cold. Very confusing hot cold. It burst and I was through the other side. I needed an extended stay in the Good Samaritan hospital like I needed another hole in my head. What should have been a routine quickie visit dragged on for two heavy weeks.

Ever since I had accustomed myself to the knowledge that I was to go back to the knife, I had imagined the worst of it. Total anaesthesia is like being dead for a while so your mechanics can be tinkered with. I was feeling like that Viet Cong suspect that the Korean captain had blindfolded kneeling on the edge of the trench, hands bound back, before loosing off an aimed burst of automatic an inch from the poor peasant's head. I was afraid I might never wake up from the needle. I got tired really quickly before I went into the Good Sam, I practised sleep, took too many drugs and painkillers. Against all advice I kept pouring down the tranquillizing beer and Courvoisier, hiding the fears that continually raised themselves to a conscious level, sublimating the traumas which no one had yet diagnosed in the daily returning veterans.

With the plastic lid installed. I could feel safe to move about, now a twig would not ruin my entire life with a casual poke. The unnerving wait to go back into the surgery was over. I would now heal completely, there was no need for any further operations. We could be in Rome for my twenty-sixth.

Linda and I went to Naples aboard an overcrowded Italian liner, the SS *Michelangelo*, where the public lavs yielded non-sputi (non-specific urinary tract infection). It meant we couldn't fuck and on a ten-day boat trip there is not a lot to do. To cap it all they charged us for the penicillin to cure it. Then we both caught the runs from the steerage-class swill, so we couldn't eat. The cabin was beside the transmission and stuffy, and I had too much carry-on baggage as usual. Even the cats, Captain Blood and Pinhead's son, born in the Hollywood sheetrock, caught a mild distemper in the overpriced, unclean kennels under the funnels.

We were underway to my new first and last promised contract, US $12,000 for the year's guarantee, eighty days, fifty fifty, *Time* and *Life*. Rome seemed at the time an obvious choice, close to Africa, which I had not seen, staying close to the Middle East, and within striking distance of England and my folks.

But Rome was alienating. I knew no one outside the bureau, which was staffed by a stuffy crew of Italians; the bureau chief,

James Bell, loathed me at first sight and I had been warned that he was a prude of the Southern School, square beyond imagination, due for retirement. I was an unwanted addition to his fiefdom where no one was interested in war stories. Then Italy worked even less efficiently than Vietnam and cost three times as much. It took three months to get a press priority phone. Every day another chunk of the car went missing and there were only eight Saabs in the town. I could go and buy back my petrol and hub caps at Porta Portezi, the thieves' market. I felt that the whole place was a conspiracy. I communicated by Italianizing my French with 'eyes' and 'ohs' declined like bastard Latin.

Linda left Rome in the summer of 1970. Blind to my own wants and needs, unsure of where or what I now was, I had agreed that when I could take care of myself again physically and we were settled in, Linda would continue on her travels of self-discovery overland to India. I had not any love in me, I had no real interest in anything, my world centred on an imaginary survival concept plagued with self-destruction. I was unable to say, Stay, wait, I need and want you. I love you. It was easier to say go, and fuck it, face the empties in the morning.

She left on an overland bus, one way, for £140. Our swarm of cats – the original two joined by assorted strays – got antsy and I started to climb the walls. The giant penthouse near the Trevi fountain seemed hollow and unhomelike. I took to prowling, screwing cheap hookers, lurking by the fountain like a paparazzo trying to find someone to talk to.

Captain Blood, an original one, had taken off from the sixth-floor balcony and survived. His son had the horrible habit of throwing up under my bed, which was large and virtually unmovable. My mustachioed cleaning lady gave up in despair.

I was rescued from total obscurity by Burt Pines, who had done an easy year in Saigon for *Time* and now had the handsome reward of the Eastern European bureau in Vienna. A slightly foppish, spooky sort of dude, Burt loved the intrigue needed to cover the countries behind the Iron Curtain. He called for my assistance. I had shot no more than eight days the whole summer. Initially I had been too busy getting set up in the penthouse, unfurnished, with an unequipped kitchen, a bare shell with not even a lamp fixture or socket outlet, prey to the mercies of the local electrician's cabal. A quick drive back to see my parents only left me sad; I was not ready to communicate there and they could never really understand what had happened. Linda's presence before had

184

complicated the issue. The memory of Terry and the twins was heavy on their minds, unsaid. Grey London was bleak as ever, Vietnam a dead subject, an occasional flash from their new colour television or rightist column in the *Telegraph*.

Paris, *en passant*, was not the same without Flynn, no one from the old days was around. Vienna awoke odd flights of freedom, new frontiers, new adventures with an old mate whose cherry in the field I had busted. I spent back-breaking weeks in the bureau Mercedes with the rotund Norbert at the wheel, doing an in-depth report on the German-speaking territories along the Oder-Neisse. Then we went first-class LOT to Warsaw. Up front on an Ilyushin still puts your knees in your chest without emergency life rafts or oxygen. Inflight service was a pot of caviar, a pack of black bread and a bottle of vodka dumped on your lap.

The Poles laid on a good time, we had a freedom I had not expected, and our interpreter was a foxy mature student from the Foreign Ministry. It was Burt's turn to show me survival: how to get by on a diet of principally alcohol. The Polish day appeared to start with a collective visit to a state stud farm or turkey farm, once to a computer factory. There the introductions were done over rounds of either vodka or Armenian cognac, knocked back traditionally, chased with beer or champagne, toasts to coexistence, fraternal bullshit and journalistic understanding. Then there would be mass traipse-out for the photo opportunity. Mercifully we were on our own for the visit to Lublin and the Lubianka concentration camp nearby, within 100 kilometres of the Russian border.

I made two of my most haunting frames inside that foreboding, concertina-fenced, barracked killing field: a single rose on the ledge above the ovens where the cadavers burned. A gladiolus on the slabs where the most useful items were removed, the gold teeth, the jewellery and the hair. Not a bird chirped in the whole mile-square place, only poppies grew on ditches where 10,000 had been buried alive. Burt, originally a Pineski, with Jewish ancestry, faced other ghosts. We crept back home to Vienna along the East German border, then through pretty Prague and liberal Czechoslovakia. I moved into the Sacher Hotel, filling up after rationed Poland on the house torte and venison pâté.

Another ten days in Warsaw followed with a swing through the industrial south. The liberal dosing of American Time Inc largesse had done the trick; we apparently were not CIA agents. We were cleared. We sank in so well this time that the interpreter took us to a party where I ended up spending the night with a Mexican student on Czech-made acid. It was not a bad Polish joke, though a gruelling plod back to the Hotel Metropole in the damp dawn, eyed suspiciously by militia patrols. Shooting the Moda Polska fashion collection was less amusing; it is hard to make a Stalinist-designed society look joyful, though the Poles are the best at breaking the ice shackles of dominance from the East. The restaurants had elaborate menus dating in style and content to the last days of the Third Reich, forlornly reduced on enquiry to borscht and chicken. Overheard at a diplomatic do at the US embassy: 'And what would happen should the Sahara turn communist? A shortage of sand.'

I returned to a cat-devastated crib, chilly, empty. Burt hauled me out of Rome a little later to cover Nixon's jaunt to Yugoslavia to pow-wow with the ailing Tito. It pissed down for just about the whole four days, and nobody, including the presidents, appeared to be having a good visit. Dour peasants stood in the thick drizzle, clutching sodden paper Stars and Stripes and Yugoslav flags. To cap it all, Nasser went and died in Cairo and everyone not on the White House zoo press plane took off south. His death dropped us off the cover of that week's magazine, reduced to two inside columns.

That was effectively my last shoot based out of the Time-Life bureau on Via Sardegna. Not half of the contracted days would be shot. I was totally adrift.

Linda's promising letters from sunny places made me want to follow. I would wait no more for her return, having borrowed money from an old Saigon Reuters hand for a Sydney–Rome ticket. The last missive had been from a tropical glacier on New Zealand's South Island.

Months later I had to go out to Fiumicino customs to retrieve a strange Balinese rug-wrapped parcel from the customs. The object, sea-mailed from Singapore months previously, was a swaddled Afghan muzzle loader. The flint for the lock was missing, the mechanism rusted over. Customs were concerned that I might use it offensively. Later still I got an airmailed boomerang and a Balinese fertility fetish godlet wanking itself. I amexed her the borrowed ticket money, praying for her return by Christmas.

I met Jan two nights after Belgrade when she came with some friends of the downstairs neighbour to a party I gave for anybody I vaguely knew, hoping to stir up some action in this unenlightened

Catholic burg. There was nothing shaking except in a cellar opposite in my Viccolo del Puterello (translated locally as alley of the little boy hookers) which was rented by six shaggy streetboys in their early twenties who wanted to be rock musicians. Their repertoire was mostly old Beatles numbers.

Jan was another lonely soul, though she had been three years in Rome. Unhappy with the life in the Pacific Northwest, she had left for southern California to crew boats, eventually ending up in Italy. She now designed knitwear for a chic boutique at the foot of the Spanish Steps, selling upmarket twinsets for the visiting matron. Grasping for her help was bad judgement. She was not easy with men for friends, a rape and a lost daughter had left indelible scars. We were lost ships in an Italian storm from which we both needed to evacuate. We matched well, though our tandem insecurities could never be simultaneously resolved. We grooved the city together, and I saw another side though I never grew to like it. A noisy, discombobulating constantly altering jumble dotted with incredible monuments around which a polluting traffic snarled. The locals lacked manners. I liked the wine and the pasta. Jan loved the cats, which were starting to go feral for lack of attention.

That winter in Rome was glum. The Trevi had snow on it, and the heating in the rooftop flat failed to keep my arthritis at bay. The contract money was nearly gone, spent on expensive drives to Paris to fit out the place from Galeries Lafayette. Except for a couple of *Elle* shoots there was no incoming and I was extravagant, especially in wooing Jan. We curled up at her place a lot, where the heating spastically functioned, playing games of argumentative Scrabble. American vocabulary and spelling could drive the sanest Brit to distraction. She also spent hours filling in simple crossword-puzzle books. Now I can ask why.

A shaft of hope appeared. Martin Stuart-Fox – newly married to Elizabeth Cavalarie, in Eltham where he had been reduced to teaching physics at the local comprehensive – arrived in a VW camper, on his way to the burgeoning crisis in Bengal. We had a plan. Jan and I would join them in India in our own truck. I would shoot and Martin would do the words. Rumour had it that Simon was going out freelancing for the Beeb and the *Telegraph*. It would be like the old days again.

Believing that marriage would automatically create a safety net and protect us from the troubles I was sliding into, I proposed to Jan. The marriage ceremony was performed by the Greek district

187

commissioner in Nicosia in August 1971. Jan had promised to visit an old Arab friend in Jerusalem. I could stay with Marsh Clark, my erstwhile chief in Saigon, now running the strategic Jerusalem bureau, and as a bonus Nik Wheeler was in the country shooting a wine piece on the once Jordanese vineyards. The bureaucracy made it impossible to get married in Israel and we flew on to Cyprus. We arrived a quarter of an hour early at the run-down government building near the old green line. A blond Israeli Jewess and an Arab gardener were in front of us on the production line. Jan decided to take off right then, and I almost had to drag her back to go limpingly through an unprepossessing civil spiel. We both mumbled nods without looking at each other and split for a cove on the north coast to guzzle overpriced warm champagne with ham and cheese sandwiches. We frolicked and coupled in the crystal, then unpolluted, water, oblivious to the momentous commitment made moments ago. The mood was shattered ominously by four figures in black wet suits who clambered down from the opposite headland, adorned with tanks and spears. We beat an undignified retreat to our abandoned gear.

There was even a honeymoon, a lull before the storm. A lull after too. Already we were spitting like the cats, returned in misery from fleablown kennels at outrageous fees. The once large penthouse now seemed overcrowded with a marital collection of two mounds of junk. We were now trapped and we voiced it. Deep down I regretted having blown the trip with Linda; this was a poor substitute for the peace in the storm that had been. I was not working and there were no prospects, already a hole was being nibbled in the first instalment of the severance payment Frank McCulloch had negotiated from the hierarchy in Rockefeller Centre. I belatedly found that I had signed all my rights away, not helped by one of the constant Italian mail strikes. This time all air mail had been dumped into boxcars and taken off to a remote rural siding to be burned. Jan's money was to remain hers, her name did not change on her passport until I defaced it with mine with a red felt marker. I planned to put the rest of my bread into a tax-free Ford Transit in Cologne, to be delivered and outfitted in Orpington, to drive to the emergent state of Bangladesh.

Our wedding present from David Sulzberger was couchettes on the Brindisi–Patras ferry on the way to the honeymoon, a little late but with David playing joker and peacemaker. In Athens we filled up with four more folks, all old friends from Vietnam where

David had had a spook job poring over statistics with CORDS, the co-ordinating office for rural development, a counter-terrorist programme run from the US embassy annexe. His father, Cyrus Sulzberger, the roving *New York Times* columnist, had turned up in Vietnam with Marina, David's Greek mother, in tow. We had taken her to Dao Island and later to the opium den while Cy had interviewed the powers behind the game. Marina had come by the hospital later in Yokohama. David had organized the Long Hai beach parties north of Vung Tau, leading the ragged convoy in his canary-yellow and black *traction d'avant quatre chevaux* Citroën. The family home was on Spetsai at the end of the Peloponnese, superbly suited to a romantic interlude. Jan and I hardly spoke, letting the others' conversation wash us together. Scrabble induced bickering again. The relationship was making the sour taste bitter. The two-week paradisical period was an emotionally draining attempt to not lose face in front of old friends who knew only too well what was going on.

Back in Rome, we packed up, shipped the cats stateside at astronomical airfares, crammed what was not crated into the Saab and autostraded north towards Cologne. My dodgy left leg, unable to release itself, did in the clutch for the fourth time near Modena. A tax-free Ford transit truck was ordered from the factory outlet with a large deposit (which *Time*'s accountants refused initially to support). We arrived at my parents, just in time to greet a five-ton Italian van disgorging our chattels into the cluttered semidetached. Jan's welded bed would not go through the door. We were back on the mattress. The whole family was uncomfortable.

Jan disappeared. I found her in Brixton; we argued, we fought, we drank, we fought. She split for Seattle. In despair I cancelled the Ford. Christmas was a month away and the plan blown. The emotional downward spiral was blacker than when Linda had left, the illusion of a supportive marriage was dust, my head a confused pain. Lots of booze, Dilaudid, phenobarb and Dilantin blurred my pain and desperation. I had no idea what to do but knew I would do something, unlike the previous winter, when I had attempted to end it.

Every time I hear the theme from *M*A*S*H* with that innocuously camouflaged jingle 'Suicide Is Painless', I have to giggle in relief. Then I had not got a laugh to look at. Funked out, on a dark, rainy, cold Roman night, alone in the cat-piss ponged marble-floored *salle*, my thoughts had meandered wild and crazy.

I got the .38 Ruger out of the bedside cabinet. When Linda and I had driven out to Los Angeles for the plastic surgery we had stopped in Arkansas with Jim Guy Tucker, a Democratic political hopeful and gun buff. I had patrolled upper II Corps with the Special Forces in leech-infested 1965. On the spur of a paranoid moment I had bought the six-gun at a pawn store, with 500 rounds and shoulder holster, for $84. For demented therapy I could hit a number eight can at 50 feet in midair. The gun was still with me. The metal glinted purposefully. I got a handful of the hollow-nosed slugs out of the Indian deerskin drawsack and counted out five. The cartridges' snick slid home in the chambers, which clicked satisfyingly home in the breech. I spun the barrel and in one movement pointed straight between my eyes and pulled the trigger. My eyes blurred and refocused on the barrel, un-smoking, a black hole, a round in the chamber either side. I lowered the message miracle very slowly and lay back, wiped out.

I was not going to lose the battle of this relationship. I was too selfishly consumed to let Jan get away. I went broke again with a one-way ticket timed to get me to Seattle for the Christmas festivities. The condition was that I was not to mention sex, drugs or war around her family. I became a land mine waiting to be triggered by enough pressure. My in-laws grooved to *South Pacific* and I was tracking to the Doors ending it. It got colder and damper, finally dumping two feet of snow over south-west suburban Seattle. My aggravated arthritis got worse, the house claustro-phobic. As the snow mushed out, it was suggested we move south to Olympia to stay with the parents-in-law, for the obsessive clan had divorced and remarried to other addicts. Their hooks were gambling and alcohol, the wives laden with cancer and multiple sclerosis. Like feuding hillbillies they lived at opposite ends of the state's capital.

Olympia is not quite a one-hearse town, not quite a city, with a standard capital building downtown surrounded by wooden-framed middle-American homes. The poorer whites tend to con-gregate in mobile-home lots on the outskirts where giant lumber dumps are interspersed with shopping malls, 7-11s, burger joints and roadside taverns. Junked autos and abandoned household appliances strew back and front yards. Many of the folks are descended from early Scandinavian settlers, their names ending in -hansen and permutations. Christianity and alcohol fuel their insecurities. Nearby Boeing in Tacoma, their principal employer, was in recession that bleak first month of '72. There were no photo jobs anywhere locally.

With the eventually returned deposit I bought a '63 red Beetle, which must have been eighth-hand with the clock turned over once, but it loved the snow and we skittered around the Olympic Peninsula in the depth of that January. The beaches were pristine, void of humanity, washed up, snow-capped logs making patterns along the shore under the crystal-blue skies. You could see clear across the Straits of Juan de Fuca to Victoria Island. We turned inland and nosed up the dirt roads carved for the descending log trains, giant tractor rigs with three trailers, dragging 200 tons of felled trees down to the boom villages dotted at creek estuaries. Up the valleys the corporation giants, Crown Zellerbach and Weyerhauser, cut magnificent 200-year-old Douglas firs. You could see the ships leaving Puget Sound, decks stacked with logs; other craft passed inbound loaded with Japanese and Korean finished consumer wood products.

The Ozette Indians, whose natural habitat this was, were mostly on welfare, a lucky few working the logging on the dangerous, denuded ancestral slopes. The tribes here were the first humans to preserve fish by smoking it. The salmon run in schools, the Humboldt Current brings seasonal bounty, the beaches and estuaries are littered with clams, oysters and the local peculiarity, geoduck, a chewy, cuttlefishy, giant razor clam. They make the best chowder in the world around these shores. The rain forest was frozen into extraterrestrial forms, misty spirits wafted among the primal pines and firs. A day's hike led to a cove with ancient Ozette hieroglyphics celebrating their hey-day.

We stayed in rough and ready but clean working men's motels, ate well of home fries, chowders, free-range eggs and fresh fish. I was chasing my beers now more regularly with a shot of whisky. We were occasionally having a good fuck and no arguments. The Scrabble I had condemned and left in Olympia.

As we got down to the Oregon border, the glamour of adventure evaporated. We clunked back to Olympia and the bitching and spitting recommenced. Now living with her haggard mother, whose whining voice penetrated the walls, Jan had taken up the trailer camp's passion of penny-a-point poker played by alcoholic blue-rinse dowagers. I refused to play cards, having no feel for them and loathing losing. I had played and lost in An Khe in 1965 and again in Rome at the Press Club, where I had tried to ingratiate myself into the foreign society. I stayed in, moaning;

191

when the card players came I went out to a tavern. A handful of Dilaudid and phenobarbs and a jug of red wine gave a confused, crashing high, paranoia, angst, white flashes. Agony of mind masked with a dirty filter.

Then the colour of the reality changed at least to a rosier tint, the edges became more pastel; the ensuing pains and hangovers jarred it back to garish bright. The aphasia that I had written off previously as nothing to worry about, just a flash of forgetfulness, or suddenly not being able to think or remember what I had been thinking, was becoming more frequent. I felt I was a failure, past it, forgotten; I thought the world owed me a living. And I had been forbidden to bring up the subject of the war. It was history, *fini, capice*? And that from the woman I was married to. Her mother whined naggingly on.

I cannot recall exactly what caused the ignition to spark, what butt lit the bush fire. It was the reverse of getting zapped. I had been plugged in for hours in front of a black-and-white television set on the nylon shag carpet with a gallon of Thunderbird, watching reruns of Indianapolis 500s. I had been stewing all day for months, probably for years, a whole pent-up mess of agony bottled tight after the corpsman at Long Binh had called my attitude. Jan and her mother got back in the dusk and an argument broke out before they had even got out of the Chrysler. My safety switch flipped off and I went bug fuck. I lashed and whirled, broke and hit and smashed. No focus, no point. I went berserk. Jan was the initial recipient, but then I focused on her mother going for the phone to call the police. Snapping the telephone cord in two, started to wrap the receiver cord around her neck, smashing her with the handpiece, Jan clinging to my back like a bug on an animal's tail.

In seconds it was done and over and I collapsed, bloodied and bruised, against the wall, surrounded by debris. The horrible aftermath of an intimate fight ensued, with pieces being picked up, conversation at best pained and polite. I skulked, unable to leave, knowing what was to happen, what I was going to do, what they were to do. I could not remember what I had actually just done or why or how, it was as though a giant hand had erased the surface of my mind's memory bank. Leaving nothing but a feeling of despondent, suicidal remorse.

A short while later, probably only minutes, the blue strobo-scopic lights of help arrived in the guise of two large sheriff's deputies, combat ready, holsters unflapped. They took in the glum scene, homing in on my bedraggled, barefoot self. To cool me off I was prodded outside at baton length and backed against the aluminium-sided trailer. They took their easy-going civic retribution with more probing jabs, standing there, four inches deep in snow, in a rosebush. Something about them was familiar, I could not quite place where and when but it was in the Nam. An eye was caught, we flashed, they hesitated and the drift was back in-country in 1965. They had been on the airboats, the ones with the big rear props, working the swamps and reeds from the Special Forces B team on Moc Hoa. I had been killing time out at Cai Cai flush on the southern border of Cambodia on the Parrot's Beak. Back then there was a lot of cross-border sneakery and few *bao chi* ventured out to the really sticky parts. We fell to rapping, going back inside. They left after five minutes, shaking my hand firmly, the incident written off as a family disturbance. End of patrol.

I was just about to go MIA. I had to get out of this place.

8

A life-time case

Struggling forward, slow
and steady, then grinding treads
in the air of a sudden precipice,
he is not unlike a tank,
steel-armoured for the
task of survival.

Susan Cahill McBride

After the incident at the trailer camp, the Pacific Northwest was
not exactly a hospitable zone. I did not turn the wipers off until
I was descending into the first olive groves of northern California.
The hitch-hiker escaping from a youth institution up near Willows
in California's Sierra foothills must have thought he was being a
cheap shrink in exchange for a lift to his cousins in Burbank. The
kid even had a little stash.

By the time Jan came to join me, I had moved five times. Back
at 1140 North Clark the rent had only gone up $30 since the
installation of the manhole cover. A paranoid Canuk ran the
joint, angel dust drifted down the central well, hookers slept it
off by the tiny T-shaped pool. Same level, just above the parking,
two doors from the old one, I at least felt at home.

Men's groups were all the rage in the mid-seventies. A collective
of survivalist soul-searchers clubbed together for consciousness
raising – or so we thought. I had been staying in the Silver Lake
district of LA with an architect whose wife was in one of the first
radical women's awareness things. Spouses and boyfriends formed
their own club to sort out their hang-ups while baby-sitting. I got
caught up in the question, 'What do you think of your father?'

There was form to it, some understood gentlemanly thing not to butt in, a calm achieved by men who had never had totally heavy crises, and who had been analysed. I got hooked, it became the only discipline I had in another spiral downtwist accompanied by paranoid lassitude. I was struck by the innocuous way that stories were related, attitudes sometimes frankly explained, and the incongruity of coughing up a life story in front of people who shifted from stranger to confidant, adviser and friend. Two went off later to become lovers. The women's group met at another venue discussing us. No one really took my story for the truth at first, but weekly the history of the disintegration of my marriage unfolded with its mindless emotions lifting me again like radar-guided SAM hits at 38,000 feet.

Jan forbade the group to meet at the Clark crib but then stormed out anyway. We should have had the ferro-concrete box foam-rubber lined. I hung macabre black-and-white prints of dead VC on the wall, their foreheads retouched with a peace sign. Jan went north for extended periods. Soon the domestic marital scene turned into a nightmare. After a series of bouts culminating in my thrashing Jan black and blue, she decided, wisely, to leave and get her own crib. She disappeared from sight, though I knew she was still in LA. All along she was living in a sunnier, bigger flat, two floors higher up. The gun-toting maintenance man eventually tipped me off about Jan's whereabouts. We became for a short period, good neighbours, right through the earthquake that left the swimming pool half dry, the balconies cracked and myself over the back fence in next door's yard half naked. I promised not to hit her again, took to honeying her Opel's gas tank instead. When I got really pissed off I'd let down her tyres. The same would happen to mine until it got boring.

The person possibly most responsible for the downfall of Nixon through the Watergate affair, Daniel Ellsberg, who took part in leaking the Pentagon Papers to the press, was playing to a packed federal courthouse in downtown Los Angeles. Back in Saigon he had come round with a couple of other friendly spooks. We had a reunion lunch in the Casa Verde, a great Mexican kitchen two blocks from the cold slabs of the court buildings. I sat through the trial to take some photos for *Time*, a little hand-me-down job that suited exactly.

There emerged a small clique of insecure *bao chi* vets in LA at that time, all grouping back into an alien, tame but simultaneously

195

terrifying challenge to what we had just captured. It was difficult to find a market for our contemptuous, somewhat cynical attitude to the editors who would be our employers. What the fuck did they know? One way or another we let that hang out and that was embarrassing to them and thus damaging to us, though we didn't always realize it. I was filed in the black list, another casualty.

I can't remember what that spark was generated by, but it went up like fifty tracer into thatch. I attacked Jan in her car. My virtually powerless left arm jolted with robotic control, ripping the antennae off the compact's wing, and as she sat frozen like a still from *Psycho*, I thrashed out any glass I could get at, starting timidly with the headlights and going big as Jan screamed and I raged. I starred the windshield twice, succumbing to a crushed toe as she gassed down for the exit. The seeing-eye door took enough time to flip itself horizontal on the steep ramp to enable me to shatter the rear window. I went into a slide of confusion and blackness, like a bad pattern on a TV screen. Breathing hard, I stood steady, a working member of the downtown press before the summoned arm of the law. I was a bad note in their book, a lodged official restraint entered on the complaint form. Case to be continued, thank you sir, have a nice day, wow, really. VIETNAM. My release was secured because the cops had visited Twickenham on the Police Department rugby side. Brits were OK. The dame was kinda crazy. Gee, Vietnam, really? My buddy was there, man, yeah, well.

Jan went south to Latin America to ride mules in the snowfields, pretending to be in that peculiar fast-forward California dream of a coup with a dangerous affair on the side, the movie script that they all want to enact. I stayed respectful of the law, hearing that she had now filed for divorce.

I spent Christmas 1973 just on the Valley side of Laurel Canyon at the house of a mob record producer. The yule tree was decorated with little pharmaceutical bottles stuffed with a spectrum of tabs, caps and pills festively decorated and labelled for each guest. A poolside clique were busily gobbling their presents, each other, and the five-star hors d'oeuvres. Back at the ferro-concrete cell a sprig of holly stood in a circle of N-gauge track, a miniature train switched hauling four stake cars and a caboose, the flats stacked with ready rolls. I tested the snow of Hollywood for the first time. Carly Simon's 'You're So Vain' followed me around at that year's cusp. I managed a lonely seduction at the club on the

196

Strip run by Filthy McNasty, the first commercial punk stop in town.

On 27 January 1973 a treaty of peace was signed between Vietnam and the USA. Well, there it goes, another war, I thought. I wept again for the fate of Dana and Sean, MIA since the Cambodian invasion, Dana now known to be dead, Flynn only later felt so. I managed to contact Lili Damita, his mother, before representatives of the government or the corporate concern of *Time* magazine, his employer at the time of capture, could make a heartless call. Sean and I had agreed, in some abstract pact when we both had felt moribund, to be reciprocal notifiers of our next of kin in the event of the unsayable.

The next day, when the bells of peace rang out, I felt empty and suicidal. Pain seemed only to be alleviated in these times by heading for the freezer for another half a pane of acid, a window to a different reality, so far from contact that there was no madness, only flow.

A lot of wartime friends passed through attempting to lift me out of my gloom. Perry Deane went by on his way gaily back to Saigon and points east for *Rolling Stone* and to finish off the research for *Two of the Missing*, his docu-drama book of Flynn's and Dana's lives, times and disappearance. We shared premonitions and tears. For the few days he was in town I felt normal without defining it. A friend bombed through, chasing substances, jobs and his erratic brother, who was piano tuning in Pasadena. I renewed friendship with the latter under some unreal black windowpane he had found in the suburbs. I was starving, bumming a day's rations, turning up at mealtimes at friends' homes. Occasional strings of work for a never ending series of failed, disparate magazines. Apartment 107 was beginning to get too much incoming fire; too many hassles, too much back rent owed, the phone on second red note then off, no stamps for mailing, a final notice from the gun-toter no longer interested in manipulating our marital mistrial.

Very close to my stamp-sized glass-fronted living room lived these strange Magyars. I never could ascertain exactly how many, it was like a resistance cell in exile from Budapest circa 1956. I suspected their business from the first. They were more than friendly to a fellow hungry alien, taking me on midnight runs to grotty complexes in Winchester under the flypath for LAX to collect mysterious packets. Their door was busy twenty-four hours, their sexual preferences a little violent, their choice

AC/DC. We did a lot of dope, chess and sharing of the goulash always simmering in their kitchenette. The first impression that grabbed you when you entered was the smell of cum, paprika, dope and foetid body laced with Rexal bargain aftershave. Dino, Paulo and Klaus were embarrassingly super people to have for neighbours, always on the bullshit, always on the cadge, but it came back in soul help and a fix when needed. I had not enough cash to get my prescriptions filled, without them I was convinced I would go into a painful fibrillative death spasm.

Vietnam was starting to get recycled. In 1973 Robert Lifkin's *The Boys That Came Home*, the first study of the mental trauma occurring in returning Viet vets, was published and then Wally Terry's Motown album *The Men Who Came Home*, an aural history of the blacks up front, hit the racks with my sleeve photo of a stoned soul arse-deep in a paddy on a 9th Division patrol near Tan An.

Compassionate Caccavo, a timid freelance man I had briefly and quietly met before the end of my war days, found me to ask me to lecture at the Arts Center out in Pasadena. He thought I was the person to relate Larry Burrow's work to his photo-journalism class. Passing on filed images for the first time in years was a luxury and the audience applauded unprompted emotions. The memory of the era would survive. The war, now a Vietnamese affair as it should always have been, became less tainted by the day. Jim Caccavo had as much pain explaining his hurts and whiplash to being here as I did. He had married an Asian girl, a Korean Catholic, Sung Hee, had married the east's wounds and woes, feeling more for that fate, of which we were all a collective – more than I could grasp. We shared sad moments, saying little over successions of fizzy draft beer in porno parlours on Western Santa Monica and Melrose where five suck'em, fuck'em movies projected simultaneously onto writhing, naked, ageing models and hookers. We had a common bond in our unhappy state, both with a sense of going nowhere with women as appendices, no story to compete with the one that had made us up. Maudlin over the Bud's froth, half-hearted hard-ons below the bar, we were too broke to buy the attention of the floor girls. Vets did not reveal themselves, the baby-killer refrain was still alive. Being with Jim was almost too cathartic too soon, no one was ready to come out yet, liberation in Saigon was another two years off. He distrusted the men's group and their phoney manners, he wanted to talk about the one consuming thing, his Nam, my Nam, *the*

Nam; I had been programmed to erase it. Suddenly I was reprinting old negs and fuelling strange psychology magazine editors' covers with vet time-bomb portraits.

It was Hunter Thompson who popularized gonzo journalism, but it was coined by Bill Cardoso, a Portuguese Bostonian side-man of the war, on the campaign trail in New Hampshire in 1968 – when he worked on *The Globe*. I met Cardoso in Los Angeles soon after Perry Deane Young had passed through. Bob Sherrill's *LA Weekly* was happening then. I think I must have worked for at least a dozen papers, magazines or journals that came and went in that period.

During the agony of separation, of divorce, out and down, I found a refuge with Cardoso (then fresh from the East Coast with twenty-year-old cat, two enormous Afghan bitches and a cantankerous wife) eight minutes' downhill walk across Sunset to behind the Safeway off Santa Monica Boulevard. We were lucky the palms were still real, in an ersatz neighbourhood. Cardoso, the prince of gonzo, hosted many passing-through hip scribes including big, bearded Tim Cahill, a senior heavy in the hierarchy of Rolling Stone. He was about to let his lovable toughness get taken by the Jesus Freaks who proselytized on Hollywood Boulevard by Grauman's Chinese. It was a brilliant piece and culminated in his rescue from the Easter sunrise ceremonies held, Moonie-like, out in Manson country near Saugus and the Grapevine north of the metro sprawl.

That happened after a visit to San Francisco on an unexpected commission that had started to lift my spirits at the end of 1972. An ex-*Esquire* writer, ex-GI, Burr Snider, had seen Mike Herr's piece about colleagues back in 1969 when he was doing his Nam stint. He had conned Jann Wenner, the publisher of *Rolling Stone*, to commission our coverage of the reunion, when the POWs, from the Son Tay North Vietnamese prison camp, would have a ticker-tape parade and three-day soireé when they got to meet the raiders who were supposed to have sprung them. (Strange that, the same Rambo colonel Special Forces type later led the ill-fated raid that ended up hostage-less in the middle of the Iranian desert.) The magazine even threw in a suite at the Mark on Nob Hill, across the street from the Fairmont where the emotional convention was staged. A bit like our reunion in New York, but their highlighter guest was John Wayne. There were separate NCO and officer frames played out in different suites. Post that gig Cahill, who lived in San Francisco, and I limped into Bel Air and back to 1140 North Clark, burning as much oil as gas, with a push rod about to poke out of the head of the dying Beetle.

The next issue of the paper contained seventeen frames I had made, printed superbly in black and white. Things were looking up. I was lured north again for the fame and possible photo-journalist's contract. It was Hunter Thompson who wrecked my recovery progress by telling the swayable Jann that I was too crazy to hold the gig. We had only spent ten hours together out of his forty-eight in town on a fear and loathing on the campaign trail saga, while he played with a Vincent Black Shadow superbike and we watched the Rose Bowl in Cardoso's salon. My relaunch on the media world, contract in hand, would have to wait until I had relocated from Southern California.

The options increased when Don Downing, then a *Time* reporter, got out of the business, having put in a year and a half in Indochina in the early seventies. His last bureau had been Los Angeles where we had drawn magnetically together to rap out our separate pains and past participles until Don had decided to put the whole thing on tape with the intention of shaping a book. An emergent editor, Dave Obst, formerly of *Ramparts*, was mildly interested in taking it to the Big Apple. The agents weren't keen and it died a slow death with no calls ever to be returned and my fantasies blown.

The Downings were to make the hop from the Palisades to leather-worker communes and welfare paradise of Marin County. Janet immersed herself in her yogananda hangups at the Fairfax Temple. Downtown in San Francisco a new gallery, the Vorpal, was to open on the Battery, run by Muldoon Elder; Don and he had met at army basic-training anti-clap lecture, and were now in partnership. This gave Don a flexible schedule. I started to spend soporific midweek weekends laid back on a west-facing bluff surrounded by fragrant eucalyptuses high above Mill Valley, alternately taping, drinking, cooking, smoking, organic gardening, trying to resolve the past through stream of conciousness, rarely prompted by my relaxed friend intent on seeing his own dilemmas emerge from my story. The rest of the week I lived on a massive bunk in Dave Edwards's front room on Pine Street, San Francisco.

Dave had a Wolfean hook with Perry Deane back to Chapel Hill, North Carolina, and Bob Sherrill who started the new LA paper was also from the Carolinas, via New York. Dave liked to cite the fact that the lowest rate of mental instability is among carpenters. He taught me post-teen woodwork as we restored Victorian houses in the city for abysmal hourly rates. (He at five and a half dollars an hour, me at an apprentice's three.) We put in long non-cheating days, consuming a virtually junk-free diet, solacing each other over our evening's well-earned beer for our recent broken relationships.

The highlights of my time in Northern California are acid etched. In Berkeley, Roger Steffens (another Vietnam vet, now a disc jockey and poet) and I had cached 10,000 windowpane hits in the icebox of the seedy student crib we were sharing hard by Sproul Plaza on Channing Way. Over the seeming years of time warp I crashed in Berkeley the block had a cast of occupants. A gay book binder, an apprentice shrink who ended up using me as his thesis, a ballerina, a stripper, an accountant and assorted anthropologists. A continual stream fresh off Telegraph Avenue, the seat of the radical and protest movements on the West Coast. Roger had somehow met the William Burroughs clan, who came to stay for a week when he was out of town, talking to co-eds. It took two days to police the pad after their departure, getting the smelted puddle of plastic bin, needles and garbage from the blackened kitchen linoleum, and scraping down the bathroom. And Junior had walked off in my only decent boots, $100 Fry's. Thereafter to O.D.

I forgot all about my marriage, the woes of down south evaporated in a haze of excess. The nights were a party blur, dawn a surprise on top of Mount Tam, Oming at the naked fireball, awakening in cabins up private drives in Marin with people only vaguely familiar hours before, now intimate. Other nights there was a mattress on the floor in a Haight commune run by a half-American Indian lady poet and folk singer. I went back to Berzerkley having been put through a total recycling campaign, my disintegrating jeans lovingly patched and embroidered in post-hippy gaud. My hair grew over the shoulders to match the folky Amie who was attempting to cool me out.

One afternoon the reverie snapped with a knock on the door. Most people usually walked right in, our paranoia was totally gone. From my couch I could dimly see through the screen officialdom, straightness, a possible threat. A pork-pie straw hat, tightly knotted tie, wash'n' wear jacket and slacks. Hitler bristle and clutching folio case. Roger groped to the door. I stayed down, heard my name mentioned. Re-adjusting my sarong, I accepted with trepidation the unknown papers. They revealed my divorce's finality.

And on 30 April 1975, Vietnam finally liberated itself.

My income in those post-Watergate years was minimal, the odd bob or two catering friends' barbecue parties paid in kind, a short stay, stash filled and a tank of petrol. Photographically it was nowhere, I shot colour courtesy of friends who donated it and bought the occasional black-and-white roll. Another dozen magazines or papers I was working for folded; *Life* itself had receded to an occasionally published special, no longer interested in my whereabouts.

Time froze on Christo's Running Fence in summer 1976. All of Sonoma and Marin counties were aware of the project; every kid was going to make a buck hanging the thing up before yet another injunction could be slapped on it. It was a beautiful ribbon of 18-foot high fabric designed as a temporary sculpture or event by the artist known for his large wrapping projects. This all coincided with some nasty pressure, having to get out of the US, at loggerheads with the immigration department, obliged to go back to London for six weeks to cop a fresh visa. Conveniently the landward end of the extravaganza terminated near Railroad Avenue in Cotati. At the seaward end whales and seals frolicked, contradicting the environmentalists' claim that the creation would disturb the ecology. The last panels of the fence were being hitched to their undersea moorings and the last legal motions were put against it. The fence ran 24.5 miles from the 101 freeway into the sea at Bodega Head, through beautiful rolling dairy and arable land, the tints of which the silvery curtain picked up and rippled uninterrupted. Its unfurling, panel by ecologically installed panel, by 500 drones was filmed from snorkel, cherrypicker and chopper. For the first time in years I clicked superbly, cadged lifts and humped the line for miles. I realized enough to stage a small show.

Tracking up and down Route 101 and Interstate 5 became a pattern of existence. The jalopies conveying myself and ever increasing amounts of meagre possessions were deteriorating to a series of problems. I spent more time underneath them than in them; disassembling gear boxes, clutches, lifting heads and rings, milking the last ounce of petrol from wheezing bangers. The Vietnamese international licence had long since expired, but the original date had been sloppily inked in with a

US Army Bic, by careful doctoring, its expiry on 17 Gieng '69 was upped to '70, '71 and each year until it caught up with me in 1976.

In exchange for a painting job at an attorney's office, I had been given a 1965 Buick which was a pig wagon to the Nth degree, with expired Illinois plates, repossessed from a convicted felon who had not remunerated my attorney. Brian Clancy, Hunter Thompson's erstwhile lawyer, was prone to moments of madness, though brilliant when lucid.

The car was uninsured and lethal. I got an urgent call to the Oakland jail and courthouse steps to photograph Eldridge Cleaver's wife on a visit. I had put in a pint of brake fluid, and was cruising easily at 50, but going for the brakes on the descent into Richmond there was nothing, nothing, nothing, pump, pump, panic. Stab the parking, emergency hand pedal – nothing. Look up, see three enormous diesel semi-rigs across three of four lanes and the light red, the intersection starting to fill with another monster eighteen-wheeler. I selected park smoothly on the auto-glide shift, a screech, burning acrid smell, but only a slight velocity impedance. I went for broke and put the sled through to reverse, more screaming sounds and smoke, we dropped to 30, still heading for a narrowing gap. Straight out of a bad stunt movie. I missed the lot, brushing through the gap to be confronted by a descending railroad barrier crossing. The wreck spun to a curling stop on some waste ground, yards short of the tracks. I used a quart of hydraulics to get the next 20 miles and returned the keys to my attorney-to-be.

The Marin County jail, albeit designed by Frank Lloyd Wright, was not where I would have chosen to spend the night of the bicentennial celebration. My antics that evening with the Buick had attracted the attention of the Highway Patrol and they charged me with drunken driving, a felony.

Although I was not supposed to drive, Clancy commanded me to take the wheel to get us from his apartment on Telegraph Hill, where I was staying, across the Golden Gate in time for court at 9 a.m. during the week-long trial. It took nearly two and a half days to select the twelve jurors. We rejected eighteen people who incongruously stated that they had never had a drop of alcohol and then driven. Our champion choice, who almost made it to foreman, was a World War II GI who swore he could drink two six-packs and still handle a halftrack.

Clancy was brilliant, raving round the little panelled, circular court room, brandishing *Life* magazines and photographs, getting the whole jury to go and see the cells where his client was humiliated after his valorous service in the quest for America's freedom of truth. The fundaments of the very constitution. He poured out a magnificant, irrelevant diatribe. The prosecutor from the district attorney's office objected only lukewarmly to the judge, who benevolently let history run its entertaining course. It was a hung jury 9–3 for conviction, not enough, and the crime was reduced to reckless driving. My expired licence was forfeited for six months, and to pay the fine I had to pawn my two last functioning Nikon Fs with their motordrives.

At that time, Clancy was flush, his practice vaguely buoyant though his owed monies were from somewhat dubious cases while Pamela, his latest ex-wife, lurked menacingly three miles out in the Sunset district. She was still wont to come and make a frontal assault in the middle of the night, awakening the fragile truce of the cul de sac, as they had in their tumultuous but passionate marriage. By this time Ibby, wife number three, had gone back to the genteel tranquillity of Louisiana, necessitating my presence to keep house and act as a buffer zone against the determined Pamela. Houseboy, guardian, Mustang chauffeur as combined job status, unpaid.

My quarters backed onto the car port and ran alongside the mid-air boardwalk that reached the front door. Having no key Pamela liked to lob logs stored on the walk through my window, for my benefactor demanded a fire round-the-clock, round-the-year. This fire was the vented fury of all his obsessions. Incoming mail was stacked accordingly. Anything interesting in one pile and bills, demands, business in another which on his usual drunken arrival in the early hours he would heave into the glowing embers. Should the phone ring out of turn, it would follow into the flames. Some nights 'the victrola' as he labelled his hi-fi, would be projected into the hearth with his favourite record, Tom Waits' 'Heart of Saturday Night'. By now he would be hurling epithets and bottles off the balcony, doing his Il Duce impersonations in pig court-Latin English, retreating to line up more snow on the mirror *Rolling Stone* had given him – or possibly purloined from Jan's office. At the height of the action he would punt an NFL football, given by the coke client Raider players, about the salon cum dining room, demanding cocktails and bacon sandwiches. It was after he passed out that Pamela would come to seduce him and wreak revenge. She usually brought Carol, her buddy, to keep me quiet.

*

I stayed at the Cahill ranch just outside Sonoma again, minus wheels this time. A vortex in another mad, mega bash funded at the ranch by *Rolling Stone*. I had earned my keep as official barbie operator and expert, roasting whole 'lambs of God', as lapsed Catholic Clancy called them, in smouldering pits dug in frenetic bursts of energy fuelled by windowpanes of fairly electric content. The Cahills put up with my syndromes of erratic extremis, fuelled by top-ups from their ever present case of Coors or whatever jug of special-offer liquor Susan had got cheap at the local gas station market. Cahill had once lived in the studio flat beneath Clancy at Alta. They both knew one-eyed Hinkle, dean of the gonzoid Bay area's semi-respectable under-ground press and founder member of *Ramparts*. Hinkle married the sister of Mark Libarle who was to back Clancy with the funds to fight the case. Libarle lived in Cotati, Sonoma County, next to the Christo fence. Bill Cardoso moved north too, to complete the eccentric circle preparing for the final low-down.

The idea of my suing Time-Life for damages came to Clancy one bright, sunny day in this newly painted twenty-second floor bureau overlooking the western part of Market Street. He was on the slide from one partnership to the next, his stationery changing about as often as the underwear he liked to leave about. Thumbing through the medical section of the Yellow Pages, he found, Mathis, Jacob, K., and a listed practice at the Rice-Davies Insti-tute on Castro, right on the fringes of the city's gay valley. The man who would open the case, replete with the same notes he had taken on that day back in April '69, one of his first in-country, somewhat hectic, was auspiciously right here in town, his whereabouts unknown to me until Brian's idle perusals. It had been a not-so-run-of-the-mill neuro op, meticulously docu-mented all the same, now totally ossified traces of grey matter and blood were still smeared across the impeccably annotated procedures. His recent X-rays of me showed indelible missile tract trace scars, lazer scorches in a healed gel of dense – what? I ask.

He stood there displaying the proof of the disaster which Clancy rightly deduced had not been reasonably compensated for and which Time-Life were supposed to have taken care of as my accreditation stipulated. I was, after all, blown away on the job. I had fantasies about a cool quarter million properly put to bed in a gnome account in Zürich. The length of the case sapped us easier than the relays of lawyers the Inc harnessed over the months and years to come. They could not believe that this was not a libel suit, merely one of industrial compensation. Typical of the media giants, they were loath to settle, fearing it would set a precedent. By serving as Clancy's major domo I was on hand for cross-examination day or night. The preparation of the original suit was a masterpiece of twenty-two clauses, every which one had to be replied to, to avoid default. Brian went off to see Mathis at the clinic and returned certain it would get to court within months.

My life started to revolve around the whims of the next legal move. Their first reply just made it inside the ninety-day limit and only challenged our statute of limitations. The bickering back and forth over the definitions of insanity, responsibility and liability took years, rising to the heights of the Supreme Court for a ruling on the oral contract in a war zone. Out there we had all taken the accreditation as gospel, the flip side of it stated that we were to be taken care of by the accrediting bodies, next to our ID pix and fingerprint. The word 'freelance' was almost damning, though officialdom seemed to want to believe that wars were covered contractually, documents exchanged prior to each excursion into the field, that this had been a war played to rules, a touch of soccer in no-man's land. In fact no-man's land was a free-fire zone, anything moving was targeted. You were told to go, you went, fragged a mission, got you a tail number on the exposed flight line and came back with the new film when the smoke cleared and another bird could frag you out. Try explaining that to a bunch of right-wingers comfortably off in distant DC. They did not want to hear about it now and had only wanted to hear it then as an antidote to their own reluctance. Vets were just nasty statistics creeping into the negative demography file, crazies in wheelchairs who invaded political conventions to protest the continuing madness in Asia. They were a national embarrassment; Time Inc believed the same of me. But none of us would go away.

Page v Time-Life was malapropically transformed, by the liberal presiding judge, Judge Peckham, into the Life-Time case. That was on the second morning, after admonishments to all parties as we commenced jury selection that he did not want to see the Vietnam War rerun in his courtroom. Ironically, though he was daily to repeat his warning to the jury to abstain from reading any

206

material pertaining to the conflict or case, a twelve-part television programme was launched nationwide on the public broadcast network to nationwide acclaim. The whole country locked into its most recent history. The mini-jury of six were unable to escape the issue at home in the evening.

I freaked out again, came apart completely at the seams, became a zombie, unable to do anything. Nightmares, weeping hysteria, confusion. Living with Brian was the most stressful thing I could be doing. Our diet consisted of beer, bourbon cocktails, fat pork, acid, smoke and coke on top of my daily handful of legit pills, all served by the ever-smouldering fire my benefactor demanded.

Clancy fixed up an appointment for me at Cal State med centre with a specialist supposedly hip to the newly identified post-traumatic stress disorder. In the First World War they had labelled it shell shock, twenty years later it had become combat fatigue. Vietnam was now in turn to gain its syndrome. This Herr Platt had me fill out all the multiphasic test forms, mindless petty exams, true or false, tick your boxes for pleasure or dislike: mechanics, magazines, mother, mayhem, masturbation. Damn it, who can decide? I ticked the lot, true and false, depending on the time of day. Clancy cackled and demanded the printouts, the crippled leading the crazed judged by the insane.

The kidnapping and murder of twenty-seven school kids out in the cow town of Chowchilla revived me from the freakout. Bill Cardoso commissioned me to accompany his cover of the subsequent press stampede to the farm belt of the central valley. Three crazed rich kids pulled the mad heist to get attention, abducting the kids from their bus on the way home from a summer school swimming-gig to vanish into the 104-degree mid-valley dusty heat. We had to take the gig.

Clancy lost the Telegraph Hill pad, forcing me to crash here and there, reviving any past affair for a bed for the night. Ike Horn, who served summonses from Brian, did research for Cahill and deep investigative stuff in bars for Cardoso. He ran the background for the case, and drove my pile of junk around between crashes. He worked as an itinerant aspiring writer on the punk circuit from Cahill's flearidden Parkside crib. At the stonecutter's pad where Cardoso existed down in the seedy Mission area a dentist's chair stood proud in the third-floor bay window, a 50-kilo cylinder of nitrous oxide propped conveniently next to an anaesthetist's stand. I learned the delicate art of releasing a balloon's worth slowly into my lungs without letting go of the rubber neck as control evaporated in to weightlessness. A spinning dissolve of brain damage, lurking on the limits of the lucid. It buoyed the case's slow progress along, but led to the harder stuff. Ike got a freelance punk column. I met the Dead and the Damned, I was deafened and doused in amyl, I rushed and rushed.

I went back to being a supported hippy in the rural redwoods of West Marin's Forest Knolls. I dropped out of the city's insanity and Clancy's clutches, seduced by a lady straight out of a *True Confessions* story crossed with *Tatler*. The blot on the landscape was a loathsome son and an ex who appeared from his ski-instructor duties to spoil an idyllic retreat in a house that had made the cover of a kitsch coffee-table number on 'butcher-block designer homes'. There was a meditation room, a pool and a sauna, all cushioned by the knowledge that support was only a phone call away to the heart of Blue Whitney eastern wealth. We wintered wisely, the drugs at bay, the bottles by the case.

On top of Larganitas Hill, Marin County in a storm I was attacked by a fish pond on New Year's Day 1977. I suffered a fractured foot and a lost Rolex, replaced with a fibreglass cast to break out of. Dulled with Dilaudid and more of the spirit that had precipitated the accident, I flipped out again. Pain and anger mounted into blind rage, I snapped the crutch at the petulant kid, Michelle screaming for help. I hid in the freezing forest while the ex stormed the yard.

I was getting short again, and the Life-Time case took a step back. Roger Steffens was newly married and had moved to Hollyweird cushioned by the prize win on a daytime game show: a showroom Buick, a year's supply of cat food and two cases of popsicles. He got me a paid sojourn to advise on a movie of myself at the behest of a couple in yuppie Venice behind LA's beach. The VVAW, the anti-war vets' angry movement, had a halfway house up the block full of gurneys and wheelchairs. The House of the Dragon.

The Life-Time case was heard next in a federal district courtroom in San Francisco. The Inc just had so much more ammunition than we did, more guns, bombs, planes, money. Daily they got transcripts, we relied on a briefing during happy hour in the tavern on the opposite corner from the court. We were joined there by the court recorders and the witnesses of the day, including theirs, those who were still friends. Outside the court I had inevitable confrontations with the hardcore Incers.

After I got zapped in the Da Nang revolutionary farce, members of the *Time* bureau had ridiculed the affair to be put rightly in place by my benefactor and bureau chief, Frank McCulloch. He had fed me work, back then, supported my habits, put up with a Flynn armed to the teeth and made sure that I got taken care of; he looked after me in his fatherly way. In the desperate seventies he had passed me a cinch job when it was needed, and recently I had copped a loan for the deposit on a short-time Eastbay crib. I knew he was a company man but believed that his Iwo Jima Marine experience would colour his testimony on the stand. I walked into court with a beaming smile for him, arms outstretched as though to greet a brother in arms. I received instead a distinctly hostile greeting. He about-faced and sat on the other side. A ripple of unease ran through the court, jury and all. Frank damned me in the name of the truth according to St Inc, my performance underrated, my reliability shot, the rumours of the blacking confirmed. It was a bit like the Tet Offensive, debilitating to both parties.

The press roots for the press. At that time the newspapers were printing the story of how CBS had taken care of its people, including freelancers. During the madness that Nixon and Kissinger decided would benefit the Khmer nation in the early seventies, newsmen were going MIA and KIA like ninepins, victims of a fluctuating front with too many combatant sides, rained upon by a stream of radar-guided B-52s, the infamous arclights. A network crew was ambushed, known dead, government troops abandoning the area. The family of the cameraman, devout Brahmin Hindus, affirmed their right to have the remains for cremation at home. The next day the Phnom Penh bureau chief had driven 12 miles to the site to find the bodies buried before beating a hasty retreat to get help in digging. It cost $20 per head and a bill for the CO to get a platoon to mount a sweep back down the highway a week later with the director of CBS news breathing hard at the Hotel Royale. The cameraman's family received the normal staff benefits and the network gave his son a job in the same role. That was responsibility, post mortem. I was a living industrial accident, job-related incapacity. Hemiplegia in the veterans' administration book received a good 75 per cent pension. Guys with skin afflictions from Agent Orange were getting 10 per cent. What I would get was still uncertain. Biding

time with the self-afflicted philosophy conjured from the nightmare that 'there was no such thing as reality, only nostalgia and
fantasy'.

9

Returns

SONG OF THE HERALDS OF SPRING

We seek our playmates
Waking them up from all corners before it is morning.
We call them in bird-songs,
Beckon them in nodding branches.
We spread our spell for them in the splendour of clouds,
We laugh at solemn death
'Til he joins in our laughter,
We tear open time's purse,
Taking back his plunder from him,
We shall lose your heart to us, O Winter,
It will gleam in the trembling leaves
And break into flowers.

Rabindranath Tagore

In 1978 *Crawdaddy*, the now defunct American music magazine, had commissioned Mike Herr, who had finally finished *Dispatches*, to do a piece on the heavy-metal circuit. It got titled 'Rock Is Hell' after he insisted I shoot the accompanying photos as we shuttled between Cleveland, Detroit, Baltimore and Bing-hampton in upstate New York, being blasted regularly by 24,000 megawatts of inane electronic pulse, loud enough to drown out the continual scream of teeny boppers and the stage-crowding nerds alive with cheap red wine and bennies. A world of groupies, roadies, fast-food joints, identical hotel rooms and deafness. It was a job out of thin air, Mike had been away from the scene struggling with his book. That first night in Detroit I got the third printed copy, feeling a glow at seeing my name enshrined mythically in print.

It was the same day the Vietnamese had enough of Pol Pot's massacring raids across the border and decided to occupy Kampuchea and rid it of the genocidal Khmer Rouge.

Over the next six months I graduated to the masthead as a contributor, with studies of southern California, existential, surrealistic life vignettes: 'Force 10 from Beverly Hills', the military-vehicles collectors' society; 'Living on the Fault Line', the Huxley town of Pear Blossom that survives upwards of 400 earthquakes a year; Frederick's of Hollywood windows, unmentionables season by season, stuffed erotica; Miss Nude California competitions, replete with starkers skydivers out in the acid Mojave; Marine manoeuvres; figure-eight banger racing; motorcycle jumping. The zaniest, wackiest events I could find. I began to push film through the camera boxes again, woefully short of gear due to hocking and theft. Nik Wheeler, now in Hollywood, passed me his agency, Sipa in Paris. They took stuff, backing an LAPD press accreditation, and a seep of pride oozed back into the system.

Ladies came and went like yo-yos. I wanted a hooker, a secretary, a lover, a mother, a nurse – superwoman – and I did not know what I had to give. Still, I was becoming more self-sufficient, my confidence ebbed and flowed again.

Vietnam was emerging into its radical-chic period, reflected in the first crop of newly angled movies, *The Deer Hunter*, *Apocalypse Now*, *Coming Home*. *Dispatches* summed up the American experience, it got the language right, the dialogue straight, and it moved up the bestseller charts. A director at the National Theatre in London proposed staging it as a piece of rock theatre. Mike flew in to work on the script. Out of the ozone I got a call proposing a spin-off of it, a possible *Arena* television programme featuring my work and life. A friend of an old friend's wife had read the relevant paragraphs in the book. Apocalypse ripple wealth spread for my flight across the big pond, a new start at the other end of a lens, to star in my own feature, 'Mentioned in Dispatches'. I could have Simon Dring's Little Venice garden flat, a swingle's dream. Chris Sykes, a Beeb science reporter, started to shoot as the play opened in the Cottesloe in the South Bank complex. Before I arrived for the dress rehearsal Mike had been building a glow of legend around the reality of the experience, the myth was larger than my own life. The only member of the cast I did not meet that night was the actor who was to take my part. I passed on to him, via Bill Bryden, the director, an old fatigue jacket as a talismanic boost.

The clouds were lifting around the whole horizon on both sides of the viewfinder. I lounged around in Simon's crib, shaving and popping pills to hard rock, boozing round the corner at the Castle. They locked that crew on my back for ten days, tracking every mistaken moment. They framed me in the garden of Farnborough rectory up to my elbows in baked-bean-packing Brownies and little old ladies pouring tea. We dissolved to an abandoned World War II RAF station deep in Hampshire, filling with the first waves of boat people, Viet refugees arriving via Hong Kong. North Drive, Orpington, hosted the circus as my parents had to rerun their arrival home on the BMW 600 motorcycle six times and then were interviewed.

Returning three weeks later from an emotional sojourn to Burgundy and the Camargue, I was totally shocked to discover that my father's lips were stone cold when I went to kiss him farewell in Farnborough hospital morgue, a cross-embroidered doily placed over his face. It was as sudden as getting blown away in the field. I had always assumed that my mother would die first. The delayed force-seven crossing on the hovercraft had put the boat train in Orpington Station at almost the same moment as his heart had stopped beating, a serene smile on his face. There was a moment when we stopped that I had almost alighted, an ungodly early-hour surprise, but I had pressed on for a champagne reunion until four in the morning with Simon, fresh in from the West Coast. Somewhere in a dry-mouthed, distorted sleep a phone was ringing. Simon's voice and a shaking on the shoulder. I already knew and took the matter-of-fact, just-off-cracking voice of my mother on automatic. My mind was bursting with confronting confusions, the rush of dealing with incoming fire, trying to run straight. I called the production secretary, Rosemary, who volunteered to chauffeur me down. Then I retreated to a deep, hot bath, where the heat released a flood of racking tears, knowing I would never really know the person who had led me to know this much.

I read Tagore at the cremation and Confucianly moved back into North Drive.

In the end, I was more spooked watching the rushes featuring the interview with my folks in the *Arena* programme than by the actual event, a ghostly presence in the raw footage, unanswerable questions passing across the cutting desk.

Walking down to Charing Cross the morning after they first aired the show, I was recognized and stopped by complete strangers four times, twice by art students who subsequently got me gigs lecturing at their colleges. Alarmingly the cinema at the ICA on the Mall was so full they were standing in the aisles and back for a talk and slide show in conjunction with an exhibition of over 100 frames entitled 'NAM'. It had replaced a projected black-and-white show on the Palestinians by Don McCullin, who reportedly was unhappy with his prints' quality. I took the stage with a can of lager to hand as the projection system malfunctioned, before fielding a painful hour of inquisition from an audience which raised difficult moral issues for the benefit of the camera. A little old lady, a Beeb plant, tried to decry the glamour of the adventure behind the fame, an unshaven street person wanted comparisons between Air Cav and Marines, and a stockbroker sought a critique of *Dispatches*. The standing ovation was as disturbing as it was pleasing, the first public recognition, a reclamation of lost ego, a moral boost in a grey winter solacing my grieving mother in a chilly semidetached, sleeping on the divan bed, retained since my departure, barely bigger than a body bag, surrounded by the artifacts of my boyhood.

Escape became a priority from the locked-in horizon of the Green Belt's middle-class conformism, the rigours of trying to maintain a suburban bay-fronted celibate normalcy. A long time ago, it seemed, I had broken free of all this shit and now here I was, locked back in. One-night stands became weekends, confusing my loyalties; a perplexed widow fielded undecipherable messages. I must have had all the Greater London boroughs covered, a deck of mildly obscene calling cards to replace the voided cheap day returns.

In April 1980 the *Observer* magazine opted to assign me to Vietnam. My partner was the witty correspondent, Dick West. There was also a man from the BBC Vietnamese world service, a French lady of part-Viet, part-Indian ancestry off to see her grandmother in Bien Hoa, a young Irish headhunting yuppie who believed he was my alter ego, and in Bangkok we were joined by the local Reuters man. We were the first group of British-sponsored tourists to hit the country after 1975, although there had already been a number of socialist European parties and occasional invited fraternal journalists in. There was to be only twelve days in-country, all but two of the nights in Saigon, renamed Ho Chi Minh Ville since the day after its liberation on 30 April 1975. Our *Gruppenführer* was a gay, overweight Scot who had somehow ingratiated himself with their tourist hierarchy. At Heathrow he started bellowing in a frustrated, wimpish way for us all to obey orders and do as he said, stamping his foot for emphasis.

In Bangkok we were woken by the airplane's PA system bleating and the machine making a tight combat turn, glimpsing the control tower near the wing's end. A tinny announcement: 'Solly, we make mistake, we try land again.' The kamikaze at the controls had attempted to put 350 tons of alloy and plastic down on the wrong end of the runway, front wheels first.

So long had passed that I had forgotten all the basic precautions to observe, all the tricks of getting by in the sweltering heat of Indochina. I fell prey to every bug in the book, not helped by copious consumption of iced, formaldehydic Thai and Vietnamese beer, cans of imported Tiger, and half-forgotten street food. I collapsed naked in the freezing air-conditioned room, the ceiling fan on low, for a siesta, instantly catching the dreaded, hard to shake, tropical indoor Asian flu. The efficiency curve for the *Observer* sponsored shoot dropped to the level of the writer, who was busy seeking out nostalgic old bars, now posing as cafés and officially barely tolerated. His luggage had been a giveaway to the nature of the trip; a plastic, old-fashioned airline bag in which he had a pair of shower shoes, a spare set of clothing, two bottles of vodka and a toothbrush. He left the carton of Salems – priceless trade goods in Ho Ville – on the JAL 747 in Delhi.

It felt strange to be back in the eighth-floor restaurant of the Caravelle Hotel, over a French planter's breakfast of papaya, baguettes and *café au lait*. I was far from ready for the emotional catharsis. Curiously, the music blasting from the cabinet stereo, a popular item at the PX in the late sixties, was all taken from Armed Forces Radio, without the crazed jingles and message which used to start, 'Now, let's talk about tracers, they sure look pretty, but they burn out barrels, so . . .' I sat mesmerized, my foot pumping, as Creedence Clearwater Revival played 'Run Through the Jungle' and 'Suzy Q' followed by Wilson Pickett and then 'Dock of the Bay'. A cultural time warp, for out on the streets the music was virtually prohibited, reactionary, there was a shortage of everything and the black market flourished. The cadres still had not got around to seizing the tapes from the same old trusted staff that used to serve us fifteen years before. It was occasionally possible to catch an eye and elicit a glance of recognition, of a conspiracy in other times.

Gradually we rebelled against Nigel the Scot as we saw the Viets disregard him, having heard from two Amerasian kids' mothers who were still hooking the streets that he had been caught with his pants down in an ex-GI hotel from where they worked. The information had cost one US $10 bill for the whole service.

Besides Fat Boy, we acquired two clapped-out mid-sixties black Mercedes saloons, two drivers and two interpreters. A seven-person party became a circus. Often the whole contingent had to squeeze into one vehicle after yet another breakdown in the middle of countryside I had passed through previously only in heavily armoured company or, naïvely, open on one of the bikes. I saw the whole trip in a fevered state, fending off the emotions of coming back and the bugs I had stupidly caught. We met the VC officer who had commanded the unit that had sprung the ambush on the 173rd Airborne, who had been the adversary on half a dozen operations. We felt a bond of comradeship bridging the years. He even showed me black-and-white frames, liberated wire-service prints, which I had taken on assignment in those initial years of the war. We ended up as brothers, arms entwined, commiserating on common losses, half-dissipated in nostalgia. It was all rushing back, not then painfully, but I could feel the seeds of exorcism being sown, the light of understanding dawning, a relief, a fascination to dig deeper.

I had never liked the Vietnamese as much as the Lao, Khmer, Burman or even the Coca-Cola-kharmaed Thai. In Laos the learning had come only easily with my squad's tutelage at USAID to the degree that I could shop, make love and function agriculturally. But during the three and some years I was in the Nam, my vocabulary had stretched to no more than a hundred or so blunt words and expressions, mainly macho military or sexual expletives and words for basic consumer items – politeness and small talk were seldom heard or required in a war. Now I was trying to take part in conversations, and catching a lot of the drift. Yet I was only a superannuated tourist, dripping cameras like a Christmas tree, hacking along with a bunch of similar guys.

The tour took us back to the beautifully forlorn beach at the old French resort of Cap St Jacques at the mouth of the Saigon River, heavily militarized to prevent more boat people leaving. Offshore, Brits were working the oil-exploration platforms where injured and sick escapees were being tossed overboard by the naval patrols. We hit town the same night as they began their monthly three-day onshore leave. The oil ministry had taken over the terrace of what was once our R & R hotel to throw a fraternal party, bringing in a busload of former bar girls in their dated finery. You paid to wine and dine and then dance with them, but not touch, and at the stroke of midnight they all upped and departed Cinderalla-like back to Saigon on the old army schoolbus. Left the oil drillers a bit testy, too.

We flogged up to the cool rain of the hill station at Da Lat, retracing Route 14 when I had been driven in early 1965, scrunched up on the back floor of the bureau Pontiac, looking for an outgoing general after an attempted coup d'état. The last day trip we took was the saddest. We went down to the delta town of My Tho and then by boat out to the Dao Island. The sanctuary of peace and sanity where I had come to terms with the war and discovered inner peace and tranquillity, the adaptable Buddhist thread to my own path, an Indochinese dharma. Now the oppressive regime had turned the peeling pagoda into a tourist trap for passing Eastern bloc tourists and the hoped for occasional group such as ours. The monks had all been re-educated and many had not returned, while their women and children chopped up the sacred coconut trees to make souvenirs to sell to the tourists. Among the gaunt few men present, I spotted Dao Phouc, who had once been the leader's personal English interpreter cum ADC. We locked eyes and made the oriental hand prayer greeting and as the others drifted off, he mumbled, 'Where Seen and Yonnie?' I found out that he had just got out of the infamous Ca Mau gulag, notorious for its use of inmates in clearing the defoliated free-fire zones of unexploded ordnance, human mine detectors in a malarial defoliated mangrove swamp, creating pineapple fields so that the new colonists could have frozen fruit in party-member-privilege shops in downtown Tomsk. I left a wad of the useless dongs with the ladies selling the coconut chopsticks and spoons outside what was to have been the peace-conference hall.

The guide bummed me out further by insisting we have our hotel packed lunch picnic on the altar of a beautiful seventeenth century Buddhist temple in My Tho. I was virtually beside myself with unventable anger, almost in tears. There was no respect any more for their traditional heritage, anything not of the new order was condemned as irrelevant and profaned. No longer was there an attempt to conceal what I thought of their system, the *Gruppen-führer* or the tour, I openly chugged beers and the pot I had scored in the Thuy coffee shop on Tu Do Street. For $20 I had got some mediocre stuff from a guitar-player who had been a rock 'n' roll performer on GI bases. He had been sent down to push pineapple four times, each commandant being charmed into releasing him as he enlivened their communal mess with traditional and patriotic songs, including the mournful protests of the war. His café repertoire ranged from 'We Shall Overcome' to the Beatles and Buddy Holly. Each time he got busted and came back, he would bring up a few keys of the Delta weed, once grown to demoralize the US troops.

I felt angered rather than assuaged at the end of the visit, exhausted by illness, unable to fathom out my true emotions, having only just reached to scratch the itch of curiosity. An air of melancholy enveloped the departure lounge at Ton San Nhut where the few folk officially permitted to leave sat forlornly on the all-American Naugahyde chrome furnishing. Our group blew its remaining dong on tepid Coca-Cola.

I did not want to leave the east again, and did not immediately have to. The gold crisis gave me a reason to revisit Burma, to highlight the contrast between the First World's artificial capitalistic dilemma and the Burmese practice of regilding their shrines, shwes and Buddhas once a year in a ceremony that stretches back 2500 years. Gold leaf is sold in little stamp books at the entrance of Buddhist sites and the locals attach this to their Buddha or other sacred object to gain merit. Once a year all the gold is washed down the drain during the monsoon season.

I focused on the Shwedagon, that marvellous pagoda, three miles from the Irrawaddy waterfront in downtown Rangoon, with its countless spires and images of the Buddha. The *poya* ceremony on the Buddha's birthday when the gold is appliquéd etched the story.

Sinking back into the Burmese way of life came easily. England seemed as far away as it had during my first visit in 1963. I was back in touch, even if only for a moment, I had drawn back the curtain and the sun was shining, gold tingeing the silvered emulsions.

Later that year Laos got revisited, the *Observer* and the *Sunday Times* both throwing me bricks of raw stock non-commitally. The airport officials gave scant attention to my visa and luggage. Laos, communist or not, was still hanging loose. I could have walked straight through the airport at Wattay and gone downtown but there was no cab or bus. A UN official gave me a lift. Everyone, except for the dour Eastern bloc technocrats and engineers, had to stay at the Lane Xang, a concrete monstrosity on the banks of the Mekong. Through it passed a backwater ebb and flow of diverse nationalities and political persuasions. It had only just been built in the years leading up to liberation which had been almost without bloodshed; you could still see half-finished plumbing and wiring in the wide cool corridors. The potholes outside had been unfilled for seventeen years. They gave me a gracious monthly rate with a river-view balcony, unfortunately beneath the only night club in town. I paid the $130 up front, a secure tenant, before going over to check in with the press section of the foreign ministry.

I had completely forgotten the ways of bureaucracy in the land of Bo Pin Yan. When I arrived at a quarter to two, the ministry was wide open, not a guard in sight. I wandered upstairs following a sign to Section Information. Two minor functionaries had pulled the hospitality-section armchairs together and were fast asleep, the *pho* pails empty on the desk. I retreated to the stairs and sat down for a waiting smoke. The minister, returning from lunch, had an aide gently awaken me where I had keeled over against the rails. Coffee was brought, then tea, fruit and candies, my itineraries planned and discussed. I was a poor fish with no budget for rent-a-wrecks or left-over helicopters so there was little to discuss. The freedom of my old haunt was mine. Another Englishman, BBC man, was due next week. *Sambai*, *kup*, have a nice day, good day, thank you.

The market next to the bus station was still in full swing, although farming had been theoretically collectivized. The government had prohibited the smoking of cannabis but it was still an ingredient for starting the average potage. There were bushel baskets in the herb aisle. The little old ladies giggled, chuffed, as they doled out a generous helping for a worthless heap of new kips.

Finding opium in Laos has always been an easy trip, even today when it is banned; it is probably Laos's highest export earner, even though unofficially and at the least only mentioned *sotto voce*. The words '*Tuc fin*' will get you led up the right stairs to an oil-lamp-lit pleasure dome. It took two days to find an opium den in the back parlour of the block cell cadre in the Chinese quarter, his daughter keeping a nervous vigil out front. Next I found Belsem, a 116-pipe-per-day ancient, who lived in a stilted house with three other old addicts, for ever clustered around their little brazier on which bubbled their sustaining weed bouillon. Consumption of opium was permitted for those aged fifty or over. His son worked in the old French Gralle hospital and often translated over an American cigarette. The afternoons when the ministry had no visits organized I would lie musing on the cool lino as the old man refuelled the pipe, dextrously twiddling the needles alternately into the flame of the glass oil lamp and then into the brown liquid until the sizzling gloop was rolled into a perfect minicone to be popped into the bowl's ivory centre. It was easy to slip back into a sixteen-pipe habit when it was only an eight-block bike ride away.

No one followed me, no one seemed to care, though I know I was observed and reported; it made no difference to the Ministry of Pointless Affairs (as the newly arrived man from the Beeb hastened to call it). They kept finding it impossible to arrange visits to the cigarette factory or the Coke-bottling works. The latter was a suspected heroin-processing plant, but turned out to be only another inefficient factory, a shadow of its preliberation productivity. Instead I went off to sit in the wats and meditate, occasionally focusing on a frame in a Zen mood. The tranquillity of the tree-shaded temple compounds transcended the current regime. The idea of a photographic pilgrimage began to form in my mind's eye: the Buddha meets Lenin. The monks and their acolyte *bikkus* took to the streets at sunrise for the *bindabat*, the collection of food and alms for the monastery, which has always been the centre of Lao life. The saffron robes were also encouraged to till the banks of the river and dispense ayavedic medicine, and the wats were now obliged to double as classrooms. Many of the precious statues had been senselessly beheaded or stolen in the first flush of collectivism.

I pottered happily around the town and the environs, confined to the range of the Chinese-built rentabicycle, often in tandem with Ed the filmmaker from the BBC whom the pointless ministry was also preventing from getting out of Vientiane. They needed as many round-eyed media types as possible to decorate their celebrations of five years in power. We were to be the Lao answer to central casting extras for the Russian newsreels. The masses were encouraged to feel better as bushels of newly printed money was distributed; everyone, including the bonzes, got Hungarian paint to spruce up the town, white or green, and the markets got unheard-of shipments of coffee, tea, cigarettes and beer, all locally produced but normally only available on the black market. The bill for the week-long bash must have run to a billion kip.

The official government orgy dissolved into a traditional *Tat Bat* at the most sacred shrine overlooking the city. Fifty thousand peasants in their best arrived before sunrise at Tat Luang, a monastery surmounted with a 180-foot newly-gilded stupa, to give their annual gifts to the clergy, here in their saffron throngs from the surrounding provinces. It was the first time in a decade the ceremony had been performed. At night an endless candlelit procession drifted around the Tat; by day it was a country fair with religious sideshows, the Buddhas bedecked with flowers and offerings, incense and candles smoking in the meditation chambers.

Martin came back just in time to join in. Somehow they let him stay at the crumbling Constellation, surprising since he was with his wife, Elizabeth, whose father was the previous, dispossesed owner. They had to come over to my room at the Lane Xang to take showers when the Constellation's plumbing system failed as per usual. We were both almost speechless greeting each other as long-lost brothers together again in the orient. Rome was a decade ago now. There was no way we could pack enough words into each minute, dense with nostalgia, tales of lifetimes to catch up on. The scene was poignantly familiar; the terrace bar opposite the same Indian sundries store where the attempted-coup film had been processed. We sat as before, a *citron pressé* to hand, a large spliff passed openly. The bartender was overjoyed, remembering our apprenticeship. Only the press pigeon holes, where my UPI cable had sat, were missing. The haunted house was unoccupied, old ghosts still unsettled, and the British compound where I had recovered from hepatitis was now the thriving Australian Kangaroo Club. The pool was full of Swedish aid workers who wished the Lao could comprehend their computer-controlled maintenance plant for the 40-ton Volvo trucks they had donated to a land still boasting no roads, a promise unfulfilled by Soviet and Viet control.

It was sad to leave again, severing another slice of the past. The truth was still the same, the lessons of calm and control relearned, an inner-peace lotus petal revealed and reabsorbed. I came out with the antithesis of the combat-drawn stare, the serene glow.

For a while I was back in London, staying in South Kensington and visiting my mother at weekends. South Ken offered the cacophony of a pub, an Italian upmarket restaurant, six shops, and gays constantly arguing in the flat opposite, overdubbed with every bus routed down the Fulham Road and the sirens of ambulances from three nearby hospitals. I shoehorned into the studio flat with a large woman. Once the building had housed the artisans and metalworkers who had done the ironwork and construction on the original Crystal Palace in Hyde Park; now it was occupied by a spectrum of art-orientated earners prone to round-the-clock partying. My first birthday there was celebrated with acid punch and chocolate brownies. A friend's two teen-agers were found camping in the mews with a fire of old chicken bones under the high rear end of a Chevy Blazer, they had preferred the grown-ups' cake to the one baked especially for them.

Flights to oriental cities from Europe usually arrive early in the morning, when the place is suffused with the first soft glow of a tropical dawn. Shrugging off the jet lag, soothed by the balminess of the climate, you want to get on with a normal day, plunge into the warmth. Sri Lanka had that immediate effect on me, despite the numerous, inefficient officials, baggage handlers and hustlers dogging the airport exit a Third World constant. I haggled the first ride downtown in a new eastern land, and the confusion of Katunayake airport faded as the ancient Humber plodded off to the Galle Face Hotel in that first light, mist rising, revealing a horizon of palms. We had left a nation glued to the 1981 royal wedding and arrived in the island the crown had ruled for 150 years as Ceylon to the same delayed transmissions.

I recollected later that over a period of three years, nearly eleven months were spent in-country and barely were a day's magical moments missed. The days began at half past four in the morning and closed soon after sunset, an optimum pastel photographic ambience for twenty minutes either end of the intense hot days. For the first time in a long space it was good to be alone in a state of tranquillity, photographically tuned up, with a self-created programme for total recovery. Shown a shoot list for a book about Buddhism and the most generalized of introductory letters, the custodian of the Golden Tooth in Kandy, after hours of babble and a *cadeau*, admitted me to its presence. 'You are not photographing casket, only chief abbot holding some object. Isn't it?' The next week was *poson*, the *poya* full-moon festival, at Anuradhapura; pilgrims swathed in white eddied around the dagoba with its crowning Burmese crystal laser glinting as the sun rose through it, above a frieze of supporting sacred elephants.

The pristine beaches had paradisiacal palms drooping along the fringe, the diet had all those spices and herbs we never seem to get enough of in the west, fiery food, endless fruit and fish, over a hundred varieties of each. Trim, tanned, tuned in, turned on, I was burning film in the hope that the guide book wanted by a Hong Kong-backed entrepreneur would be published. A surfeit of good frames, temples, shrines, and bos. Every turn in the new road, winding over tea and rubber plantations, evoked another tale from the man at the wheel, Asoke. I got to know his country through his eyes. He was a proud man with the normal Lankan prejudices, once caught for Tamil-bashing before it became fashionable and wrecked the holiday paradise. We covered over 10,000 miles in a country marginally bigger than Ireland, but virtually impossible to cover end to end in an average day. The pace is that of the buffalo, hopefully of the bicycle; most of the motor fleet, accidentally chic, dates from the fifties – Zephyrs, Snipes, Hawks, Standards and Gazelles have all found their last lease of glory in Serendip. The national retort is the rhetorical 'What to do?' It excuses without loss of face, it explains the slow passage of progress and the inevitability of the seasons. The land at that time was still at peace, the Tamil-attempted accession brewing. Jaffna and the north were inhospitable and bleak, no decent hotel or beach; the opposite end was lavish with tourist facilities, the trade booming. A whole colony of Brits had found a sixties alternative retreat around Kandy and Galle.

I had to return to the west for the Life-Time trial in October 1981. After endless appeals and finally a supreme court precedent ruling on the grounds of the process, Clancy had managed to get it officially docketed although he was still unable to pay his bar fees to plead it. By now, the Vietnam War was presented almost as a radical-chic event that one should have attended. Veterans who had previously been reduced to fall guys in paramedic and police dramas, found themselves heard out as Dow Chemical was obliged to establish an endowment for those affected by the debilitating defoliant, Agent Orange. Plans for the memorial in Washington, the wall, had been approved, construction underway.

I arrived in the courtroom with a feeling of righteousness, of knowing the cause was right, the path ordained. I felt I was on a solo flight and the other actors were supplementary; only I knew my side of the story, could describe the whole picture. It was

223

fantastic to see old friends, and surprising to be at peace with Jan; I virtually applauded as she dramatically burst into tears on the stand. Later I stood for a Chinese spread, she raising a sake cup to our day.

Like the Vietnam War won and lost, so too was the Life-Time case, both sides claiming victory. Moral victory is always hollow and, like the Vietnamese, I was broke in my victory. It was good to stop fighting and be home by Christmas, a chequeless victory in our pocket and clippings to prove it. We flew out with a promise of an accounting and forwarding of funds.

Finally I had to get another attorney. The Inc had coughed up and somewhere in northern California was a substantial sum with my name on it. But so far there had been no divvying up, only an argument about the lawyers' cut, which had crept from 30 per cent to 40 per cent with attendant expenses, due, they said, to pre-trial costs. Yet some of our witnesses, my friends, had not been reimbursed their travel costs. Haggling long-distance on the phone did not work. Via the headhunter from the Nam tour group I found an attorney who knew an attorney supposedly astute in dealing with Anglo-American lawyer squabbles. I made a call, and the new guy winged a contract back from Sausalito, action guaranteed. That winter was a limbo phase of life, with the restlessness of not being able to go out and enjoy the spoils, not getting back to Lanka. Spring that year brought a first lump, immediately dispersed on debts; Richard Herndon, my newly retained lawyer, had levered most of the settlement out of the court, paying off Clancy and his partner, Mark Libarle.

The real victory was the boyhood fantasy of walking into the ultimate toy shop and being able to pick anything off the shelves and leave as the paid-up owner. The Pacific Watch Company in central Hong Kong gained forty big red G notes as I staggered out into the cluttered alley to find a cab back to the Singapore Hotel, a scuzzy breeze block in Wan Chai. What they had not got in stock, frantic second cousins were dispatched to retrieve from relatives' concessions. Outfitted like a *National Geographic* shoot, I business-classed back to Bangkok with a wad of travellers' cheques to repay the stalwarts who had supported my previous visits. Like a GI on R & R scrambling out of bed hung over, abandoning a strange bar girl, with twenty minutes to make the 0830 flight back to Colombo.

This time base camp was established in a bungalow up on the

top of Udawatakelle, the botanical reserve overlooking the lake in Kandy. There was a framework for a Lankan photographic book to work on the bones for a Buddhic opus to follow.

The next trip out to Lanka was timed to make the April *poya* on the full moon up Sri Pada, climbing the roughhewn stone stairs to the peak where Christians, Muslims and Buddhists believe that the footprint of Adam, Mohammed or Buddha is embedded. For colonial convenience it is known as Adam's Peak and on this *poya*, moon festival, the summit is mystically projected as a holographic triangle; as the sun rises further the shadow comes closer and then passes through you and the sun is up. Lemming-like, white butterflies flutter from the length and breadth of the island in the mountain's direction to die on its slopes as pilgrims flock for the three-day festival. During the six-hour climb at night one is constantly passed by scrambling little old grandmothers hand-in-hand with toddling grandchildren and devout families lugging suitcases.

Near the Japanese shrine at the bottom of the descent are traditional massage sheds where Tiger Balm is pounded into cramped muscles with a cascading stream icily running outside. Collapsing in the rest house in Dikwella I lay, flaked out, awaking to the worst tropical bites I had ever received. Tiny spiders, mites, had turned my whole body into a scabies-itching series of inflamed pinpricks. A day later I was in Jaffna for the Tamil New Year. A giant silver peacock was about to burst forth from its main Kovil of Nullur Kandaswamy. I staggered about with 103 degree fever, shooting the faithful embracing the sacred flame and smudging their foreheads, until I retreated to a room where the power cut turned the place into a sauna, and succumbed to the onset of a dozen a day squitters.

The old 404 Peugeot, originally a rental, was now Asoke's own, courtesy of the dribbled funds from Sausalito. I was ploughing the winnings back with a resolution of beating back the old labels – freak, cripple, junkie, war photographer; boring labels. Coming off the mountain clean was an exorcism, a slice of Kerouac's *Dharma Bums*. I had a supreme feeling of getting solid again, centred and at an energy peak not reached for a dozen years. Problems were dissolving on contact. Serenity seeped from the island into my soul. It was a re-greening.

Outside the Paddington ground-floor flat window was a bleak block of council flats and a four-way intersection. I was locked up with half an ounce of black, the same of Leb and six Thai sticks. For entertainment six porno movies and a quintessentially sixties record collection of jazz and pop. My deadline, sprung on me as I deplaned from Colombo, had initially read seven weeks, shrunk to five, and finally squeezed into three weeks for a complete retrospective text to accompany the book of war pictures, *Nam*, now going into print. Some days I bounced mastubatively off the walls, devoid of ideas; other days I could not put the words down fast enough. I hardly even reread it, handing it in a day late, homework finished on the morning's number 51 bus ride to school. The war was done, packaged and dispatched. The city was closing in around me, a soured air in the studio as I emerged.

The fighter bombers made strafing runs in Technicolor, dropping napalm and high explosive, tanks trundled and the horizon blurred with pain. The most intense set of migraines hovered in my head from the moment I awoke to the time I was able to slip into a pheni-induced sleep. The worst of bad dreams screeched in my mind until I woke up exhausted. The agony was barely dented by the rescue rings I threw in the form of synthetic smack and morphine tablets. The hand reached for the bottle, hoping to numb out of the inner battlefields. The firefights continued with full illumination. I wanted to crawl into a foxhole to die. Weird fright patterns boiled in my brain, overheating cells popping with some strange post-op residue. I suspected cerebral malaria, but there were no sweats, and knocked back another handful of painkillers with a swig of wine. Swallowing all pride, freaked out, I called Mathis in San Francisco, embarrassed to disturb him; the demigod status I had bestowed on him had only been reinforced by the trial. An examination was appointed for five days later. Meantime I got to see the GP, whose father had been our family doctor since before I was brought home, nineteen days old. Cold turkey on the alcohol, painkillers and coffee was the local answer, deeper prognosis reserved for that most hideous of drums and needless pain, the brain scan. All this was going to cost a small fortune; I was broke again, the new attorney, Herndon, not responding to calls, cables or letters for the last three months.

In Mendocino I caught the fourth of July parade from the balcony while in the kitchen my new counsel served pure Peruvian flake out of a five-pound Folgers can. I had not the slightest inkling I was paying for the show. The invitation to go north, a three-day boogie, had been too good to refuse, my promised accounting still unsatisfied. Off duty I hoped to get the truth.

226

Initially all had been cordial, a joint in the office, dinner on the dock, sympathy, promises and a cheque to cash on Monday morning. The Bank of Sausalito put me on hold while they perused the proffered slip. The account did not exist; Mr Herndon's personal account was overdrawn and no, sorry, they could not help. By the time I got back to his office, he had taken off. I befriended the screeching secretary, who had not been paid for as long as I, and lay in ambush, placated by this weekend.

The good news emerged after the battery of tests that proved there was no sundry rubbish still lying around in the grey matter. Dr Jake said I would need to ingest five times the amount of anti-epilepsy pills to keep things straight; what I was taking bounced right off. Provided I stayed off the booze and caffeine, I could come off the medication for good. Benignly he enquired into my consumption of marijuana, 'Still daily, I presume? Well, in your case it probably does some good.' He prescribed a muscle relaxant and a regime of detoxing over three months from the heavy shit I was now hooked to – beholden to, I believed.

At first I could only discern slight liftings of the veil, but as the thirteen years of addiction receded, a life tempo picked up. The smell of alcohol, the whiff from open pub doors became repellent. Put to test in towns renowned for their hard drinking the decision stayed proven. I boringly consumed sodas in the small hours on Bangkok's Pat Pong, I survived San Francisco, the Apple and DC. There were no more arclights or tracers ricocheting in my head.

From its inception in the late sixties as the anti-war wing of Vietnam Veterans Against the War, VVA had become the organization responsible for the Moratoriums and changing the whole confused attitude of Americans towards the dilemma the conflict had created. A nation still split and divided over the issues was as troubled by its conscience as those who had participated in the nightmare. VVA had raised the capital and organized the building of a suitable monument for the over 58,000 killed, and a year after its unveiling they were staging a convention in Washington. It dawned that I must attend.

The black marble wall is a soulful slash angled just so, near the Lincoln Memorial. The names of the dead are etched into its surface chronologically, the wall tapering to surrounding green lawn. It is best seen at sunrise, the sun reflected in the marble with a backdrop of the Cenotaph-like Washington Memorial. Early-morning joggers slow their pace, hesitate and stop to read

227

the names, locked in the timewarp that the wall emanates as an ambience. Offerings are placed at the foot of the panels and roses lodged into the interstices of the slabs high up, next to a remembered one's line. All day long there is a procession of mourners, some in old fatigues and camouflage suits, who come to make rubbings of a remembered name.

The mist rising at that early hour revealed a lone Vet in a Zen meditation on the grass facing the wall. His mood, the wall's vibration, filtered into my mind and reflected my own confusion about the past.

The convention, a gathering of 4000, was based at the Shoreham Hotel, another faceless mega-roomed inn catering for optometrists, grocers, Rotarians, but never before such a multifarious lot as this. Some looked like lost rock 'n' rollers with shoulder-length hair, some as though they had just left the parade ground; there were the limbless, blind, wheelchaired and the crispy critters, the deformed ones, the aftermath of our own napalm and white phosphorus. They were seated over on one side of the hall so as not to disturb the mainstream, but next to the press table and information point.

Upstairs in Suite 210 was a scene from a dorm party, the three rooms occupied by two camera crews, a director and his assistant while I crashed on sofa cushions in the lounge area. John Giannini, a GI turned photographer, was orchestrating a documentary. During the court case he had been a saviour and morale booster. Now I chowed down with a ten-strong team and was accorded the same status as a delegate; I drifted from room to room, basking in the newfound comfort of acceptance. My tales of woe and recovery paled against my peers', though their stories reassuringly parallelled my own. Sharing them we stroked each other's horrors out of a tangle to a calm, straight meaning. Nam was being exorcised.

On the last morning, ex-Marine Bobby Muller, now a wheelchair-bound paraplegic, the newly elected president, mentioned John's crews and then paused and introduced me to the assembled hall. I was asked to rise and the whole assembly rose with me. Befuddled, overcome with emotion, I sat down crying, my hands steepled in a thanks to my generation. A hand touched my shoulder in reassurance and I turned to look into the mutilated face of a once Negro, now surgically unrecognizable as a face, which murmured, 'It's OK, man, you can let go now . . .'

*

Peace meant no more cities: I wanted to get away from the pressure, the noise, the madness and competition, not to mention the dogshit. The owners of the Bell House, a restored Victorian school building, needed a paying housesitter for their idyll overlooking my old Wealden cycling grounds. Boughton Malherbe can be translated as scarp of the bad grass, a Norman name. The grass that was nurtured in the sublet half acre got us evicted. The owners returned unannounced on an unscheduled leave from their African posting, completely freaked out and told their son, who had been living a blissful libertine life, awaiting university, to burn it.

A year had passed in meditative retreat with only occasional maddened crowds at weekends. The crowning event of the year was a feast, albeit in a downpour, to celebrate my fortunate arrival into my fourth decade, an ounce of black for each one in a chocolate gâteau nearly psychedelic in performance. A year of gathering thoughts with an eighteen-year-old boy as a brotherly companion, enough trips to assuage the traveller's itch and a renewal of affairs. I watched the Weald through the seasons, the logs' embers in the hearth and the fields harvested, then burned across the lane. I had found my spot, a rainbow's spectrum across my own nature, a slot I had craved for too long. In a middle-class way I was still a tenant in Mrs T's expensive 80s *Britlag*, flashing on what Hunter Thompson had said, that the sixties were for the experience, the seventies for survival and the eighties for paying the mortgage.

Royalties from my war book had unexpectedly started to materialize, but ceased as a character I had photographed smoking a pipe full of Cambodian red in 1968 filed a libel suit out of the blue from Augusta, Georgia. The frame was a full plate in *Nam*, which was prominently displayed in the bookshop in the shopping mall where he worked as a salesperson in a jewellery store, and was surprisingly allowed to carry a weapon. A dropout who packed a .45, who as a GI had graduated no higher than E6 after six years, who had been fired from a detective agency in the Carolinas, a small-town police force in the Virginias and sundry food- and chicken-packing plants, now had some quasi-qualified shark urging him to sue me for three quarters of a million. Ironically, it would cost more to defend oneself and win in a federal court district area where the jury would have military overtones (Fort Benning, the home of Special Forces and Airborne, is right up the interstate) than to cough up enough to satisfy his fantasy. Our private eye, a retired colonel, Homer

229

Pickens, assured us that all the kid wanted was a kit to build an autogyrocopter. In America you are guilty should you fail to respond to the suit, and there was no way I was going back into a federal courtroom.

I hit the track to Thailand instead.

A bizarre reunion of mufti-clad warriors and former mercenaries had assembled in early 1984 for a lecherous reunion. They had represented the real spook side of the war, the clandestine shit, the heavy, deep-penetration missions across the border, as well as the hardcore Air America flyers. Since the post in Thailand was one in exile, unrecognized by its US parent, it had become the magnet for all the civilian construction workers and contractors whose role during the war was always dubious and overpaid. The writer William Shawcross and I were being overpaid by a New York women's magazine to cover their convention. We were eighty-sixed, thrown out for their view of William's political persuasions and lived out the story on the fringes, hanging out in their bars and employing other ex-Nam press as runners after Willy was ousted from their grotty headquarters, Lily's Tiger Den.

Afterwards, I flew up to the Golden Triangle to truck around the opium villages with Macbeth, an ex-pat Kiwi, my junior by a day and Thai-fluent. The smack epidemic was running riot in comprehensives the length of the British Isles and we had a United Nations development Thai liaison lad as a guide. I fell through the bamboo landing of the *fumerie* in Son Pot hamlet and Kodak trashed all but two rolls of film. The dope crisis was resolved. Bangkok was then a catchment for a lot of people who had fought in, studied or covered the American Indochinese period. Half a dozen of them, headed by the doyen of the press corps, Neil Davis, regularly got back into Vietnam with little hassle. Conversation kept returning to the magnet, our *raison d'être*, but the gulf had been widened since 1980 by communist distrust. Neil had Hanoi's complete confidence and said it could be done. He had taken over a year and a half to organize a direct transmission to take place from Ho Ville on the tenth anniversary of the South's liberation. Reunification ragtime blues would be sponsored by live *Today* show spots intermixed with cereal commercials on an NBC breakfast programme, hosted by a black one-time sports commentator who had never before been in the Far East. I could ride a lot of surf on the ripples of the television extravaganza planned in order to appease the American conscience.

*

The Thai Airways jet flew in on its final approach over a series of symmetrical round holes dotting the landscape. Hanoi's perimeter is littered with unfilled paddy ecosystem, residue of the bombing campaigns. The severe formality of the arrival lounge and the inefficiency of multiple uncarboned forms let you know that you are still basically the enemy, though officially an invited guest.

I had posed as a tourist to get an invitation to shoot a book, climaxing in their extravaganza down Thong Nhat Boulevard in downtown Saigon, now renamed, for the day the T-34s rolled in, 30.4. My title would read, in a sixties-group time warp, *Ten Years After*. I bought, reluctantly, another package tour, resolved to leave it as soon as we got in-country, the twelve-day swing descending by air to Da Nang and then overland down to Saigon.

The tourist ministry refused me access to their foreign department colleagues, leading to my first and last sit-down strike, a reflection of the coal problems at home which made the headlines here, outside the gates of Ho's old Hanoi residence. I was on strike under giggling guard in the orderly room for an hour. The white-uniformed honour guards spoke no English or French and had not a cigarette or writing implement amongst them, though we had a perfunctory natter in Lao before I wandered off to the shade outside the KGB headquarters. I got to see the main man forty minutes later.

Meeting with Duong Minh, I confessed to three crimes: loving plastic, smoking dope and telling the truth. He had been a deep mole for years, as an attaché in the southern regime's old London embassy. We chatted of Kensington and our mutual histories as the chilly dusk descended on the salon of a once resplendent French villa. The allotted twenty minutes amicably stretched to two hours and dinner. My request for an extension and approval to return for Tet would be most favourably considered. Over lunch in Da Nang two days later the reply was received by the miracle of a working phone. The party-liner tour guide reluctantly conceded that I was now a government guest and not simply a tourist; he no longer had to command me not to photograph bridges, ferries, official buildings, soldiers or anything remotely military in a country with the fourth largest standing army on the planet.

Once in the south our dollars bought comfort and service much as they had done in the war. I was auspiciously assigned room 401 at the Caravelle where my first *Life* assignment had been transacted, the room my mentor Larry Burrows habitually had used. Lam Song Square at the hub of downtown Ho Chi Minh Ville, the centre precinct of which is still called Saigon after the river, used to host demonstration parades and military machinations; now it is the parking lot for vehicles of the privileged staying in the neighbourhood. Between them, raggedy, homeless kids play an endless game of football. The opera house – which became the Senate of the American-run regimes – is now an art palace and occasionally a set to stage show trials to which the outside media are invited. The Continental Shelf overlooks the square. Now there are more bikes, fewer clients, the East-bloc types shunning the unlit, uncooled interior – for the marvellous, lethargic ceiling fans have ceased to turn. The hotel upstairs is a transient officials' quarters while the Caravelle behind the opera house across the way, renamed Dong Khoi (roughly, Revolutionary Fervour), still has many of the same room boys and waiters, even the half-Indian elevator lad. This was my firebase at peace for ten days.

I went home large with images of the havoc of Agent Orange, the residues of conflict visited in homage. Once again I had sunk into the soft light, the mellow greens of the paddies, the rhythms of Asian life. The people were now desperately poor though proudly trying to recover from the longest modern struggle. You had to hand it to them, with pitifully little they had rebuilt a lot, always looking north over their shoulders towards China, Vietnam's age-old enemy, whom they had fought for a millennium to escape a dynastical doctrine. Foolishly they still drained their energies in neighbouring Cambodia, having saved that country from total genocide under Pol Pot, and received for this only excommunication from the Western powers.

As I documented their agonized recovery, the jigsaw of my own started to form a recognizable shape. Tears of remembrance of another time streaked the vision I was trying to create. I was trying to turn my whole self inside out, like looking for a piece of disturbing gravel in my sock.

Reflectively I returned from that reconnaissance trip to find the disaster on the scarp of bad grass forcing a relocation, boat person back to trendy city, to take refuge with a former lady friend in downtown Wandsworth. All I knew of the place was that a lot of red double-deckers overnighted somewhere there. I was relegated to a subtenant, emotionally the relationship had become a business.

I scrambled back to Vietnam in time for Tet in two towns,

jetting anxiously down to Ho Ville on their surviving malserviced 707 from Ha Noi. We all had a fat New Year and they acclaimed me as number-one champion consumer.

In theory the plane takes three hours from Ho Ville to Hanoi, the train takes three days and the mahouts on the two Kampuchean elephants I passed on the street – the old Rue Sans Joie – between Hue and the old DMZ thought they would take three months. They were ferrying the beasts from Phnom Penh to Hanoi, a democratic fraternal gift, people to people. The first time I made the passage it took thirteen days in a jeep.

After much persuasion the authorities decided my trip down to Buon Me Thuot would be that of a guinea-pig, the first foreign media visit to the first town of consequence that had been liberated in the onrush during the spring 1975 offensive. Even today, the road past Play Cu, Rte 14, is insecure; remnants of FULRO (a revolutionary independence movement among the despised Montagnards) still ambush vehicles, especially those containing round-eyes, presumably Russians or Eastern bloc 'technicians'. Six weeks previously they had sent a rocket propelled grenade through a blue Gaz Russian-built jeep, identical to the one I was trundling around in, now sporting GB plates and christened Blue Max. With this in mind higher authorities had assigned me a young man as additional security, though what he could have done against incoming rocket and automatic-weapon fire with his 9-mm Tokharev pistol was never discussed. Tang turned out to be an affable lad who had studied English in Australia and carried a party card; he was moonlighting for internal security on top of his post at the ministry of foreign affairs, foreign-press section. His last job had been working with a German-based American NBC cameraman and his English soundman. This team had endeared themselves to their companions with copious gifts, virtually converting them to out-and-out capitalism.

Tien, whose father was the ambassador to Algeria, was my minder, interpreter and guide for the duration. Benefiting from the overseas contact, he was wearing blue jeans and sneakers and had a sizeable collection of Beatles records. In his English library he had Kesey and Kerouac. He was being briefed, I suspect, to understand the hip quadrant of any visiting media. He was mine to groom, ending our few months together keeping the seeds from the Thai stick he had dutifully gleaned out, hopefully Hanoi now has a small patch of golden green. We would bump and rumble, with no major breakdown, nearly 12,000 kilometres from one corner of the country to the other. Their brief, my programme, ever changeable, was to try to revisit the locals I shot to two decades ago plus exploring the Tonkanese hinterland.

Between them Tang and Tien composed a litany to overwhelm recalcitrant committee members in the provincial ministries, each one a duplicate of its brother in Hanoi. They introduced me as *bac si*, paramedic, or professor Can Sa, man with hole in his head, who do most famous antiwar book. Whereupon they would whip out a copy of *Nam* and get the assembled members' selection of number-one picture. Meanwhile I got on with taking unremarked, unbothered frames.

Amicably we ambled north laden down with trade goods, camouflaged as a market bus. Tang and Tien perched on the back seat, puffing on Marlboros, sipping Heinekens and Cokes, occasionally bumming a joint off me. In Ho Ville during the tenth-anniversary party days, Tang had, at the behest of his Aussie-educated interpreter mates, requisitioned my man Tien to score some of my ganja, which they had heard was from Thailand. I secured a lifetime base of conspirators inside democratic Vietnam's higher society. In reality the grass had come from Kampuchea, compliments of Neil Davis of NBC, to whom it had been thrown by an old Khmer friend while their truck cruised downtown Phnom Penh. We were ostensibly trying to follow the Unification Express, the train on which Noël Coward had written 'Mad Dogs and Englishmen' in the thirties. The story of the country's reunification was mirrored in the progress of restoration of 1800 kilometres of track which had been subjected to the most vicious interdiction campaign ever waged. Our efforts were complicated by the total lack of a timetable the length of the line. No doubt a state secret. It was known that one train left daily from Hanoi and Ho Ville on opposite headings with five locomotive switches in between, but all enquiries were treated with utmost suspicion even after our official internal *laisser passer* was produced. In Hue, where the station master hardly wanted to admit that the train outside was actually the train, Tien introduced me by a new title, Bao An. I was, in best Hanoiese, a progressive radical photographic artist, no longer *bao chi*.

The road is no longer a narrow lane. Since that final wounding in April 1969, US technology had carved a regular graded highway two and half lanes wide from the coast up over the col to supply the Central Highlands bases that we had known as accessible only by air, even then usually by STOL or chopper. During the last days of the war, it had been badly knocked about until the communists consolidated their position, needing to open up the Cordillera plateau to colonize from their overcrowded, impoverished Tonkinese cities. The new immigrants squatted near to ancient posts, SF camps and ARVN/US firebases, which provided local security, their ranks swelled by demobbed *bo dois* (North Vietnamese GIs) gradually subjugating the rebellious indigenous populace. Nothing had changed in the way that the lowlanders, the Vietnamese, be they from Tonkin, Annam or Cochin, treated the locals; racist as ever, they called them *moi sau*, meaning savage pig. The poor Montagnards imbued with animism in the way the Burmese are with their *nats*, the Lao with their *pis*, all-embracing spirits, all to be revered for fear of upsetting the balance of nature, had been enslaved by the French who needed endless free indentured labour for their tea and coffee plantations. Under American rule they had hunted whomever paid the highest. Liberation for Vietnam in 1975 had not spelled freedom for the ethnic minorities, only a certain degree of autonomy within their own districts and only within the restrictions of dogma and committees. These aborigines of Indochina, harmonious with nature, had lived communally for longer than the Viets had strugged to free themselves from Chinese suzerainty.

The first of the 'ethnic minority' resettlement villages was clustered around the old 1st Air Cavalry base near An Khe, known once as the Golf Course. The Cav used to have 650 helicopters there. The Special Forces post had crumbled into the earth again; the road to the erstwhile ambush climbed past well-tended yards in front of small brick and stucco porched houses, each one with a red star and its year of construction modelled over the lintel on raised plaster. Gone was that foreboding jungle screen. In fact, it was difficult, peering at the passing details, to recollect the past.

Leaving the township, climbing into the foothills, curving up the Red Ball Highway, once an artery of petrol bowsers, semi-trailers, trucks and jeeps, where so much history had flowed, it was disillusioning to see the wasted, off-green hills with blackened stumps spiking up, the victims of intense defoliation. Grass that grew here once towered up to two and a half metres, but now reached only two feet. The bends began to look familiar and I am fairly certain I spotted the exact location where we had pulled those sticky bodies out of the battleground.

It was eerie, I was waiting for something to happen this time. Nothing did, save for a shadow of sadness for all that innocence raped, all that time, all those friends gone. I think my three-man Viet crew sussed this and we climbed in silence. The Blue Max thudded past log trucks to the top of the col. The French graves had gone, obliterated ignominiously in an arclight. The view back down to distant An Khe was denuded of a decent-sized living tree, the hairpins were cluttered with wrecked trucks. This time the twisted, rusting remains were Chinese or Russian. It was *déjà vu* and hopelessly sad. The ghosts of past horrors and concealed nightmares were being exorcized under a sky uncluttered with fighter bombers and helicopters, crystal-clear blue, with post-monsoon, high, white clouds scudding along. An Asian day of the kind I had known and to which I had become addicted and was still mainlining.

The challenge was suppressing the rush of nostalgia, seeing a familiar place now stilled, the people at peace. It was now possible to see how incredibly beautiful the country was, to see the Confucian heritage, the layers and veneers of various colonial powers, the core of what had drawn me to the region originally.

There were times, plugging along at no more than 50 kilometres per hour, that I would have popped champagne for a good old US Huey chopper. The only ones visible were squatting discontentedly beside the flight line at Ton San Nhut, bamboo pushing through the floors, rotors drooping, cannibalized for spares or bits for the new Japanese-sponsored electric-fan works. The Vietnamese recycled everything. I was busy working on my emotions, the photography on automatic.

Returning to Hanoi after each foray south was almost a home-coming, the same Eastern bloc and PLO barflies in the Thong Nhat hotel, where they kept putting me in different rooms. My basic reserve was stashed at the Australian ambassador's house, where I sought refuge from the winter *crachin*, the seasonal chill and damp, over debriefing chess evenings, Dylan lyrics amplifying our mood.

Apart from the emotional trauma of revisiting Vietnam, I picked up an excruciating ailment each time. I realized that a land soaked in defoliants and explosives is not going to produce a very nutritious diet. There were also too few dong about to guarantee for the Viets the fertilizers and insecticides that we take, like toothpaste, for granted. Large chunks of my feet started to fall off from the dust, heat and wet. Subsurface Dioxin at work.

During the build-up to the May 1985 bash we programmed in a visit to find the ultimate destination of the endless war scrap.

With foresight the Taiwanese, US allies, had built a recycling mill north of Ho Ville on the country's only four-lane expressway, the Bien Hoa Highway. During the war the wily Chinese spirited away the spent brass as well as the profits; the metal often came back in the NVA's linked belts, Hong Kong being the entrepôt. Now in 106-degree heat, the foundries and furnaces were going full blast. At the centre of the antiquated mill, where one in ten had a hard hat, scampering round the molten metal in flip-flops, the temperature soared to the 140s. The din was as dense as the air. Half-naked people wrestled with jammed, toothed mechanisms. I almost fell off the gantry way high up. I climbed off the dodgy gangway and zoomed back to the corner NBC hospitality suite run by Neil Davis, air-con cool, cold Cokes, baguettes topped with imported pâté. I awoke from a prolonged siesta back up the street at my hotel with a case of congested lung that only aggravated as we headed north up the trail to the damp of Tonkin.

As I went to put on my underwear in the light of the flickering bulb the day before the Ilyushin would leave for Bangkok, my back went. I crawled to the tiled bathroom, frightening the cockroaches, to throw up. I returned to Don Maung doubled over, Tien and company had dragged the 100 kilos of gear aboard in Hanoi, Tan the trusty NBC man sliding me back to Neil's klongside care. The next day, my birthday, morphiated, I lay dumbly by the pool at MacBeth's apartment complex. I boiled over in a fever, drowned later in champagne. Bangkok was culture shock after seven weeks, the longest anyone not carrying a red card had spent in Vietnam so far. An overstocked bustle hard to relate to, retired master sergeants running veloured girlie bars on the strip.

Going back to Wandsworth, first class, courtesy of Imelda's airlines, was a bigger downer. Now there were clients to satisfy and 300 rolls of colour to condense for French, German and American editors' attitudes. The catharsis was in the editing more than it had been in the shooting; now there was time to mull over tastes and colours, the tortured landscape and the saddened people projected in the security of south London. The project opened again like a lotus in dawn light, the selection was a main line to the soul, the gaps in the shoot became obvious. I had a tremendous feeling of control, a Zen master's feel of the brush for a perfect stroke, knowing I ruled my destiny for a while and it was not just happenstance, stumbled reactions to accidents.

Tet '86 was auspicious. They had put my embezzler, Herndon, in the same jail I had spent the bicentennial, where he graduated to chef. Only then did the bar association decide to consider disbarring him and my case could be closed. Even then it took them a year and a half to cough up. The only straight guy I met in the American law business, a photographer and author of a book on GI justice, Bob Rivkin, promised to phone as soon as the cable and then the cheque reached his hands. I had already spent it, and paid my debts.

In 1987, after five and a half years, I finally got the nub end of my settlement, awarded after a five-year battle to get my case to the federal court, fifty-three days therein, embezzlements, thefts, strikes fraud and mayhem. It didn't make me rich but I could breathe deeply once again. Never mind that I had dropped a couple of hundred G on the trail. Another fight done with, another battle behind.

Since 1986 there has been a personal landing zone, a far too small eighteenth-century cottage high on Windmill Hill on the Downs above the Weald of Kent. Outside there are, once again, Turner skies and scudding hurricanes, barely two miles along the same ridge from the Bell House. Osteopathically I have almost been released – no, liberated – from the last traces of paralysis. Dream-like I imagine I am running as I walk to the corner post box, and the legs pick up weightless and it happens. The cat sits on the mat in front of the fire; his name is Phoung and he is the colour of a *bikku's* first robes. The lady with whom I thought the impossible would never happen, love at first sight, will soon walk through the door, now as my wife. And I will look up, Enderby-like, each morning in contemplation. The thought Bhadra bestowed on me during the reawakening on Sri Lanka is over two and a half millennia old: with no ifs and buts.

> *We are what we think having become what we thought*
> *Like the wheel that follows the cart pulling ox*
> *Sorrow follows an evil thought*
> *And joy follows a pure thought*
> *Like a shadow faithfully tailing a man*
> *We are what we think having become what we thought.*

Gautama Buddha Mahinda

Epilogue

The wheel turns yin and yang, time cycles, most of us are still alive, greyer haired, families fathered and zones changed. The nexus of our fraternity, especially the bonds and friendships formed chez Frankie's House, still endure. The survivors are probably closer, though farther physically apart now than then. Maturity has suited us all. Our heads are held high of the past, paralleled in individual ways into a nostalgia never forgotten, a brotherhood intact.

Last Christmas saw the cramming of the cottage with half of them. The dearest of them all, Steve Northup, flew in from his hand-sculpted adobe house in New Mexico where his artistic photograph stymies *Time's* corporate imagery. Frère Minimus had to be collected from the Vlissingen/Sheerness ferry, his 18-year Ph.D thesis on Bali complete, rewarded with a sojourn at Leiden's Asian Studies Centre, to collate a bibliography on his adopted land. Simon Dring arrived stately in a classic, pristine Rover, albeit with dented grille, out of the hard news business, now workaholically selling Sport Aid. Inconsistent to the last, Simon did manage to interrupt his latest mission.

Those who could not make it, we had all heard or seen in the past year. Tom Corpora is now a hot shot political news director with NBC in DC, virtually next door to Joe Galloway who is heading the foreign desk at US News & World Report and lives on a farm whose creek his grandfather fought over in the civil war.

Robin Mannock, lost opiatedly for years in Laos writing the definitive novel, was last heard of editing Beirut's English language daily, *Inshallah*. That report came from Jack Lawrence,

239

now an ABC TV correspondent London based. Jim Wilde tenuously maintains his sanity still for the Inc, a Conradian outcast in Nairobi. Then there's my original older brother, ever-studious, ever-respectable Martin, living with an extended, enlarging, Lao family and expanding his house in Queensland, holding the chair of history at the University there, Elizabeth beautifully beside him.

The Tu Do flat never quite generated the same esprit as Frankie's, we were never more than a fire team and it did not last long after I was hit. Nik Wheeler, destiny always sunny, landed in the Hollywood Hills. He was last seen, tanned by the pool, with a new son paddling and a sensitive corporate colour shoot around the corner. Perry Deane was last heard from locked up with his amour in San Diego, crafting his fifth book. We are all still waiting to act ourselves in the movie from his first book *Two Of The Missing*.

Louise Schmeisser Stone sadly languishes with MS in Kentucky, and confirms that news of Dana's death is never likely to be forthcoming. Sean is still MIA and my attempt to check out rumours of his death in transit as a POW in the tri-state area of Laos, Northern Cambodia and Vietnam revealed little, even though I got really tight with the Chief Foreign Ministry bod in Hue, now the governing city of that region. Six months after his capture, I sensed his talking to me in pain, later reports said there was an '*en claire*' NVA transmission that a POW on the way north had been hit during an arclight. They requested emergency medical evacuation. A later signal cancelled it as the patient had died. On the west coast, I had felt that. It nags not to really know.

The seventies dissipated people a lot, all the energy went into the surviving of an era gone blah, media facing its honesty in a Watergate mirror. The folks that weathered that one are less tight, less prone to renewed kinships. Since *Dispatches* and then *Apocalypse Now*, Mike Herr has dug his family bunker in England's greener pastures. Linda, the lady who saved me declining from that moment in Long Binh, stayed on the road after Rome, until the lures of the east trapped her in India. She has been a Sanyasin of the Bhagwan for a decade. My ex, Janice Ann, beavers away in her native state, refurbishing a 125-room skid row hotel in downtown Seattle.

The Prince of Gonzo called at an ungodly hour a few weeks back, the Life-Time case's money man, Marc, hovering at his highside, cheerful insinuating platitudes on their tab for half an hour. They gave a Four Corners, Idaho map reference for Brian, my erstwhile guardian and counsel.

I pray that under California's bamboo legislation overstaffed with lawyers, that my embezzler is not back in business. Doctor Jake strives on perfecting the techniques of sorting out traumatic brain dysfunction, his treatises on missile trajectories in the grey matter are the definitive, while out in the mesa sticks of Colorado, Bill and Velda Hoke run a forty-five acre mountain, he still in the saddle with stars and stripes-covered prosthetics. Leaving his porch in a brotherly hug, his parting shot was, 'I only git radical, these days, when I cain't go fishing!' Going there to see him, the lifer sergeant who was atop the 350-lb mine back that April, whose belt of M16 ammo had cooked around his waist, who, legless, had summoned help, who died then awoke in a bodybag, and lived now, so dear that my own life was reflected dear.

Down south between the astro-turf divides of Los Angeles, Roger Steffens poetizes to a reggae beat, the AFVN voice doing duty on the romantic upsurge of period movies.

The ones who did not make it are still with us all in spirit, their collective kharma echoes in our minds, an inspiration. We grieve not, we smile with life.